Fashion and Fiction

Cultural Frames, Framing Culture

Robert Newman, Editor

Fashion and Fiction

Self-Transformation in Twentieth-Century American Literature

Lauren S. Cardon

University of Virginia Press · Charlottesville & London

University of Virginia Press

Printed in the United States of America on acid-free paper

First published 2016

9 8 7 6 5 4 3 2 1

Library of Congress Cataloging-in-Publication Data

Names: Cardon, Lauren S., author.
Title: Fashion and fiction : self-transformation in twentieth-century American literature / Lauren S. Cardon.
Description: Charlottesville : University of Virginia Press, [2016] | Series: Cultural frames/ framing culture. | Includes bibliographical references and index.
Identifiers: LCCN 2015037819| ISBN 9780813938615 (cloth : alk. paper) | ISBN 9780813938622 (pbk. : alk. paper) | ISBN 9780813938639 (e-book)
Subjects: LCSH: American fiction—20th century—History and criticism. | Clothing and dress in literature. | Fashion—Social aspects—United States—History—20th century.
Classification: LCC PS374.C565 C37 2016 | DDC 810.9/355—dc23
LC record available at http://lccn.loc.gov/2015037819

For my mother and my grandmother,

who introduced me to the world of fashion

Contents

Illustrations

Acknowledgments

I have many people to thank for their assistance with this project, whether they helped by reading and editing chapters, aiding in the research process, or just talking with me and providing moral support. I began this project as a postdoctoral fellow at Tulane University, and both Tulane and the Newcomb College Institute played an enormous part in the project's early stages. I want to thank Professors Felipe Smith, Joel Dinerstein, and Molly Rothenberg, who read and edited sections of the manuscript and have mentored me since the project was just an idea. Professor Molly Travis, also from Tulane, generously took on the role of respondent for one of my chapters during a works-in-progress series organized by Professor Patricia Burns. I am very grateful to the Newcomb College Institute for providing research funding that aided me in my initial research and providing me with an outstanding research assistant, Britta Aden-Buie. My fellow postdocs and former director, Professor T. R. Johnson, provided constant encouragement and moral support. I owe a thousand thanks in particular to Professors Anne-Marie Womack and Elizabeth Kalos, who have read almost the entire manuscript, offering their edits, providing suggestions for content and wording, and helping me brainstorm changes and developments.

Since becoming an assistant professor at the University of Alabama, the amount of support and encouragement has continued, and I am deeply grateful to my new colleagues. In particular, I want to thank Professor Fred Whiting for leading the Americanist Workshop, and thereby affording me an opportunity to present part of my manuscript to professors in a range of disciplines. I also want to thank Professor Anton Smith and members of the Americanist Workshop for reading chapters, and for offering kind and thoughtful words of encouragement. I am grateful for the Emerging Scholars Program at Alabama, which provided me with a freshman research assistant, Shae Tate, who conducted archival research for the project. In 2014

I was fortunate to secure Research Grants Committee funding through the University of Alabama. This generous grant allowed me to conduct research in New York City and Washington, DC, and to visit exhibitions that aided me in my research and writing. The grant also gave me the opportunity to work with a graduate research assistant, Chris Emslie, a talented poet and insightful literary scholar.

I am grateful to the librarians and administrators at the Howard Tilton Memorial Library at Tulane University, the Stephen A. Schwarzman Building and Schomburg Center for Research in Black Culture of the New York Public Library, the Metropolitan Museum of Art, the Smithsonian Institute, the Condé Nast archives, and the Amelia Gayle Gorgas Library at the University of Alabama. Emma McClendon, Assistant Curator of Costume at the Museum at FIT, and Jacqueline WayneGuite, Fashion Study Collection Manager at Columbia College of Chicago, assisted me in finding historically significant gowns and images for the book. In addition, I want to extend my gratitude to Erica Garber at Art Resource, Melissa Marra-Alvarez at the Museum at FIT, Rachel Jacobs at Waddesdon Manor, and Kyle Tanner at Condé Nast for their assistance in securing permissions for the illustrations featured in this book.

I would like to thank Lacee Drue Nisbett, Administrative Specialist in the Department of English at the University of Alabama, and Barb Ryan, Executive Secretary of the Department of English at Tulane, and the other members of the English department's administrative staff at both Tulane and Alabama for helping to make my research trips and other scholarly pursuits connected with this project possible.

During the process of researching this book, I have been privileged to be a part of various scholarly communities. My colleagues in the College Language Association, the Southwest/Texas Popular Culture Association, and the American Culture Association offered their valuable questions and feedback when I presented portions of the manuscript at their annual conferences.

I would like to extend my deepest gratitude to the University of Virginia Press's Cathie Brettschneider, who first took an interest in my manuscript and was instrumental in getting it published. Anna Kariel, Acquisitions Assistant, and Ellen Satrom, Managing Editor at the press, have provided me with patient and diligent guidance in seeing the manuscript through the various stages of production.

I want to thank my dear friends and family for their continued love and encouragement, including Megan Holt, Elizabeth Kalos, Anne-Marie Womack, Patty Burns, Rachel Stephens, Bart and Joya Elmore, Patrick Frantom, Nigel Seaman, Eleanor Finnegan, Jen Drouin, and Michelle Bachelor Robinson, among many others, who have provided the moral support that kept me focused during the writing of this book. My mother, JoAnn, and my stepfather, Ron, always motivate me to succeed in my personal and professional goals through their love and their confidence in my work ethic. My sister, Caroline, and her husband, Casey, parents of my precious nephews, have offered their encouragement, as well as room and board, during multiple research trips to Washington, DC, and my brother, Aaron, inspires me through his hard work and intellectual curiosity.

Finally, I want to thank Thomas Altman, my partner in life, for his patience, love, and support throughout this project.

Fashion and Fiction

introduction

Fashion in the Land of the Free

> It was the Russian Jew who had introduced the factory-made gown, constantly perfecting it and reducing the cost of its production. The ready-made silk dress which the American woman of small means now buys for a few dollars is of the very latest style and as tasteful in its lines, color scheme, and trimming as a high-class designer can make it. A ten-dollar gown is copied from a hundred-dollar model. . . . Nor is it mere apish copying. We make it our business to know how the American woman wants to look, what sort of lines she would like her figure to have.
>
> —Abraham Cahan, *The Rise of David Levinsky*

In the above epigraph from Abraham Cahan's *The Rise of David Levinsky,* the protagonist, David Levinsky, depicts the purchase of a fashionable gown as an intersection of ethnic, class, and American concerns. He suggests that it took a working-class Russian immigrant to dismantle the hegemony of elitist Old World fashion and make it accessible for working and middle-class Americans. These immigrant designers could accomplish such a feat because they had grown skilled at observing American modes of style and behavior so that they might adopt them and assimilate into the mainstream American culture, securing privileges for themselves and their families by erasing markers of otherness. In other words, by yearning to become American, immigrants would ultimately help transform the American fashion industry and democratize a system that had historically catered only to the very wealthy.

The rhetoric of Americanization dominates the institutions associated with fashion (especially catalogs, advertisements, and fashion journalism) during the late nineteenth and early twentieth centuries. In their 1992 book *Channels of Desire: Mass Images and the Shaping of American Consciousness,* Stuart Ewen and Elizabeth Ewen describe the United States' first clothing catalog, Montgomery Ward's "The Great Wish Book," as "a perfect vehicle for 'Americanization': the pictorial images spoke an easily understood, universal language, demonstrating what an American appearance was all about; actual transactions could be performed in one's language of origin" (42). This catalog, appearing first in 1873, represented a bridge between a social elite (those who traditionally had exclusive access to high fashion) and a broader American populace. Like the immigrant Russian designers described by David Levinsky, these early catalogs and other hallmarks of the American fashion industry—magazines like *Harper's Bazaar* and *Vogue,* department stores with dazzling displays of samples and accessories, and the earliest sales of ready-made garments during the industrial era—seized an arena reserved for the wealthiest classes and channeled it to the working class, to people living in rural regions, and to different ethnic and racial groups.

Since the late 1800s, American fashion has negotiated a balance between reinforcing a longstanding socioeconomic hierarchy and promoting the dissolution of this hierarchy through manufacturing and mass marketing. In his comprehensive study of advertisements in *Vogue,* the fashion illustrator and historian Daniel Delis Hill observes how American fashion has blended the emphasis on mass production epitomized by British manufacturers of utilitarian clothing with a Parisian emphasis on high fashion, or haute couture (4). The fashion industry in the United States, in other words, strove to preserve the glamour and luxury of Parisian couture while convincing all Americans that this luxury was within their reach through mass-producing and advertising affordable versions of high-end looks. Hill articulates "a symbiotic, tripartite relationship between clothing mass production, fashion journalism, and mass-media advertising" that generated the consumer-driven clothing industry that began in the late nineteenth century and remains a key element of the U.S. economy today (ix). In both its American and European formats, mainstream fashion journalism offers its readers an ever-changing assortment of garments and accessories they can purchase to appear part of a fashionable elite; indeed, in his iconic 1967 book *The Fashion System,* Roland Barthes focuses not on actual garments (or "real clothing") but on the "written clothing" of fashion magazines, which signal to a reading public what purchases will connote the abstract, ever-fluctuating concept of fashion.[1]

One of the most prominent distinctions between the European and American journalistic formats, however, is the American focus on affordability, accessibility, and personal style. Fashion journalism in the United States does not seek merely to promote consumption of trendy items, but to encourage a kind of consumer identity construction that will, ultimately, lead to more consumption. A magazine "Get the Look" collage will guide consumers to "sparkle like Daisy Buchanan" by presenting a list of beautifully photographed items for purchase: not only the gown, shoes, jewelry, and accessories but also a bottle of perfume, a crystal vase, a nightstand clock, and a set of highball glasses.[2] American popular media still present us with fashion icons wearing expensive, inaccessible designer clothing (e.g., journalistic coverage of the royal wedding, the Academy Awards red carpet, or the inaugural ball) worn by an American or European elite (royalty, political figures, or pop culture celebrities); conversely, department stores and other retailers present fashion-conscious Americans with affordable versions of haute couture, and journalistic coverage helps citizens feel connected with the social elite.

Yet fashion journalism has come to play another role besides promoting the American consumption of ready-made clothing: it teaches citizens about *style.* Fashion journalism tells Americans "what not to wear";[3] it stigmatizes wealthy celebrities and politicians who lack style with its worst-dressed lists; it instructs consumers on how to capture a particular look or lifestyle through clothing (telling us an ensemble says "debutante" or "bohemian" or "jet-setter"); it delineates which pieces are classics, which are trendy, and which are out of fashion. Like the Montgomery Ward catalog, American fashion journalism teaches consumers which pieces will help us blend in, and which pieces will make us outsiders. During the period of mass immigration from the late 1800s to the early 1920s, fashion print media helped Americanize newcomers.

The concept of Americanization, of shedding ethnic origins and physical signs of otherness to embrace a constructed prototype of American identity, mirrors a common theme in American literature and social rhetoric: a theme of self-fashioning, upward mobility, and rising above one's circumstances. This theme surfaces in a wide range of American literary, political, and sociological texts ranging from narratives of Jamestown to immigrant memoirs, from slave narratives to *Gone with the Wind,* from *Ruth Hall* to *The Great Gatsby,* from *The Bell Jar* to contemporary transgender autobiographies, from the writings of Horatio Alger to those of Barack Obama. Twentieth-century and contemporary American literature frequently features an individual striving to quit his or her current socioeconomic sphere to move into one deemed more liberating or socially superior. Physical appearance is integral to this canonical theme—usually because it presents an obstacle to social mobility. In George Schuyler's *Black No More* (1931), Max Disher's skin color prevents him from merging with white society and from dancing with the woman he desires. In Anzia Yezierska's *Salome of the Tenements* (1923), Sonya Vrumsky's humble clothing and hand gesticulations identify her as a Russian Jewish immigrant. In Theodore Dreiser's *Sister Carrie* (1900), Carrie Meeber's poverty prevents her from purchasing the fine clothing that would unlock a world of better career opportunities and more desirable suitors. For many of these protagonists, clothing surfaces as a skeleton key to enter alternate social spheres, allowing the individual to transcend barriers of class, race, ethnicity, and even gender. The authors linger on the details of clothing—on materials, on displays and mannequins, on accessories, on fine gems and luxurious furs, on the condition of the pieces—to indicate a character's finesse with reading and adopting social signifiers.

Clothing, in these texts, becomes a mechanism through which authors conflate the historical, economic, and sociological realities of the American fashion industry with the genre themes of self-fashioning and transformation. American authors present several archetypal elements at work: (1) a desired elite group, (2) a protagonist outside of or on the fringes of this elite, (3) either an implicit code to ensure outsiders stay outside the group or members of the elite who police its barriers, and (4) an implied American mythology that promises upward mobility as a reward for hard work and ingenuity. The authors use fashionable clothing to narrate their stories of social mobility. I argue, through a broad-spectrum study of fashion in early twentieth-century American literature,[4] that the authors map an evolution in the fashion industry beginning with its earliest signs of diverging from European conventions: the industry adapts over time, they suggest, to maximize fashion's performative function in order to encourage individual identity construction that jibes with a nationalistic sense of belonging.[5] By promoting experimentation and alternative modes of personal style, the industry engenders mass consumption of goods, providing consumers with a sense of individuality even as their sense of civic or community affiliation is reinforced.

In this book, therefore, I argue that the authors use clothing as a barometer for achieving American ideals of upward mobility and the pursuit of happiness, defined here as the pursuit and expression of individual desire. I focus on the early divergence of American fashion from a Parisian haute couture–dominated global industry, beginning with the restrictive fashions of the Victorian era and running through the rise of American designers and Hollywood style in the 1930s. I employ the term "democratic fashion" to convey the expression of American ideals of freedom and democracy through the American fashion industry, as reflected in the accessibility of fashion to all citizens, in fashion's facilitation of individual self-expression or personal style, and in the comfort and ease of the clothes themselves, allowing for freedom of movement for the wearer. The authors suggest that fashion is a set of signifiers that can be adopted or manipulated, and their knowledge of both fashion and style (terms I define below) serve as tools to develop their protagonists—to predict their relative potential to break down social barriers. The characters' ability to transcend such barriers thus rests not solely on hard work, merit, and talent (as the Horatio Alger version of the American Dream would suggest) but on their ability to read and manipulate surfaces, to blend, and to perform. As the American fashion industry develops, these characters have more options for using physical signifiers to construct their public identities; however, having too many options leaves some characters lost, disillusioned, and alienated.

While most of these narratives focus more on women's fashion, and therefore so does much of my analysis, at certain historical moments men's fashion becomes equally significant in stories of transformation and plays a similar narrative role (e.g., in Jewish immigrant fiction, or in postwar counterculture narratives). However, most of the authors indicate that men's fashion has had more of a utilitarian emphasis than women's, whose fashion history has by and large been dominated by aesthetics.[6] This distinction mirrors the more "decorative" role women have historically been expected to play within a patriarchal culture reinforced by a patriarchal fashion and beauty industry. Women's social mobility, therefore, often necessitates a more thorough understanding of physical signifiers, especially as they pertain to dress and style.

The characters I examine reveal a knowledge of American fashion and style as they draw from these signifiers to strategize their social mobility. While the early twentieth-century works focus on the limitations of democratic fashion in transcending class boundaries, other texts expose how understanding fashion and style opens possibilities for characters to explore different classes as well as different racial, ethnic, and gender identities. The texts map a trajectory of American fashion and identity from a glorification of an Old World European elitism to a celebration of American entrepreneurship and consumerism. However, they also show how fashion is a means to an end rather than an end unto itself. While many authors depict disillusionment with the American Dream as a promise of happiness and fulfillment (a nice house and a steady job are ultimately materialistic goals and fail to fulfill a more spiritual human need), they also show the unsustainable elation deriving from fashion, clothing, and glamour. In some ways fashion is more intoxicating than the white picket fence vision of American success and happiness, for it offers a fleeting sense of pleasure, even ecstasy.

As American fashion grows more democratic, the characters in these works are allowed more experimentation; it becomes easier to transform themselves, and therefore their performance can be a temporary rather than a permanent role. Fashion allows characters to experiment with alternate social circles rather than committing to them for life: they avoid more permanent choices—for example, a marriage of convenience or, as in the case of many turn-of-the-century novels, forswearing one's family and passing as another race. Fashion knowledge becomes an opportunity to explore alternate personas. The value of the temporary performance is not in escapism, as modernist criticism might suggest, but in testing alternate identities in a quest for self-discovery.

A Definition of Terms

While in American vernacular we often use the terms "fashion," "style," and "dress" or "clothing" interchangeably, for the sake of clarification I make careful distinctions among these terms. Like Barthes, I use the term "fashion" to refer to a fluctuating system that deems certain looks, textiles, pieces of clothing, accessories, or other aspects of attire in style and others out of style.[7] However, I find the system less abstract than Barthes suggests: it's largely governed by the aforementioned collaboration between fashion journalism, high-end designers, and advertisers; it establishes new trends yet also revives older ones, deems some pieces classic (and therefore *always* stylish), and tends to value clothing aesthetics over utility. Being part of the system requires knowledge, research, and maintenance: knowledge of fashion rules (What fabrics are appropriate for evening wear? Can I wear white after Labor Day?), research of current trends and any changes or updates to the fashion rules (we no longer have to match our purses to our shoes), and maintenance of that knowledge as well as the pieces themselves (regular wardrobe purges/updates, repairs to clothing, visits to the tailor, dry cleaner, or cobbler). For the sake of this study, I assert that fashion is the system; the fashion industry is the governing body that controls the system.

At the pinnacle of the fashion system is haute couture, which, according to N. J. Stevenson, "means 'high sewing', and the artisan's work that goes into the production of a couture gown justifies its price" (5). In order for a house to gain recognition as an haute couture fashion house, it must be accredited by the Chambre Syndicale de la Couture. In her book *Couture and Commerce: The Transatlantic Fashion Trade in the 1950s* (2001), Alexandra Palmer explains that to gain this classification, the house has to meet a list of standards, including the following: "at least twenty-five models had to be created in-house every spring and fall and a sample garment for each made to measure on a live mannequin. . . . The collection was then to be presented on live mannequins in an 'appropriate' setting in the haute couture house, which had to be situated in Paris" (15–16). Today, only a few thousand people in the world buy haute couture; typically, they go to fashion shows, select pieces, and have the designer tailor-make those models. On average, one outfit runs \$20,000-\$60,000 and takes 150 hours of work, though an evening gown may take as many as 1,000 hours. Palmer attempts to correct a common misuse of the term "haute couture" as a designation of any high-end fashion; to avoid this misnomer, I use "high-end fashion" to designate the creations of higher end designers (not necessarily those within the Chambre Syndicale) *including* their ready-to-wear collections. A \$4,000 dress designed by Valentino available for purchase at Saks Fifth Avenue, for example, would be considered high-end fashion, but it would not be haute couture.

Scholars of the social and economic dimensions of fashion have tended to follow different theoretical approaches—approaches that offer not only a clear perspective on fashion's function in a postindustrial society but also an analysis of how fashion changes and evolves. Georg Simmel, for example, offers a class-based theory in his seminal 1904 article "Fashion": "The elite initiate a fashion and, when the mass imitates it in an effort to obliterate the external distinctions of class, abandons it for a newer mode" (541). His theory echoes Thorstein Veblen's theory of conspicuous consumption and emulation,[8] but while Veblen focuses on emulation within the upper or "leisure" class, Simmel focuses more on emulation of the wealthy by the poorer classes. In contrast to Simmel's "trickle-down" theory, Barthes suggests fashion emerges not from specific social classes but from the makers and producers of fashion in conjunction with fashion journalists (xi–xiii).

In 1984 Pierre Bourdieu presented a theory that offered rebuttals to Simmel's, explaining that the working class cannot simply imitate the upper class—not merely because working-class citizens cannot afford the clothes, but because their clothes are partially dictated by lifestyle: "The tastes of working-class men would be based on a 'culture of necessity' characteristic of that class, in other words, clothing that was practical, functional, and durable rather than aesthetically pleasing and stylish" (Crane 8). Those who moved into the middle classes would be expected to adopt the clothing and behavior of that class "but would not exhibit the same levels of taste and refinement owing to insufficient socialization and education" (ibid.). Bourdieu acknowledges the role of fashion in upward mobility yet characterizes changes in dress not as the gate keys to different social echelons, but as necessary signifiers of embracing a new status.

The problem with all these theories is that they cannot be universally applied: fashion functions in various ways in postindustrial nations across the globe, as well as at different historical moments. In addition, as the cultural studies scholar Jennifer Craik has observed, fashion is not even "unique to the culture of capitalism" (3) and is not explicitly concerned with consumption.[9] Even within the United States, fashion has emerged from different wellsprings and has held different symbolic meanings from decade to decade. Applying Veblen's theory of fashion among the leisure class, for example, does not adequately explain the character of conspicuous consumption among the leisure class during the Gilded Age in New York. In *The Age of Innocence,* Edith Wharton—a critical observer of women's fashion—depicts the contrast between members of New York's "old society," who wait several seasons to wear their Parisian couture dresses, and the nouveau riche Regina Beaufort, who wears the newest Parisian designs as soon as they debut (258). The women of the New York aristocracy imply that they find Regina's choice vulgar, even though it represents the latest fashion and connotes high economic value. The example shows the difficulty in detaching the value of fashionable clothing from longstanding rules of style and taste.

Similarly, the theories fail to account for fashion inspiration derived from a different country, culture, or counterculture. When asked where fashion comes from, many people within the industry will simply state "Paris"; however, during the 1950s the premium on beautiful leather goods and new textiles helped to launch Italy to the apex of the fashion world, and in the 1960s the youth culture of London dictated new modes of fashion and style. Today, fashion does not hold the same cachet that it did a century ago: few women remain slaves to seasonal trends but instead adopt a few trend items into a wardrobe of classics. In fact, many Americans during the recent economic recession have come to denigrate the conspicuous consumption of wealthy citizens: during the 2008 presidential election, for example, people admired Michelle Obama's accessible yet stylish wardrobe (often featuring pieces from J. Crew and H&M) while condemning Sarah Palin's $150,000 wardrobe budget for campaigning. In the United States, style has gained greater civic value and regard than fashion.

"Style" is often used interchangeably with "taste," but I want to draw a distinction. Taste, in this context, refers to the ability to recognize what is appropriate and elegant. Style is the embodiment of taste in one's attire and carriage. In other words, the stylish woman not only recognizes what pieces are tasteful but also knows whether they will suit her—her lifestyle, her figure, her coloring, and so on. Taste might direct a woman to a particular scarf and pair of jeans, but the woman with style skillfully pairs that scarf and pair of jeans with the perfect jacket, leather satchel, and ankle boots. The resulting look is deliberate, put together, and appropriate. If the look also feels consistent with the woman's personality, then the woman has personal style: she expertly uses clothing to express something about her personality and lifestyle.[10] This concept of personal style dominates contemporary popular culture and fashion journalism. As an example, the popularity of the television show *Sex and the City* (1998–2004) delineated four distinct constructs of personal style that became crucial in defining the four main characters:

the fiscally irresponsible free spirit who blends vintage finds with high-end pieces (Carrie), the old-fashioned romantic who wears Dior-inspired classics (Charlotte), the career-driven alpha female in tailored designer suits (Miranda), and the hypersexual public relations executive in skin-revealing, cutting-edge fashions (Samantha). While later series episodes and the two *Sex and the City* films obscured the show's initial fashion and style aims with their promotion of specific high-end brands (Manolo Blahnik, Louis Vuitton, and Hermès, for example), the show's initial fashion focus fell on personal style, not high-end fashion.

Personal style has become a hallmark of American democratic fashion, representing the freedom and savvy to customize one's look by selecting from an endless range of options. Even though the garments and accessories may be mass-produced, their availability does not limit personal style: the stylish consumer finds innovative ways to wear any given piece, as well as new combinations that work with her chosen public identity.[11]

In addition to these key terms, I use "clothing" and "attire" interchangeably to refer to the garments themselves (whether a thrift-store T-shirt or a haute couture gown). "Attire" refers to anything worn as part of an ensemble, whether clothing or accessories. Lastly, "dress" denotes a particular mode of clothing associated with an occasion, an occupation, a ceremony, or some other subcategory in which observers can spot identifiable similarities in clothing (as in "women's dress during the Gilded Age"). In his sociological work *Fashion and Focus* (2011), Tim Edwards notes that while fashion fluctuates, "dress remains relatively static" in comparison; as an example he says that while "what is in or out of fashion" may change seasonally, "the distinction of formal from informal or casual dress" (3) remains the same, with only minor changes over the years. In order for the fashion industry to continue its relevance and its hegemony over a nation of consumers, then, it has to function symbiotically with the rules that dictate style. Over time, the industry may break some of these rules (e.g., the recent popularity of winter whites has shattered the traditional label of white as a summer color). Nevertheless, having some consistency in dress across fluctuating fashion seasons helps to uphold longstanding social conventions and class barriers—even if those barriers become permeable.

The Origins of American Fashion

The novels and memoirs I discuss in this book span the late nineteenth to mid-twentieth century, limning a full spectrum of American fashion from its early reliance on Parisian designers to the emergence of distinctly American style in the 1930s. In each chapter, the authors under discussion distinguish between mere imitators of fashion and interpreters of fashion. The imitator knows through social conditioning what fashions are stylish and appropriate, and she purchases them; the interpreter, however, who has mastered the semiotic power of clothing, can use it to maneuver for greater privileges and freedoms. Unsurprisingly, with each passing decade, characters have more clothing options despite their socioeconomic conditions. At the same time, they have to become even more acute in their understanding of what various garments, accessories, and combinations will signify in a public arena.

Before discussing these characters in depth, it is important to offer some foundational information about the American fashion industry's past. The fashion industry as we know it today originated not in the United States but in France. France became the fashion capital of the world because it produced the best silks,[12] and the earliest couturiers used this luxurious fabric to realize their artistic designs (Palmer 13). Most scholars of fashion deem Charles Frederick Worth the father of haute couture. As the evening gown in figure 1 shows, Worth's clothing was impeccably tailored, with intricate hand-sewn details and luxurious materials (in this case, silk with velvet scrollwork). According to the fashion writer and stylist N. J. Stevenson, "When Charles Worth shaped haute couture into a definite industry in the 1860s, he gave kudos to the dressmaking trade by attempting to place fashion into the realm of fine art" (5). Worth opened his showroom to a wealthy elite of female clients, who would observe his one-of-a-kind pieces on live models. His fashion house became famous because of its workmanship and "its use of opulent textiles and trimmings" (Kelly 16), as well as its consolidation of textile selection, design and pattern making, construction, production, and tailoring under one roof.[13] Worth is also famous for putting his name on his clothing in the form of labels (thus elevating the status of the dressmaker or, in this case, designer) and for establishing the first Chambre Syndicale in 1868.

In the United States, the wealthy elite of the nineteenth century had their clothing made by the best tailors and seamstresses, and the very wealthy

Figure 1. An 1898 silk evening dress designed by Charles Frederick Worth. Silk textile. (Metropolitan Museum of Art, Costume Institute; gift of Eva Drexel Dahlgren, 1976, 1976.258.1a,b; image courtesy of Art Resource, NY)

would order their clothing from Paris couture houses (as May Welland does during her honeymoon with Newland Archer in *The Age of Innocence*). Ewen and Ewen observe, "The opportunity to wear a skillfully crafted garment symbolized a status within society—the status of one able to afford the employment of those whose long labors and intricate touch could be mobilized to construct an appropriate public or private image" (115). The expense of fine textiles and craftsmanship reinforced circles of privilege during the nineteenth century, when most Americans made clothing in their own homes (116). Early American fashion thus relied almost exclusively on Paris for design inspiration and trends, and fashion itself was confined to those who could afford to buy expensive clothes and those living in proximity to major cities or centers of fashion enterprise. While access to haute couture would remain a privilege of the wealthy for the foreseeable future, access to fashion would not, as I show in my first two chapters.

In chapter 1, "The Free Spirit in the Gilded Age," I discuss the attempts by two Edith Wharton heroines—the Countess Ellen Olenska and Lily Bart—to flirt with the boundaries of propriety in their searches for happiness and fulfillment. In *The House of Mirth* (1905), set in the 1890s, and *The Age of In-*

nocence (1920), set in the 1870s yet ending around 1900, Wharton canvasses early American fashion's mimicry of a European elitism. These early periods, she suggests, represent the strictest of social boundaries for women: movements were restrained, with very little allowance for individual expression (it was more important to show good taste and breeding). Accessibility to fine clothing was limited to the wealthiest classes, and upper-class women's clothing and behavior were closely monitored for anything unconventional or risqué.

The Age of Innocence reveals the way high fashion restricted personal style and ease of movement during this period (underlining the clearly defined, socially acceptable roles for women of the time), and how this restriction of movement echoed the limitations on personal freedom. *The House of Mirth,* meanwhile, reveals the nearly insurmountable economic barriers surrounding elite New York society at the turn of the century. Although *The Age of Innocence* is set during an earlier period, because the novel concludes at the turn of the century, Wharton writes with a degree of historical hindsight, exposing the increasingly liberal trajectory of American fashion over a period of thirty years. In both novels, the heroines are savvy interpreters of high fashion; though living at a time when elite fashion had extremely strict rules of propriety, these women enjoy the luxury of personal expression through fashion at a high personal and social price.

Though Wharton portrays the before and after in her later novel, she does not account for the sociohistorical events that catalyzed these changes. The first change came with the circulation of fashion print media, including the first publication of *Harper's Bazaar* in 1867 and the first clothing catalog in 1873. The mass circulation of women's fashion magazines during the late nineteenth century gave women outside city centers and the upper classes access to fashion, as did the concurrent invention and distribution of paper patterns. In 1899 *Vogue* began running paper patterns, allowing readers in rural areas to re-create high-fashion designs in their own homes—often from "illustrious" Parisian couture designers like Charles Frederick Worth (Hill 3–6). These patterns, along with the invention of home sewing machines, would allow women to "experiment with fashion at home" (Craik 74). The 1890s also saw the mass production of corsets (145), making high-end undergarments (and by extension, high society silhouettes and posture) accessible to lower income women. The biggest factor in shaping what would become American fashion, however, was the rise of the ready-made garment.

The late nineteenth century marked a period of rapid industrial development in the United States, bolstered by an enormous influx of working-class immigrants from eastern and southern Europe from the 1880s through the early 1920s. The development of production technology and a steady arrival of immigrant labor fueled what would soon become a thriving garment industry. Ready-made garments had existed before—usually for laborers who wore crude fabrics, or for slaves (Ewen and Ewen 119–21). Yet by the 1880s, women's fashions were mass-produced as well, and the early 1900s saw the mass marketing of women's shirtwaists (131–32). In *Twentieth-Century American Fashion,* Linda Welters and Patricia Cunningham reflect on the significance of this mass production of clothing for American civic identity, noting that "Americans in the early years of the Republic often sought to distinguish themselves by revealing their belief in democracy and liberty through their clothing" (2). Whether the rise of ready-made clothing resulted from such ideology or from an enterprising body of manufacturers working in collusion with marketers and journalists, the industry grew and now extends to all socioeconomic classes. We know "ready-made" now as "ready-to-wear" or "off-the-rack," and even the most illustrious designer houses like Dior and Chanel now produce ready-to-wear lines to reach a wider customer base. The ready-made garment ultimately allowed for the rise of democratic fashion.

It wasn't enough, however, to manufacture these pieces. Somehow American consumers—and not merely those in the highest circles of society—had to hear about them. Advertisers and retailers seized the moment: magazine print ads increased, and the first department stores opened during the mid-nineteenth century. The stores opened in busy urban centers like Chicago and New York, populated by individuals from all walks of life—including newly arrived immigrants. Many of these stores, like Lord & Taylor, originated as dry goods stores and were reinvented during the late nineteenth century as the palaces of consumption we know today. City-dwelling Americans could purchase garments from department stores, while Americans living outside the metropolitan area could read about current trends in fashion magazines, learn about different brands through mass-media advertising, and either purchase items through catalogs or purchase patterns to re-create pieces themselves. With the rising popularity of shirtwaists and skirts during the 1890s (Hill 23), fashion became even more affordable in that consumers could mix and match different pieces—the first separates had entered the fashion marketplace, and consumers could now create multiple "outfits" with the same items.

Chapter 2, "The Social Climber in the Era of Ready-Mades," chronicles some of these commercial, industrial, and social shifts through the literature of the naturalist writers Theodore Dreiser and Abraham Cahan. Rather than focusing solely on actual clothing and design in this chapter, I also look at the changing American industry behind the clothing, as well as a modified nationalist ideology born from this manufacturing and marketing revolution. Dreiser's *Sister Carrie* (1900) and Cahan's *The Rise of David Levinsky* (1917), both set during the Victorian and Edwardian eras, map two major developments at the turn of the century: the rise of department stores and, concurrently, the beginning of women's outfits (using individual pieces, like shirtwaists, for multiple ensembles), which would allow for more class maneuvering through the strategic use of fashion.

The fashion industry did not solely reward women who had financial means; rather, it rewarded those with style, charm, and cleverness. Both Carrie and David possess these qualities, and both are expert interpreters of fashion. Cahan shows how knowledge of fashion and the fashion industry allows an individual to transcend class and ethnic identity. Dreiser, meanwhile, indicates that access to clothing (i.e., wealth and class status) is not enough: through Carrie, he shows the value of a sense of style—how she wears the clothes, how she understands which clothes will best showcase her beauty, and how the proper deployment of clothing can influence her fate. Both novelists also depict, through the increased accessibility and display of clothing and accessories (in shopwindows, catalogs, advertisements, and a more public city life), a new paradigm in consumerist mentality, a conflation of the American Dream with heightened access to luxury and material goods, and the ultimate disillusionment that stems from these changes.

With a wider consumer base for fashion innovations, American manufacturers could explore new avenues for fashion design, production, and retail. The United States would contribute to the transatlantic development of modern fashion in many important ways that I outline in the chapters that follow. With his 1909 purchase of *Vogue,* Condé Montrose Nast would transfer the magazine's focus from fiction to fashion and set the global standard for fashion journalism. That same year, fashion editors began challenging American designers to compete with their Parisian contemporaries and to create fashion that better suited the American lifestyle (Hill 17). By 1924, according to Hill, Paris looked to American sports clothing as inspiration for its couture (38), and by the 1930s, both Lord & Taylor and *Vogue* were promoting American designers. Today, Paris perseveres as the global fashion capital, yet American designers like Michael Kors and Marc Jacobs, among many others, have gained a prominent footing within the global industry. And, while fashion capitals have developed throughout the world (including Milan, Tokyo, Barcelona, São Paolo, and Johannesburg), the recognized most powerful figure in the global fashion industry is the London-born editor in chief of American *Vogue,* Anna Wintour, who allegedly determines, single-handedly, what fashions will dominate for a given season. Despite her influence, fashion in the contemporary world has splintered: few women across the globe buy haute couture, and while a larger percentage of women worldwide do keep up with seasonal fashions, more American women concern themselves with cultivating a personal style.

Modern American Fashion

The literature between the world wars chronicles American fashion from the advent of mass consumerism to the development of a uniquely American style. My third chapter, "The Immigrant in the Era of Simplicity," features characters who read the minimalist fashion of the post–World War I period as an opportunity to assimilate, to collapse barriers of class and ethnicity. I rely predominantly on the fiction of Anzia Yezierska to articulate the revolution of fashion embodied by the minimalist approaches of Paul Poiret and, later, Coco Chanel, who simplified women's dress and unwittingly made it easier to copy. Yezierska's immigrant narratives reveal the transition from the prewar opulence of Edwardian fashion to the postwar simplicity of early modernist fashion. Her heroines learn to contrast the simple luxury of upper-class fashion with the bright and gaudy ready-made clothing that appealed to immigrants and the nouveau riche. She suggests that while access to haute couture is confined to the wealthy, even the poorest woman can have (or at least acquire) a sense of taste, just as even the wealthiest women can lack a sense of taste. Yet Yezierska's fashion-focused tales are cautionary: like Dreiser and Cahan, she reveals the dangers of attaching too much meaning to the clothes themselves and the materialism they represent. Her heroines' performances as women of taste often come at the expense of family and community ties.

The simpler styles of the post–World War I era paved the way for experimentation in style during the 1920s, when women's fashion began to draw inspiration from non-Western cultures, from working-class dress and uniforms, and even from menswear. In "The Modern Woman and the Slim Silhouette," chapter 4, I look at some of the most prominent writers of American modernist fiction (F. Scott Fitzgerald, Ernest Hemingway, and William Faulkner), and their depiction of the modern woman. While the protagonists in the first three chapters turn to clothing to secure or attain a higher class status, the women discussed in this chapter wear more androgynous clothing to blur boundaries of class, race, gender, and sexuality. I argue that rather than maneuvering to secure class privileges, these women maneuver to escape more personal limitations on behavior, often represented by belonging to an old money family or being a housewife. The characters resist the restrictions of high society by flirting with a bohemian lifestyle, and the restrictions of white womanhood and heteronormativity by acting or dressing like men and, in some cases, through race performance.

Specifically, I look at the characters Jordan Baker in *The Great Gatsby* (1925), Brett Ashley in *The Sun Also Rises* (1926), Patricia Robyn in *Mosquitoes* (1927), and Catherine Bourne in *The Garden of Eden* (1986). Through these women, the authors engage questions of physical beauty and body type alongside the political and social messages encoded in contemporary fashions. They expose how 1920s fashion both liberated and constrained women—it increased mobility and comfort, yet it also demanded a slim, boyish body type that made larger and more mature women feel excluded from style. The authors portray the modern woman as resentful, seemingly attributing this resentment to the illusion of liberation symbolized by their clothing: that is, a woman's democratic style makes her hyperaware of the restrictions that remain, thereby making her a destructive force.

In chapter 5, "The Black Middle Class and the Primitive," I examine the bipolar pressures of the fashion industry on African American, middle-class women during the late 1920s and early 1930s, drawing from literature of the Harlem Renaissance, in particular Nella Larsen's *Quicksand* (1928) and *Passing* (1929), Carl Van Vechten's *Nigger Heaven* (1926), and Jessie Redmon Fauset's *Comedy: American Style* (1933). These novels feature black middle-class female characters who attempt to emulate the simpler styles of white middle-class fashion, as well as characters who enjoy the exotic styles of primitivist fashion and performance, fetishized by modernist literature, art, film, and theater.

During this historical moment, American fashion steered black women in two directions. The earliest periodicals aimed at a black female readership,

Ringwood's Journal and *Half-Century Magazine*, sought to distance a developing black middle class from an enslaved past—particularly from white stereotypes of black female hypersexuality. Magazines targeting a black female readership therefore encouraged women to dress conservatively and modestly, to avoid bright colors, garish trimmings, and the more exuberant modernist styles. At the same time, mainstream modernist fashion drew inspiration from African themes, indulging in primitivist fantasy through the vehicle of clothing and accessories, and celebrating performers like Josephine Baker. The heroines of these novels, to some extent, share a desire for upward class mobility yet falter when attempting to negotiate among conflicting societal messages about self-presentation and racial politics. In many ways, these pressures force them to choose between showcasing their physical beauty in its most exuberant light and adopting a more muted appearance for the sake of evading both sexual and racial fetishism.

The Depression may have brought an end to the Harlem Renaissance, and it may have abruptly halted an era of heavy consumerism; however, the economic crash also brought about some important changes in the American fashion industry. By the time of the crash, Parisian designers had already begun responding to the lucrative American market and, to some extent, letting American tastes dictate their designs (Buckland). As an example, in 1924 many Paris collections were inspired by American sports clothing—kilts, culottes, and pleated skirts appeared in multiple collections (Hill 38). Yet the Depression, ironically, would catalyze American style and American designers. During the early 1930s, American retailers and citizens alike could not afford Parisian imports, and retailers began championing American designers more than ever before (Buckland). Making one of the most influential decisions in American fashion history, in 1932 Lord & Taylor vice president Dorothy Shaver showcased and promoted American designers, making them household names and championing them as the next leaders in fashion (Hill 56). Though American consumers would continue to view Paris as the bedrock of cutting-edge fashion, retailers' responses to the heavy tariffs on Parisian imports, combined with *Vogue*'s Americana editions in the late 1930s (Hill 58), helped elevate American brands and American fashion.

I therefore conclude this volume by arguing that the Depression set into motion two important patterns that would change American fashion: a greater reliance on American designers, and the rise of Hollywood-inspired fashion. In the conclusion of this book, I reference several "Hollywood novels," particularly Nathaneal West's *The Day of the Locust* (1939), to articulate the emerging "California style" of the 1930s, and I discuss how film adaptations of novels like *Gone with the Wind* and Raymond Chandler's *The Big Sleep* (1939) would generate major fashion trends during this period. Although the post–World War II period would see a renewed infatuation with Parisian designers and haute couture, this early assertion of American fashion independence would help engender our contemporary enjoyment of multicultural fashion and personal style. The Hollywood novels represent a pinnacle of the American fashion industry: characters in these novels wear American designers and showcase a thriving industry during a time of economic devastation. American designers would continue to thrive during World War II, when imports from Paris were practically nonexistent. The fashion of this period thus epitomizes a brief midcentury moment when American fashion came into its own. Although the end of World War II would bring about a resurgence of expensive, restrictive Parisian designs (heralded by Dior's famous New Look of 1947), during the 1930s and 1940s American fashion embodied democratic ideals: it was affordable, comfortable, versatile, and adaptive for work and leisure; moreover, it gave women a range of options and personas to try on as they constructed their public identities.

one

The Free Spirit in the Gilded Age

She was so evidently the victim of
the civilization which had produced
her, that the links of her bracelet
seemed like manacles chaining her
to her fate.
—Edith Wharton, *The House of Mirth*

In the famous tableaux vivants scene of *The House of Mirth,* attorney Lawrence Selden observes Lily Bart's choice of costume for her display: "The noble buoyancy of her attitude . . . revealed the touch of poetry in her beauty that Selden always felt in her presence, yet lost the sense of when he was not with her. Its expression was now so vivid that for the first time he seemed to see before him the real Lily Bart, divested of the trivialities of her little world, and catching for a moment a note of that eternal harmony of which her beauty was a part" (171). The scene is one of several in the novel in which Selden focuses not on Lily's expensive clothing and jewelry but on her natural beauty. Such scenes tend to occur when the pair walk out in nature and converse privately, beyond earshot of their high society friends. By responding so passionately to Lily in her unconventional costume, Selden comments on conventional high fashion: it can be stifling, binding, and exorbitant; like the society it represents, it smothers natural beauty and celebrates wealth and taste. Only when women have more freedom with their dress for personal expression and for revealing their natural shapes can their beauty emerge.

The world of the New York elite that emerged during the nineteenth century, including its fashions, tempted women with its luxury and beauty yet placed strict limitations on any freedom of individual expression or desire. In Edith Wharton's novels of manners, *The House of Mirth* (1905) and *The Age of Innocence* (1920), the novels' heroines, Lily and Ellen, use clothing as a tool for constructing a public persona—and thus it is also the means through which each woman either asserts her will to conform or, however temporarily, voices her defiance. Lily and Ellen cope with fashion's limitations on their self-expression in different ways. Having limited finances, Lily relies on her physical beauty and charm to navigate her elite social circle and to secure a position for herself, while Ellen pushes the boundaries of propriety in her fashion choices, assuming that her loved ones will accept her eccentric public persona. Both means prove problematic, bringing a series of unexpected problems. I argue that Wharton reveals, through these two characters, the tension at the core of the fashion world that would foster the more democratic American fashion industry.

The emerging American elite preserved the exclusive and expensive traits of the Parisian fashion scene. The emulation of a European fashion elite depicted in these novels seems the very antithesis of democratic fashion. The stiff, binding, and costly clothes reflect the rules of behavior embraced by model citizens like the character May Welland in *The Age of Innocence.* These rules could only be bent by women who were so rich or engrained in old society that sycophantic friends or husbands could obscure their flawed behavior. A woman had little freedom of expression in her physical appearance except in the guise of a performance like the tableau vivant, and the clothes were affordable only to a limited few. Situating her novels during the height of the Gilded Age and at the genesis of what would become, essentially, American royalty, Wharton intensifies the pressures acting on her heroines to belong to this elite world.

A novelist recognized for her naturalist style, Wharton frequently placed her colorful heroines within the strictly governed, conventional setting of New York City in the Gilded Age. The Gilded Age spanned from 1870 to 1914, and in northern cities was associated with the decadence of an "old money" elite (Kelly 10). During the Gilded Age, Wharton suggests, the fashion industry aided in deifying the upper-class elite, as though they ruled by divine right. Wharton characterizes this elite as beautiful and elegant on the one hand, and exclusive, parochial, and even oppressive on the other. The landscape of old New York, with its heavily draped drawing rooms, horse-drawn broughams, and perfectly trimmed and tailored Parisian gowns, serves as the setting for *The House of Mirth* and *The Age of Innocence.* The free-spirited women of these novels must contend with the old New York landscape, and as in many naturalist novels, their setting is ruthless and unsympathetic to suffering, rewarding the hustler and punishing the naive. At the same time, the world of old New York is beautiful and full of promise, suggesting that a more glamorous life hovers in close proximity.

The Gilded Age period, encompassing both the Victorian and Edwardian eras, preceded the shift toward mass consumption of ready-made fashions by America's upper classes and therefore maintained strict lines between those who could afford to participate in an American aristocracy and those who could not. Because of the residual old money attitude toward ready-made fashion, members of New York's social elite ordered their clothes from Paris or from the most illustrious dressmakers in New York; they adorned these clothes with expensive jewels, hats, and other accessories. To give a sense of the expense of maintaining a fashionable wardrobe, the $9,000 that *The House of Mirth*'s Lily Bart owes Gus Trenor for her lifestyle supplement would equate to well over $200,000 today. It was normal (and is, today) for women of Mrs. Trenor's class to spend this amount on a single season's wardrobe—sometimes on a single gown. Such an emphasis on luxurious fashion made upper-class women obsessed with what women were wearing in Europe, and indeed what the major fashion designers were creating for European royalty and nobility. In fact, this attitude helped bring about the first publication of what would become the leader in fashion journalism worldwide: *Vogue* magazine.

Vogue spotlighted the American aristocracy with a kind of journalistic idolatry, and it circulated their fashions and doings to a wide American populace. On the cover of the first issue of *Vogue,* which appeared in December 1892 (fig. 2), the Albert B. Wenzell illustration features a young debutante posing in a Victorian evening gown and holding a bouquet of flowers in her right hand (Kazanjian 6). Flower petals swirl around her, and a butterfly flutters its wings above her left shoulder. Above her, two sylph-like women lounge against a scrolled banner reading "Vogue." The effect elevates the young socialite and other women of fashion, rendering her more like an ethereal goddess than a young lady making one of her first social appearances. The image set the tone for the early years of *Vogue.* Its founder,

Arthur B. Turnure, aimed for the magazine to keep its audience abreast of what clothes, home decor, activities, and people were in fashion that season (Hill 6–8). According to the writer and journalist Emily Esfahani Smith, pre–Condé Nast *Vogue* was conceptualized "by and for the new New York aristocracy—the Vanderbilts, the Whitneys, the Astors, the Stuyvesants, etc." She explains that not only would the wealth of these families "be spent on lavish fashions and opulent homes, which *Vogue* could (and did) feature in its pages, but it also created a need for social models." The magazine helped to delineate an American style and grace that matched, and yet was distinct from, the style and grace celebrated by a European elite, and helped distinguish the fashionable old money set "from the vulgar *nouveau riche.*"

The new American aristocracy included the notorious Four Hundred, allegedly named for the number of people who could fit in the ballroom for Mrs. William Backhouse Astor's illustrious Winter Ball (E. E. Smith). *Vogue* positioned the Four Hundred as the group that everyone wanted to join yet few could. Their parties, travels, and milestones (weddings, etc.) were announced in *Vogue*'s society pages, and the magazine was littered with photographs of their events and gowns as well as detailed descriptions of their clothing. Because of its visibility, the group was subject to constant scrutiny and evaluation, constant gossip, and constant policing for violation of social convention—and for scandal.

Edith Wharton was born on the fringes of this elite, and even as she critiqued it, she too looked on it with awe. In her biography of Wharton, Katherine Joslin notes that the author's ancestry dated back to the Dutch settlers in New Amsterdam, and that her mother's family was part of "The 400" (2). She explains that Wharton had to learn the social conventions and values of the New York elite; despite her later rebellion against them, Wharton understood that "identity is bound" to these conventions and values (2). This world and its manners, Joslin asserts, would provide raw material for Wharton's writing as she assumed "the role of realist writer and novelist of manners." Wharton does not simply dismiss the New York elite as superficial or predatory. In fact, she often dwells on its delights and temptations, its aesthetic beauty and cultural wealth, celebrating good taste in dress and decor even as she depicts the psychological impact of these displays on society's have-nots. Nor does she glamorize the working class—indeed, some scholars have exposed an implicit eugenicist bent to her writing.[1] As a realist author, she does not assign moral rectitude to a particular class, but instead

FIGURE 2. First *Vogue* cover, December 17, 1892. (A. B. Wenzell, *Vogue;* image courtesy of Condé Nast)

focuses on how different individuals grow within their given circumstances, in an era dictated by the glamorous surface of conspicuous consumption. Wharton may maintain a critical distance from the elite, but she also seems to worship its beauty, and she never questions its divine right.

Wharton therefore shares the plight of her characters: she can critique the social limitations on behavior and dress, yet she also craves acceptance and admiration. In celebrating good taste and aesthetic beauty within the New York elite, Wharton reveals a central facet of her early identity: her self-proclaimed "desire to love [and] to look pretty" (*Unpublished Writings* 185). In her unfinished and unpublished autobiography, "Life and I," Wharton explains, "I always saw the visible world as a series of pictures, more or less harmoniously composed, & the wish to *make the picture prettier* was, as nearly as I can define it, the form my feminine instinct of pleasing took" (ibid.). Wharton often visualized her society in terms of cohesive images—aesthetic tableaux composed of backdrops, people, and their costumes. The contemporary interest in staging tableaux vivants and costume balls (discussed below), or the practice of wearing one's new Charles Worth gown in the opera box at the beginning of the winter season, mirrors Wharton's view of her society as both visual and performative.

Much of the scholarship on *The House of Mirth* relates the novel to Thorstein Veblen's *The Theory of the Leisure Class* (1899), published only six years prior. Veblen's analysis of gender relations, conspicuous consumption, and dress are especially pertinent to this discussion. He explains that men of the leisure class, like their "barbaric" predecessors, must not only assert themselves as strong and aggressive but must also assert their leisure, wealth, and taste. They must spotlight their wealth through their consumption of tasteful, expensive, and high-quality goods, and certainly fashionable clothing is one of the most conspicuous examples of these goods. Here, however, Veblen indicates an apparent paradox. Not only must fashion for the leisure class be opulent as evidence of its wearer's wealth, he argues, but it must also boast its wearer's inactivity (170), and therefore must be "inconvenient" (173) and uncomfortable. In other words, the clothing must illustrate both "conspicuous waste" (because fashions change so quickly, and old styles are simply discarded) and "conspicuous leisure" (181). Paradoxically, however, men cannot wear uncomfortable clothing, because it marks them as infirm and of inferior strength, and thus they must depend on their wives to wear this uncomfortable, conspicuously wasteful clothing (182). Veblen's analysis is helpful in characterizing the limited, restrictive roles of women during the Gilded Age. Veblen likens women in high society to chattel, citing as evidence "the high heel, the skirt, the impracticable bonnet, the corset, and the general disregard of the wearer's comfort which is an obvious feature of all civilised women's apparel" (182). Whatever restrictions women of this world faced in their social interactions were only enhanced by their fashions, which restricted women economically owing to their fleeting value and high price, physically owing to their physical discomfort, and even aesthetically, for as Veblen notes, if fashion were getting more beautiful with each passing season, a given trend would not be viewed as "grotesque" only a few years later (178).[2]

In *Displaying Women: Spectacles of Leisure in Edith Wharton's New York* (1998), Maureen E. Montgomery notes that as New York society became more "heterosocial," women had to engage in increasingly public displays of their husband's wealth, wearing their finery "in boxes at the opera or various shows at Madison Square Garden" or "in fashionable restaurants" (10). As society magazines like *Vogue* gained popularity, she continues, women paid more attention to and more money for clothing and opportunities to display their Parisian gowns—for example, at "fancy-dress balls and *tableaux vivants*" (10). Society media of the time would often photograph and chronicle these events, titillating a mass audience with glimpses of the aristocracy's elaborate amusements while mentioning the names of high society's prominent members.

Given the emphasis on public display in late nineteenth-century New York, Wharton was acutely aware of the need to manage one's public image—even if this image failed to reflect one's interests, personality, or genuine desires. Referencing Erving Goffman's theory "that gentility is a performance," Montgomery compares the upper class to performers in the theater—actors who must convince their audience that they embody their assigned characters (13). This connection between intention, appearance, and context helps explain the behavior of Wharton's characters: within her literary world, clothing and physical appearance can merely aid in one's overall impression. Her characters must dress impeccably and exhibit excellent taste, but they must also have costars (approving social allies who will vouch for their respectability), a setting or respectable home, and a consistency of performance. This type of performance should not be confused with the performative function of democratic fashion I have described—in fact, it is the opposite. In its most democratic form, American fashion allows the wearer to experiment, to perform multiple identities and try them on as part of identity construction. In contrast, Wharton's heroines are channeled into scripted roles that they must perform flawlessly. The cost of deviating from these roles—whether the script or the costumes—is social ostracism.

Wharton's heroines Ellen Olenska and Lily Bart know their place. Both women understand their decorative role in society, a role that helped dictate the rigidity of Victorian and Edwardian fashion.[3] These heroines manage a tension between their free-spirited personalities and their need to meet the strict standards of social convention for their own sakes as well as for their loved ones. They struggle to maintain their footing within New York's social elite because of both their violation of behavioral codes and their inability to meet standards of dress: Lily cannot meet them because of her limited financial means, and Ellen has grown too accustomed to the more daring, less restrictive styles of dress typical of her bohemian European friends. The tensions Ellen and Lily experience comprehending their own identities in relation to social conventions are paralleled in their romantic dilemmas: Ellen's rejection of her oppressive, philandering husband and quasi affair with the socially entrenched Newland Archer, and Lily's attraction to progressive-minded Lawrence Selden and attempts to attract the socially established and wealthy Percy Gryce. Both characters flirt with freedom within their tightly bound circles, allowing their free spirit identities to surface in small, seemingly safe ways. These moments are echoed in their selection of clothing and self-presentation.

The House of Mirth

The House of Mirth is set slightly later than *The Age of Innocence* yet was written as a contemporary novel, thus containing less historical hindsight and fewer details of dress than the latter. Published in 1905 and set in the 1890s to turn-of-the-century period, the timing falls within the middle of the Gilded Age and captures the transition from Victorian fashion to the even more opulent Edwardian era. If Victorian fashion was characterized by tightly laced whalebone corsets, impeccable tailoring, heavily layered skirts, and stiff fabrics (all of which heightened the sense of a woman being both restrained and protected), Edwardian fashion screamed opulence and excess: women wore more delicate fabrics like silk with a wealth of ornamentation, trimmings, and stand-out accessories (Hill 20–21). Women of fashion would change their attire at least five times in a given day.[4] In addition, despite the reinvention of the corset by Mme. Gaches-Sarraute, ostensibly for the wearer's improved comfort and health, the resulting S-bend corset gave women an awkward, pigeon-like posture and caused pain in the spine and lower back (Hill 19–22). During this transitional period, therefore, the look and silhouette of clothing changed, but the degree of discomfort, restraint, and expense that burdened women of high society did not.

In *The House of Mirth,* Wharton conveys the tensions of this period through her heroine, the beautiful Lily Bart. Lily is well connected to New York's social elite, yet her limited financial means and lack of a husband keep her on the fringes, desperate to secure her position for the future. The novel's plot is indirectly driven by high fashion, for Lily uses her clothing and style to make herself appear younger and to dress the part of the prospective wife. Yet when Lily has all but snared the dull but wealthy Percy Gryce, her personal desires drive her to sabotage her chances. Unable to sustain her lifestyle and expensive wardrobe, Lily charms a friend's husband into helping her out financially, thereby setting into motion her own social demise.

Lily Bart's limited financial means and tenuous place in the first circles of New York society force her to use her cleverness and beauty to achieve what she believes she wants: a more secure social position through a practical marriage, the clothing and jewels to best accentuate her natural beauty and charm, and the resources to participate in the social life of high society (playing bridge, taking trips to Europe, having a summer house, etc.). She has been raised physically and mentally to aspire to this elite by her socially ambitious mother, as well as her conservative patroness Mrs. Peniston. In addition to breeding Lily for this socioeconomic echelon, Mrs. Bart has placed a burden of duty on her daughter, cultivating Lily's beauty to secure her place in high society and to resurrect her own: "Only one thought consoled her, and that was the contemplation of Lily's beauty. . . . It was the last asset in their fortunes, the nucleus around which their life was to be rebuilt. She watched it jealously, as though it were her own property and Lily its mere custodian; and she tried to instill into the latter a sense of the responsibility that such a charge involved" (69). Wharton provides this backstory to show the urgency pushing against Lily's free-spirit instincts, a sense that she is only suited to move within New York high society as a decoration to a wealthy husband, and an additional pressing obligation to fulfill her late mother's unrealized hopes.

The novel's central tension revolves around whether Lily really wants to belong to this social elite. Her free spirit, moral compass, and romantic interests (for Selden too, as an attorney, lives on the fringes of the group) all steer her away from this group, but her driving sense of purpose instilled at such a young age and the mesmerizing beauty of the elite world convince Lily she belongs nowhere else. Lily has so thoroughly convinced herself of the correctness of her breeding that she is easily seduced by the symbols of the elite world—she worships at its altar even as she longs for freedom from its constraints. During a wedding scene, for example, Lily looks upon the bridal jewels with a sense of deep longing, the jewels bewitching her into believing such embellishments represent happiness and fulfillment: "The glow of the stones warmed Lily's veins like wine. More completely than any other expression of wealth they symbolized the life she longed to lead, the life of fastidious aloofness and refinement in which every detail should have the finish of a jewel, and the whole form a harmonious setting to her own jewel-like rareness" (126). Lily perceives the fashions and jewels of the elite as the appropriate showcase for her natural beauty. Both Lawrence Selden and, ultimately, Lily herself question whether this assumption is true.

Even in the first pages of the novel, it is clear that Lily questions whether the high society life would actually bring happiness. In her conversation with Lawrence Selden in the novel's opening, she reveals her delicate position in her social circle, made even more delicate because of her sex. After observing that Selden's coat is "a little shabby," she tells him, "If I were shabby no one would have me: a woman is asked out as much for her clothes as for herself. The clothes are the background, the frame, if you like: they don't make success, but they are a part of it. . . . We are expected to be pretty and well-dressed till we drop—and if we can't keep it up alone, we have to go into partnership" (46). Her words reveal her resignation to feminine conventions, yet they also reveal her wit and intelligence—two assets that go unappreciated by most of her circle. Lily knows she must remain adaptable, using her clothes to blend into the necessary scene (e.g., avoiding her more risqué dress when she tries to impress the puritanical Percy Gryce), while also repressing her inner urges for independence and even her intelligence.[5] Lily's fastidious dress is therefore not necessarily the outward expression of her spirit and personality, nor her position in society, but instead the "frame." The clothes allow her to perform the role of the high society wife to which she aspires.

The fashion of the Gilded Age is therefore both a major cause of Lily's financial woes and the means by which she can secure her interests. Her propriety in dress stems from a studied practice of emulation, yet Lily's advantage lies in her knowledge of her own beauty and best features, and how to use clothing to simultaneously blend in and stand out. In the novel's opening, Lily's clothes highlight her in the midst of a crowded station, prompting Selden to spot her and invite her to tea with him at the Benedick: "Selden had never seen her more radiant. Her vivid head, relieved against the dull tints of the crowd, made her more conspicuous than in a ball-room, and under her dark hat and veil she regained the girlish smoothness, the purity of tint, that she was beginning to lose after eleven years of late hours and indefatigable dancing" (37–38). This early moment shows Selden's understanding of Lily and her knowledge of how to use clothing and accessories to showcase her features in the most flattering light. Yet he also sees that

Lily hides any signs of aging, any fearful hint that she is losing her "girlish smoothness." The scene exposes Lily's heightened sense of urgency in cementing her place: these subtle allusions to her aging make her search for a husband feel more desperate and rushed.

Wharton makes it clear that Lily has the means to secure such a husband in the figure of Percy Gryce. Her social maneuverings, her charming conversation, and certainly her more subdued clothing choices at Bellomont indicate her intention to attract him and catch his interest in her as a partner. Her friend, the wealthy matriarch Judy Trenor, even tries to help Lily secure a permanent position in her social set, frequently inviting her along on weekend trips and other excursions, playing matchmaker, and monitoring what she wears—"Don't wear your scarlet *crêpe-de-chine* for dinner . . . !" (81). Lily heeds her friend's advice, for she wants to mark her place in the elite, and yet, conversely, she wants to assert her unique natural beauty and personal desire—both of which speak to her as an individual rather than part of a group. Lily's free-spirited nature ultimately pushes back against such a resignation to fate, and she sabotages her own attempts to secure Percy. Instead, she looks to stall having to marry for convenience, still hoping to strike a balance between personal freedom and social conformity. For Lily, delaying marriage means finding an alternative source of money, funding for her expensive wardrobe and social activities. She turns to her friend Judy's husband, Gus Trenor.

Lily's conversation with Gus in the Bellomont illuminates the financial strain of keeping up appearances in high society. Discovering Lily's dour mood, Trenor remarks, "Why on earth should you ever be out of spirits? Is your last box of Doucet dresses a failure, or did Judy rook you out of everything at bridge last night?" (118). The Doucet reference serves to exemplify the expense of remaining part of the Trenors' social set,[6] and Lily goes on to paint a woeful picture of her attempts to sell herself in marriage to men she does not love. Knowing that another of her friends, Carry Fisher, borrows money all the time from Gus, Lily believes she can manipulate Gus into giving her money out of charity simply by flattering him into the position of her savior. Gus offers to invest Lily's money and make her a fortune, a deal she knows is a sham. However, she underestimates his rapacious desire to "collect" on her debt.

Lily's bargain with Gus allows her to delay her need for a husband and to enjoy her social interactions, including her intimate friendship with

Selden. Nevertheless, her position remains tenuous, since she knows that her finances will eventually run out, and she will once again face the decision of whether to sell herself in a marriage of convenience or lose her social position. As a character who "only fits into one hole," as she claims in a conversation with Selden, Lily does not have the luxury of trying on alternate identities, and we see her struggle with her own limitations for personal expression throughout the novel.

The one instance in which Lily is allowed to perform herself, to don a costume that fully expresses her spirit while simultaneously allowing her to joyously showcase her beauty, is in the tableaux vivants scene. In this scene, Lily participates in a party where women dress up and pose to re-create famous works of art. Lily chooses Sir Joshua Reynolds's portrait of Mrs. Richard Bennett Lloyd (fig. 3), an image of a woman in nature wearing a loosely draped, ethereal gown. Wharton does not portray Lily's own thought process in selecting the painting and her clothing, but instead describes her appearance from Selden's point of view: "She had shown her artistic intelligence in selecting a type so like her own that she could embody the person represented without ceasing to be herself. . . . The impulse to show herself in a splendid setting . . . had yielded to the truer instinct of trusting to her unassisted beauty" (171). Wharton calls attention to the style of the dress, a draped look more reflective of the aesthetic style I discuss in the next section than of Victorian style. While Lily normally wears tailored, opulent, and restrictive clothing in keeping with the current fashion, here she wears simple, comfortable, draped clothing and unveils her inner spirit.[7]

This scene confirms that Lily's high society self is her performance, and her tableau vivant performance is in fact the real Lily—Lily as she would exist without the confines of her social role. Wharton offers glimpses of this authentic version of Lily earlier in the novel—for example, during her private conversation with Selden at Bellomont. The chief irony, of course, is that to achieve even the glimpses of personal expression and identity, Lily has to do so in the guise of a costume. By pretending to be someone else, Lily becomes more herself: daring, vibrant, passionate, and free-spirited. The tableau vivant marks the only instance in which clothing is both liberating and expressive for Lily.

While Lily's choice of clothing in this scene strikes some viewers, like Selden and Gerty Farish, as stunningly beautiful, it sparks judgment in others, and in Gus Trenor it engenders an angry possessiveness and an irra-

FIGURE 3. *Joanna Leigh/ Mrs. Richard Bennett Lloyd (b. 1758) Inscribing a Tree,* Sir Joshua Reynolds, 1775–76. Oil on canvas. (Private collection, image courtesy of Waddesdon Manor, The Rothschild Collection, Rothschild Family Trust)

tional belief that she has been borrowing from and sleeping with other men while denying him his claims to her. His response alarms Lily: she has underestimated his sense of entitlement, believing that as her friend's husband he would let her keep the money without any expectations. In this scene, Wharton links the fashionable clothes for which Lily has indebted herself to a larger gender commentary. Gus does not mind furnishing his wife's wardrobe, for she functions as a decorative and social accessory for his lifestyle—she is his possession. Similarly, he does not mind furnishing Lily's wardrobe and social activity—because he expects to possess her as a sexual object.

Lily's confrontation with Trenor during his attempted sexual assault initiates a series of desperate attempts to regain her slippery social footing and to repay Trenor. In her analysis of the novel as a naturalist work, Bonnie Lynn Gerard observes how "Trenor's attempted rape signals the relentlessness with which New York society will devour Lily Bart, as if in accordance with an implacable natural law that dictates the victimization of those who threaten the power of others" (414). Given the relentlessness of the social elite, Lily's attempts to maintain her social position become more desperate, her decline more dramatic. She tries to borrow from her aunt without success (prompting her offended aunt to leave much of her inheritance to Lily's cousin Grace Stepney); she then tries to reestablish her social position in the European social scene but is set up by Bertha Dorset, who claims Lily is having an affair with her husband. Lily then tries to live independently back in the United States while remaining part of a respectable social set, yet fails at this, too. She struggles to remain a part of the social elite with the aid of Carry Fisher and a newer crowd of socialites who embrace Lily, but her financial woes ultimately compel her to seek employment and, eventually, less respectable lodgings.

Lily's reduced circumstances force her to realize that the balance she hoped to strike between personal freedom and group conformity was never really possible. Her circle of friends had given her the illusion of such freedom. Lily's spiteful rival, the securely married Bertha Dorset, is free to act on her instincts, even having affairs with younger men and flirting openly with them, because her position is secured through a pragmatic marriage: "the mere thought of that other woman, who could take a man up and toss him aside as she willed, without having to regard him as a possible factor in her plans, filled Lily Bart with envy" (60). Perhaps one of the more interesting and unconventional characters, Carry Fisher exercises a fair amount of wit and social liberty; as a divorcée she is somewhat of an anomaly in high society, yet her connections secure her permanence within that group, and her current marital status enables her to borrow money from her friends' husbands. Selden's cousin Gerty Farish represents perhaps the only alternative life for someone of Lily's financial means and connections. She lives independently as a philanthropist, connected to New York society by her cousin, yet without real aspirations to entrench herself in this world. She attends some of the social functions yet never dresses the part. Despite Gerty's apparent happiness, Lily rejects her lifestyle as an alternative when she criticizes Gerty's clothing: as she notes "the 'useful' colour of Gerty Farish's gown and the subdued lines of her hat," she considers that "it is almost as stupid to let your clothes betray that you know you are ugly as to have them proclaim that you think you are beautiful" (125). Lily's judgment of Gerty's clothing as "useful" underlines the uselessness of her own clothes in contrast. Gerty as a character mirrors the usefulness of her clothing—at several moments throughout the novel Lily turns to Gerty for aid, for comfort, and even in grudging admiration. Yet despite the possible balance between conformity and self-expression that Gerty represents, Lily rejects this role, for she has not been bred for it. Late in the novel she confesses to Selden, "I have tried hard—but life is difficult, and I am a very useless person. I can hardly be said to have an independent existence. I was just a screw or a cog in the great machine I called life, and when I dropped out of it I found I was of no use anywhere else. What can one do when one finds that one only fits into one hole?" (348). With its strictly delineated markers of class, Lily's world runs with a machinelike consistency, and in her confession she realizes the futile choice before her, for she cannot enjoy her personal freedoms and belong to her desired social elite.

Once Lily has been shunned by her former social set, she gains a new vantage point on her former circle—the view of the outsider. Like the readers of *Vogue,* she now possesses only the fantasy of that beautiful world as she is forced to join the ranks of the working class at a milliner's shop. Initially, Lily is asked to be a model or "displayer of hats," but rather than display herself in this way, she prefers to learn the milliner's trade.[8] Whereas early in the novel Lily performs the role of a proper society woman to secure a wealthy husband, here she attempts to distance herself from the tragedy of her social decline by performing the role of a worker, by continuing to imagine her place in the workroom as temporary role-playing. Indeed, Lily cannot even imagine herself as one of the women workers, as evidenced by her observations of their physical appearances: "There were twenty of them in the work-room, their fagged profiles, under exaggerated hair, bowed in the harsh north light above the utensils of their art; for it was something more than an industry, surely, this creation of ever-varied settings for the face of fortunate womanhood" (321). Wharton acknowledges that the women work in a "fashionable millinery establishment, and were fairly well clothed and well paid," yet she characterizes them as "dull and colourless as the middle-aged" (321). Never one to reflect on her own physique as "dingy" or "colourless," Lily maintains her distance from the group—a distance deepened by her incompetence as a milliner and her having once belonged to the world "of fortunate womanhood," the very world for which she and her fellow workers now design and manufacture.

Lily is reminded of her liminal status, belonging to neither the world of fortunate womanhood nor the world of the working women, as she listens to the workers discuss Mrs. Trenor and Mrs. Dorset:

> It was the strangest part of Lily's strange experience, the hearing of these names, the seeing the fragmentary and distorted image of the world she had lived in reflected in the mirror of the working-girls' minds. She had never before suspected the mixture of insatiable curiosity and contemptuous freedom with which she and her kind were discussed in this underworld of toilers who lived on their vanity and self-indulgence. Every girl in Mme. Regina's work-room knew to whom the headgear in her hands was destined, and had her opinion of its future wearer, and a definite knowledge of the latter's place in the social system. (325)

Wharton notes that the women initially seem interested in Lily as a former member of this set, yet they quickly lose interest, being "awed only by success" in terms of "material achievement" (325). Lily is the only character who gains the double sight of both a member of and an exile from New York society, and this unique position allows her to see the lofty requirements of membership to this exclusive elite as well as its intense fascination for outsiders.

Incidentally, the workers' fascination with Lily's former set mirrors the *Vogue* audience's voracious interest in the gossip surrounding high society and its prominent members. From the magazine's inception to today, *Vogue* has catered to an audience easily dazzled by what a celebrity wore to a star-studded red carpet event, what bridesmaids wore for a royal wedding, how a billionaire playboy decorates his "bachelor pad," or how a young starlet formerly adored for her chaste persona has fallen into scandal. This last example, more reflective of tabloids than fashion magazines like *Vogue* or *Elle,* helps to establish the fleeting interest the women workers show Lily, likely out of schadenfreude. Her former glory and her disgrace make her interesting for only a moment. Once the conversation has passed, she becomes a social outcast, unworthy of even being discussed.

Lily cannot accept this fate, and her failure to adapt to her changed circumstances ultimately leads to her death. On the night before her death, Lily looks through her possessions, characterizing her "few handsome dresses" as "survivals of her last phase of splendour": "The remaining dresses, though they had lost their freshness, still kept the long unerring lines, the sweep and amplitude of the great artist's stroke, and as she spread them out on the bed the scenes in which they had been worn rose vividly before her. . . . She was startled to find how the atmosphere of her old life enveloped her" (356–57). Wharton imbues the dresses with a corporeal presence, as though they embody Lily's life before her scandal and contain her physical memories. Before she takes her fateful overdose of sleeping medicine, Lily gazes at the last dress in her trunk, "a heap of white drapery which fell shapelessly across her arm" (357)—her famous tableau vivant dress. The dress has the same ghostlike quality of the others in her trunk, only it calls forth a stream of her happiest memories—those involving her interactions with Selden at the tableaux vivants and the fountain at Bellomont. After putting the dresses away, Lily receives the long-awaited estate check from her late aunt, and she immediately writes a check for the full amount owed to Gus Trenor. Soon afterward, Lily takes her medicine, goes to bed, and dies in her sleep.

The dresses in this scene recall Lily's conversation with Selden at the beginning of the novel, particularly her assertion that her clothes are "the frame," the costume she dons to perform a role for their social circle. When Selden discovers Lily, her clothes are put away, and he is left alone to observe and read her as he had done when she was alive—only without the costumes. The final pages of the novel show his difficulty in understanding her even when the performance has disappeared—he lingers over her "only traces of luxury" and tries to ascertain what transpired between her and Gus Trenor by glancing through her checkbook. In her interpretation of this moment, Jessica Van Slooten asserts, "In the final scene between Lily and Selden, Wharton reveals that though they share a mysterious and quasi-romantic connection, he is not the man to fulfill her desires because he, too, judges and underestimates her. His late arrival and assessment of the final correspondence on her writing table attest to his inability to truly see the 'real' Lily Bart" (262). Selden's inability to read Lily may stem in part from his own prejudices—his unacknowledged susceptibility to gossip and social convention—but it also stems from Lily's inability to reveal herself. The tragedy of the scene is not merely the thwarted romance, or Selden's recognition of his poor timing, but what it exposes about old New York: high society demands a repression of individual expression and identity for the sake of embracing an acceptable public persona, and such a performance makes real intimacy between a man and a woman (or even between two women) impossible. The dresses, for Selden, show that contrast between Lily's self-exposure at the tableaux vivants and the persona she donned for public life. Just as the expensive gowns drained her resources, the public performance they represent has drained Lily of her vitality.

Lily's erratic behavior in *The House of Mirth* illuminates the appeal and limitations of New York's late nineteenth-century aristocratic society. Its appeal lies in its exquisite beauty (represented in the spectacle of the tableaux vivants, the Van Osburgh wedding jewels, the natural landscape of Bellomont, and the stunning designer gowns of Lily's friends), its aesthetic and epicurean luxuries (attending the opera, touring Europe, summering at Newport), and its promise of security in the form of a wealthy husband and steady income. Its downfall lies in the limitations placed on one's personal freedoms: the freedom to follow one's vocational interests, romantic interests, and personal interests, as well as the freedom for individual expression. The desires of the individual spirit counterbalance the pressures imposed by social convention, and because Lily can commit to neither, she cannot survive in this setting.

The Age of Innocence

In her letters, autobiography, and novels, Edith Wharton voices her fascination with the social conditioning that forces women to perform a public self for the sake of family, friends, and even society journalism. In her autobiography *A Backward Glance,* she describes her nostalgia for the beauty of old New York and her social education: she understood that to take part in this beauty, she had to manage her public identity by practicing a perfection of speech and "good breeding" (52) and by adhering to social mores.

The beauty of this world is captured by Wharton in a childhood memory of elegant women practicing archery, which she narrates in *A Backward Glance:*

> [A] pretty sight the meeting was, with parents and elders seated in a semicircle on the turf behind the lovely archeresses in floating silks or muslins, with their wide leghorn hats, and heavy veils flung back only at the moment of aiming. These veils are associated with all the summer festivities of my childhood. In that simple society there was an almost pagan worship of physical

beauty, and the first question asked about any youthful newcomer on the social scene was invariably: "Is she pretty?" or: "Is he handsome?" (46)

In this memory, Wharton focuses on the image of veils, items referenced repeatedly in both *The Age of Innocence* and her later collection *Old New York.* The veils add to the ethereal beauty of the scene, and they add a connotation of concealment—what a woman must keep hidden from public view. Wharton articulates the way women seemingly engaging in sport and activity were actually participating in a socially sanctioned public display that includes their donning of contemporary fashions. She continues: "Those archery meetings greatly heightened my infantile desire to 'tell a story,' and the young gods and goddesses I used to watch strolling across the Edgerston lawn were the prototypes of my first novels" (47). Wharton returns to this moment in her childhood to delve into the beautiful display, peek under the veils, understand what lies beneath the surfaces of the "gods and goddesses" in the pretty picture.[9]

This characterization of New York as "heaven" and its society members as "gods and goddesses" governs the narrative of *The Age of Innocence,* as does the archery motif. The motif functions symbolically in two ways. First, this activity so closely associated with Wharton's youth connotes the gorgeous landscape of Victorian New York and Newport, the old New York of Wharton's privileged childhood, showcasing its inhabitants with a grace and elegance nearing aesthetic perfection. Second, the motif establishes the concept of aiming and trying to hit one's target, or goal in life. Either one aims for a secure, respectable position entrenched in the old New York social world, or one aims for something loftier, the more abstract goals of bliss, love, or the sublime. These loftier ideals are constrained within the confines of Victorian New York. The most successful Wharton archers, therefore, are those who aim for convention and security. They have the advantage of being surrounded by a host of other individuals wishing to preserve the same illusions in the interest of upholding a longstanding social order. The novel's protagonist, the symbolically named Newland Archer, successfully finds the wife, connections, and profession to secure his social position, but he falls short of his target when he decides to aim for something more fulfilling.

The veils of the archers are merely one of many articles of clothing that convey the need for women to hide and restrain any trait that marks them as different. The clothing of the female characters signals to the reader their ability to navigate the social norms of their world. In *The House of Mirth,* clothing and fashion are employed as a way of revealing economic barriers (high fashion is too expensive for Lily) and barriers of decency (Lily cannot wear her daring red dress, and she can only show off her figure as part of a tableau vivant). In *The Age of Innocence,* Wharton dwells less on the economic barriers of high fashion and more on these barriers of decency—especially as they concern individual expression, sexuality, and mobility.

It is Newland's wife, May, who in her tightly laced corsets and luxurious fabrics recalls the image of goddesses from Wharton's youth and therefore best represents the old New York that arouses Wharton's nostalgia. After their extended honeymoon, Newland and May attend an August meeting of the Newport Archery Club at Julius Beaufort's summer estate. Wharton offers some historical context: "The sport, which had hitherto known no rival but croquet, was beginning to be discarded in favour of lawn-tennis; but the latter game was still considered too rough and inelegant for social occasions, and as an opportunity to show off pretty dresses and graceful attitudes the bow and arrow held their own" (205). Late nineteenth-century periodicals corroborate Wharton's assessment of archery's popularity, and one *Vogue* editorial explains, "It is a beautiful, graceful and healthful sport, and one which shows off to great advantage pretty gowns and handsome wrists and arms" ("Features: Adopted Golf" 270). By participating in sport, May in no way threatens her conventional persona; rather, archery was an acceptable arena for her to showcase her new wardrobe, her poise, and her aim. Unlike Newland and Ellen, May maintains a steady course throughout the novel, always hitting her target and always sustaining the flawless visage of her public self. Her participation in this ritual helps to portray the aesthetic appeal of old New York society and her comfort within that landscape, among a bevy of like-minded women in "pale muslins and flower-wreathed hats mingled in a tender rainbow" (211).

Wharton wrote *The Age of Innocence* nearly fifteen years after the publication of *The House of Mirth,* this time writing with the gift of hindsight. She paints a picture of 1870s Victorian New York society, with its dress, its tastes, and its strict modes of behavior. Newland Archer, recently engaged to the kind, beautiful, and obedient May Welland, finds himself transfixed by May's mysterious cousin: the Countess Ellen Olenska. For much of the novel, Newland is torn between a sense of loyalty to his fiancée/wife and his love for the free-spirited Ellen. Ellen expresses her individual spirit through her selection of clothing, believing that her confidence and the protective love of her family will afford her the freedom to be herself. Having had a taste of the conventional path, Ellen pursues the sublime, cultivating a bohemian identity while trying to maintain her place among family and friends.

As the wife of a European baron and a titled member of a more longstanding aristocracy, Ellen dresses in a modern and unconventional style that distinguishes her from her New York friends and family, but not in the way she intends. They read her clothing as risqué, the costume of a mistress—which, to some extent, is the role she comes to embody. Ellen uses her clothing to project what she perceives as her authentic self. Unfortunately, throughout the novel she must struggle against those whose entire lives are performances: according to their dogma, individuals must play their proper roles or be cast out.

The novel begins at the opera, the setting for the opening of the winter social season in New York City during the 1870s and 1880s (Montgomery 19–20). When Ellen Olenska is first introduced, Wharton describes her as "a slim young woman, a little less tall than May Welland, with brown hair growing in close curls about her temples and held in place by a narrow band of diamonds. The suggestion of this headdress, which gave her what was then called a 'Josephine look,' was carried out in the cut of the dark blue velvet gown rather theatrically caught up under her bosom by a girdle with a large old-fashioned clasp" (9). Rumors of an affair with her husband's secretary circulate about the Countess Olenska, yet her daring ensemble draws just as much attention as her reputation because of the way it defies convention. Ellen exposes her décolletage and even seems to showcase it by wearing a clasp "theatrically caught up under her bosom." She is contrasted with May, whose cleavage is covered by "a modest tulle tucker fastened with a single gardenia" (6). The contrast between these two women's exposure immediately configures May as modest and proper, and Ellen as sexually available.[10] Ellen thereby fans the flames of gossip, unknowingly giving credence to rumors of her questionable past.

Ellen's dress in this opening scene is significant not only for its sexual implications (i.e., how her observers *read* it) but also for what Ellen likely intends to project: the persona of a bohemian and a European, and the independent spirit of a woman recently liberated from an oppressive husband. This disconnect between the intention of a look and its interpretation mirrors Ellen's conflicts throughout the novel (e.g., her arrangements with the baron's secretary to leave her husband, or her attempt to file for divorce). In her book *Edith Wharton and the Making of Fashion,* Katherine Joslin articulates this pattern of clothing being misinterpreted: "At first blush, it would seem that Ellen wears décolleté to lure the men around her; she is, after all, a woman who has left her husband and may be in the market for another man. . . . At the same time, the would-be heroine seems oblivious. She does not consciously expose her body, and it is precisely that confusion over fashion that moves the action of the novel" (120). While clothing may not govern all the novel's plots, in this scene at least, it sparks a collective attempt to govern Ellen's character. The tension generated by this moment initiates the conflicts among the novel's central characters.

In addition to implying Ellen's sexual availability, her clothing is also misread as old-fashioned. However, Joslin suggests that the clothing is contemporary and even fashion forward. She notes how Ellen's clothes echo the aesthetic style promoted by dress reformers, who "advocated various styles that brought the unstructured comfort of a nightgown or wrapper, even the soft textures of lingerie, into public spaces. . . . Aesthetic dresses were made in soft, flowing fabrics and in unconventional colors such as reds and ambers and blues" (123). Though these dresses still required restrictive boning (yet they did not have the appearance of being corseted), they flowed more naturally over women's curves, were made from more comfortable fabrics, and took color and structural inspiration from nature. Given that Wharton wrote the novel nearly fifty years after its temporal setting, her knowledge of later fashion trends allowed her to characterize Ellen as forward thinking and modern. As Joslin notes, Newland's sister "describes Ellen's blue velvet opera dress as a tea gown, a style that was only beginning to be respectable in public fashion in the 1870s" (125). Figure 4 shows an example of a Liberty & Company tea gown, a gown inspired by the aesthetic dress style in its soft draping on the bodice and flowing fabrics. These styles first gained popularity in Paris during the 1870s (around the time of the novel's setting), and they became the signature look of Liberty & Company, first founded in London by Arthur Lasenby Liberty in 1875 (134).[11] Joslin argues that Ellen's dress "signals a desire for freedom. . . . Ellen makes the argument that fashion ought to be a matter of individual taste and desire: exactly the point of Liberty's advertising message" (136). Though Ellen may not, as Joslin suggests, be making a statement about how fashion should function, she does show how it functions for her—as a natural extension of herself.

FIGURE 4. Liberty & Co. tea gown, ca. 1885. (Brooklyn Museum Costume Collection at the Metropolitan Museum of Art; gift of the Brooklyn Museum, 2009, 2009.300.3384; image courtesy of Art Resource, NY)

The difference between Ellen and Lily Bart, in terms of how they use clothing, is that Lily draws from the performative function of clothes to blend into her elite circle, whereas Ellen draws from this function not to blend in but to make a profound statement about the woman she wishes to be. Ellen's style of dress more closely reflects the performative function of democratic fashion—that is, she uses the clothes to embody an identity that she chooses. Wharton indicates that Ellen's bohemian nature has been cultivated since childhood, rooted in her character and encouraged by her education:

> She was a fearless and familiar little thing, who asked disconcerting questions, made precocious comments, and possessed outlandish arts, such as

> dancing a Spanish shawl dance and singing Neapolitan love-songs to a guitar. Under the direction of her aunt . . . the little girl received an expensive but incoherent education, which included "drawing from the model," a thing never dreamed of before, and playing the piano in quintets with professional musicians. (59)

Returning to New York, away from the watchful eyes of her husband, Ellen initially feels free to further entertain these interests and values. She frequents the home of the controversial Mrs. Lemuel Struthers, who throws Sunday night parties with "smoking and champagne" (86), and she even transforms her home into a staging area for this new self.

Ellen's home mirrors her fashion and her personality, as Newland quickly detects: like her clothing, Ellen's home is the public projection of her persona. When he first enters her house, he detects a change in mood, something both inviting and exciting: "The atmosphere of the room was so different from any he had ever breathed that self-consciousness vanished in the sense of adventure" (70). Wharton continues Newland's reverie by offering details of the room's décor: "He had been before in drawing-rooms hung with red damask, with pictures 'of the Italian school'; what struck him was the way in which Medora Manson's shabby hired house . . . had, by a turn of the hand, and the skillful use of a few properties, been transformed into something intimate, 'foreign,' subtly suggestive of old romantic scenes and sentiments" (70). As a careful studier of home décor, Wharton outlined her preference for intimacy and natural lighting in her first published work, *The Decoration of Houses* (1897), coauthored with the architect Ogden Codman. She laments the Victorian dissonance between architecture and décor (xix–xx), and, as Montgomery notes, the authors "argue for a consistency between interiors and façades" that emulates "a consistency between the inner and outer self" (*Displaying Women* 67). The harmonious interior of Ellen's home is intimate and romantic: later in the novel, Newland finds himself longing for her drawing room the way he longs for Ellen. He is able to read Ellen in the arrangement of her belongings and her choice of furnishings.[12]

Ellen fails to see, however, that her carefully nurtured, bohemian persona will be read by her new circle as defiance, as spitting in the face of those loved ones resolved to help her reestablish herself as part of New York society. Each time she makes a move, whether through action or symbolically through her clothing, her move is checked by family members and friends, her identity suppressed. As she detects this pattern she laments to Newland, "Is there nowhere in an American house where one may be by one's self? You're so shy, and yet you're so public. I always feel as if I were in the convent again—or on the stage, before a dreadfully polite audience that never applauds" (132). She realizes she must play a role selected by her family, and the role has little to do with her personality.

In the novel's opening scene, Ellen is contrasted with Newland's betrothed, May Welland, to establish a counterpoint for female dress and behavior. If Ellen represents the woman of the future, the liberated bohemian who aims for more than convention, May is a paragon of convention. She is beautiful and kind, but in a way that is perfectly consistent with social mores. Wharton amplifies the contrast between May's conventionality and Ellen's free-spiritedness through their selection of clothing, which the reader observes through Newland, a careful interpreter of dress. When May is first introduced, she is described as "a young girl in white"; he watches as a "warm pink mounted to the girl's cheek . . . and suffused the young slope of her breast to the line where it met a modest tulle tucker fastened with a single gardenia" (5–6). Descriptions of May's clothing often feature words like "modest," "starched," or "tightly laced," an indication that she chooses clothing consistent with the conventions of the 1870s, Victorian-influenced fashion typical of New York's old society. After her wedding she visits Paris to select an elegant, appropriate wardrobe from the Parisian couturiers, including Charles Frederick Worth, who makes over her wedding gown (194). Worth's work was known for its luxurious materials, elaborate workmanship, and impeccable tailoring. Though he would later create gowns similar to Ellen's Empire style (Joslin, *Making of Fashion* 134), during the 1870s his dresses epitomized the Victorian mode, with its tailoring, heavy material, and expensive trimming, as in his 1872 silk ball gown pictured in figure 5. When compared with the style of figure 4, Worth's gown feels more elaborate and tailored, more structured, and it has a less natural silhouette. The silks and embellishments, as well as the bustling, make the garment seem heavy, whereas the draping and simplicity of figure 4 make it appear lighter and less cumbersome.

Newland's observation of May and Ellen at the opera awakens a deep conflict within him. Ellen's choice of clothes may represent her experimentation with a new, independent identity, but her clothing and demeanor have the added impact of injecting Newland with awareness—awareness that he, and everyone around him, is part of a grand performance, and that none of

FIGURE 5. Charles Frederick Worth, silk ball gown, ca. 1872. (Metropolitan Museum of Art, gift of Mrs. Philip K. Rhinelander, 1946, 46.25.1a–d; image courtesy of Art Resource, NY)

the performers are free, or real. At this moment, however, Newland does not yet grasp the magnitude of his new perspective. Instead, he focuses his awareness on his betrothed: "With a new sense of awe he looked at the frank forehead, serious eyes and gay innocent mouth of the young creature whose soul's custodian he was to be. The terrifying product of the social system he belonged to and believed in, the young girl who knew nothing and expected everything, looked back at him like a stranger through May Welland's familiar features" (42–43). When Newland insists to his friends that "[w]omen should be free—as free as we are," he fails to comprehend that a woman like May would never willingly "claim the kind of freedom he meant" (43). As he reflects on the difference between May and Ellen, he finally reaches this realization.

Newland's early interactions with Ellen show the disparity between the world of convention and the world of individual expression. Initially, he seeks to aid in a collective effort to legitimize Ellen and curb her odd habits. Ellen believes that she has escaped the oppression of her life with her husband, that she has returned to New York and the protection of her family. Yet she does not comprehend the way this world operates, how her family and friends have already endeavored to soften scandal, refute unpleasant rumors (though never directly), and establish Ellen's respectability lest she reflect ill on any of them. We see this behavior in Newland's decision to announce their engagement early as a distraction from Ellen's unexpected presence; in Newland's successful effort to convince his very wealthy and influential cousins, the Van der Luydens, to invite Ellen for dinner; and in Ellen's family's choice to seat her in their opera box at the beginning of the winter season right next to their daughter May. Newland takes an additional step when, urged on by his employer and his own interest in avoiding scandal, he discourages Ellen from suing for a divorce.

It is at this moment, when Newland persuades Ellen, that she comprehends her new social environment—and at the same moment, Newland begins to develop deep feelings for her. Until now Ellen has remained immune to the pressures of convention, feeling that her family's love liberated her to be herself in public. Newland forces her to see the social acrobatics to which her unconventional behavior has driven them. Ellen looks at Newland and asks, "But my freedom—is that nothing?" (110). As Newland aspires to become freer, more like Ellen, Ellen begins to perceive the futility of her self-assertion, for she does not want to hurt her family (least of all her cousin May), she knows she cannot return to her husband, and she needs to have enough money to provide for herself and her aunt, Medora Manson. At this moment she proclaims her desire "to become just like everybody else here" (107), and Newland listens with a tinge of regret, and with a sense of empathy.

The shift in Ellen's attitude is echoed in her clothing. We never again see her appear among friends in risqué or bohemian dress; in fact, when Ellen next appears, she garners surprised admiration from Newland's gossipy sister and conservative mother: "'She had on a black velvet polonaise with jet buttons, and a tiny green monkey muff; I never saw her so stylishly dressed,' Janey continued" (151). Though Ellen still wears her signature velvet and fur, she does so in a more restrained fashion—newspapers and magazines from the time show that her ensemble would have been considered extremely stylish and respectable both in Paris and New York.[13] When Newland last sees her at the dinner hosted at his home, Ellen's arms are uncovered—only this time, her bare skin conveys vulnerability rather than sexual daring. Newland notes her paleness and senses a change in her demeanor: "she had wound several rows of amber beads about her neck. . . . The amber beads were trying to her complexion, or her dress was perhaps unbecoming: her face looked lusterless and almost ugly, and he had never loved it as he did at that minute" (333). Though Ellen no longer wears her colorful, daring clothes, so pleasing to Newland in past moments, he reads her choice in this scene as self-sacrificial—a choice that goes so completely against her character yet is necessary to preserving Newland's reputation and her family's contentment. Her clothing, though unflattering in Newland's eyes, is protective—she wears it to shield, not herself, but Newland and May from the peril of scandal.

During Newland's honeymoon with May, he comes to an understanding about the role of fashion among women of his social circle: "'It's their armour,' he thought, 'their defence against the unknown, and their defiance of it.' And he understood for the first time the earnestness with which May, who was incapable of tying a ribbon in her hair to charm him, had gone through the solemn rite of selecting and ordering her extensive wardrobe" (198). His statement speaks to the security of wearing the appropriate ensemble, of knowing one is properly dressed for the occasion and will not incur society's judgment. Victorian fashion displays the wealth and taste of its wearer but masks the persona. An especially beautiful piece is more of a testament to the skill of the designer and the social class of its wearer than to any individual's dreams or desires. The clothes, Wharton suggests, are a costume, protecting a woman from scandal and making her public persona more convincing.

In *The Age of Innocence,* Ellen is a pioneer of democratic fashion, for her clothes express her personal style and allow her greater ease of movement. Wharton shows how such bold tastes are suppressed and even punished by respectable society. Just as Victorian fashion connoted expense, heaviness, binding, and impracticality, so did the social atmosphere of the American aristocracy during the late nineteenth century. Fashion in this era was confined to a small, wealthy elite: the masses had access to clothing, and their looks could be favorably described as neat or clean, but not stylish or fashionable.

Additionally, the fashion of this period exemplifies how the fashion industry strove to preserve distinct class lines and to segregate an aristocratic, old money set from the masses, for the Victorian style signified that its wearers did not require much movement or any labor; the costly embellishment, material, and tailoring ensured that only the very wealthy could purchase it; and the emphasis on corsetry, binding, and coverage ensured the protected chasteness of its wearers.[14]

Twenty-six years after parting with Ellen, Newland confronts a more progressive time, represented both in his son's more lax attitude toward his father's feelings for another woman and his daughter's less restrictive wardrobe. Newland observes how "Mary Chivers's mighty feats of athleticism could not have been performed with the twenty-inch waist that May Archer's azure sash so easily spanned. And the difference seemed symbolic; the mother's life had been as closely girt as her figure" (348–49). Mary's body type sounds reminiscent of the Gibson Girl ideal popularized during the 1890s, and her clothes imply an increased ease of motion. Perhaps Newland's daughter would also enjoy an increased freedom of expression in personal style, and in her life choices.

Both *The House of Mirth* and *The Age of Innocence* conclude with a sense of loss, of dreams unfulfilled. Yet while the ending of *The House of Mirth* is tragic, *The Age of Innocence* is more hopeful, hinting at greater liberties to come. We see this promise in the contrast between May's portrait and her daughter's, in the acceptance of Fanny Beaufort by Newland's family despite her father's unsavory reputation, and in his son's freedom to pursue a woman he loves and a profession that allows him a sense of creativity. Wharton also alludes to important technological developments, including the telephone, which would eventually eradicate the time-consuming ritual of "calling" so central to Victorian society (Montgomery 29). Reflecting on the new generation, Newland muses, "The difference is that these young people take it for granted that they're going to get whatever they want, and that we almost always took it for granted that we shouldn't" (353).

Fashion would adapt to these rapidly changing times. The turn of the century, when *The Age of Innocence* ends, was not an era of open choice and personal style, but it was one in which the American fashion industry was beginning to move in that direction. The development of the garment industry in New York, the continued influence of dress reformers, the rise of ready-made clothing, and the assertion of new standards of beauty all contributed to a shift toward fashion slightly more consistent with American promises of democracy and individualism. The popularity of the Gibson Girl, an illustrated figure created by Charles Dana Gibson that began appearing in popular magazines during the 1890s, marked a change in a beauty ideal from a more demure, stationary, and delicate woman to a bolder, more athletic, and "defiant" prototype (Hill 23).[15] The emergence of the Gibson Girl also "heralded a new approach to clothing and fashion," for her simple shirtwaist and skirt ensembles "could be reproduced simply and cheaply" (Craik 74). According to Daniel Delis Hill, the invention of the safety bicycle also dramatically changed women's fashion (22). The invention further increased the public mobility for women referenced earlier by Montgomery,[16] but it also created the need for greater utility in fashion. Many women switched to shorter, less restrictive corsets, while some stopped wearing corsets altogether. Designers began shortening hemlines, and this era saw the rising popularity of the rainy daisy skirt that fell three inches above the ground (Hill 22).

Perhaps the most significant stylistic change of this period was the rising popularity of the shirtwaist: a mass-produced, blouse-like piece of clothing (often associated with the Gibson Girl) that came in a range of styles, fabrics, and prices. More important than the accessibility and popularity of the shirtwaist, however, was its status as a separate.[17] Now women could wear the same shirtwaist with different skirts, jackets, hats, and neckties. The same number of pieces of clothing could create different *outfits,* which made fashion more economical but also more individualized.

Granted, shirtwaists could be costly when they were tailor-made with luxurious materials and costly trimmings. The change from the Victorian corset to the Edwardian S-bend corset was nothing to celebrate, and the Edwardian era of fashion (1900–1909) proved one of the most expensive, opulent periods in American history. Nevertheless, Edwardian fashion had to compete with a continually rising public appreciation for ready-made garments, a shift that threatened to seize fashion from its exclusive elite and deliver it to a mass American populace. As I show in the next chapter, this steady move toward the democratization of fashion would only accelerate with the rise of the American department store.

two

The Social Climber in the Era of Ready-Mades

The riot of prosperity introduced the fashion of respectable women covering their faces with powder and paint in a way that had hitherto been peculiar to women of the streets, so I pictured civilization as a harlot with cheeks, lips, and eyelashes of artificial beauty. I imagined mountains of powder and paint, a deafening chorus of affected laughter, a huge heart, as large as a city, full of falsehood and mischief.
—Abraham Cahan, *The Rise of David Levinsky*

Carrie passed along the busy aisles, much affected by the remarkable displays of trinkets, dress goods, stationery, and jewelry. Each separate counter was a showplace of dazzling interest and attraction. She could not help feeling the claim of each trinket and valuable upon her personally, and yet she did not stop.
—Theodore Dreiser, *Sister Carrie*

In the opening passage of Abraham Cahan's *The Rise of David Levinsky* (1920), his protagonist laments, "My present station, power, the amount of worldly happiness at my command, and the rest of it, seem to be devoid of significance" (3). In a similar passage, at the end of Theodore Dreiser's

1900 novel *Sister Carrie,* the omniscient narrator addresses the title character: "In your rocking chair, by your window dreaming, shall you long, alone. In your rocking chair, by your window, shall you dream such happiness as you may never feel" (487). Both characters have risen from humble beginnings to achieve fame, career success, and excessive wealth. Both characters have arrived at their success through their ability to read and manipulate appearances, to speak the language of fashion and style. Yet both characters, as these passages indicate, find themselves restless and unhappy: not because they cannot have something they want, but because they do not know what else to want.

These two naturalist novels depict protagonists who rise from abject poverty and dependence to a life of resplendent luxury. Both novels situate their narratives during a time of rapid industrialization, when fashion no longer belonged only to a privileged few but fell into the realm of the middle and working classes, thereby mapping the launch of ready-made fashion and mass consumption. The characters navigate their landscapes of consumption with awe and naïveté, easily transformed by the influences of conspicuous consumption, fashion advertising, and the spectacles of shopwindows and department stores.

Ready-made fashion, ready-to-wear, clothing catalogs, department stores—all of these things seemed to hail a new dawn of democratic fashion, promising to collapse physical barriers of class by making fashionable clothing accessible to all Americans. In some ways, the American fashion industry began to deliver on that promise. Before the Industrial Revolution, any item of clothing represented high cost and extensive labor—in fact, most members of the working class owned only one full suit of clothing (Crane 3). The many items we take for granted now that make fashion production easier—the sewing machine and paper patterns, for example—did not enter the American marketplace until the mid- to late 1800s (Daves 22–25), and fashion magazines and clothing catalogs did not have much relevance to the masses before people were buying ready-to-wear. By mass-producing fashion, the United State seized multiple opportunities: a surge of new profitable markets and industries, an enormous immigrant labor force, a cost-effective system of contract labor within the garment industry, and a surge in various forms of print media (clothing catalogs, fashion magazines, women's journals) that connected the clothing produced in urban centers with individuals of various classes and from different regions.

In the late nineteenth century, the American fashion industry was a commercial mechanism that derived many design aesthetics from Europe; until around 1909, American designers mainly "copied" French designers rather than pioneering their own visions (Hill 17). Even then, few American designers were household names. This phenomenon did not change remarkably until the Depression, when the cost of imports forced more Americans to turn to local designers.[1] Production costs, labor shortage, lack of technology, limited access to Parisian high fashion—all these factors kept American fashion confined to a small circle of privilege and wealth.

During the last decades of the nineteenth century, many changes would alter the face of American fashion. In *Cultures of Opposition: Jewish Immigrant Workers, New York City, 1881–1905,* Hadassa Kosak explains how the invention of the sewing machine and various other technological advancements in garment construction "ushered in a new era of mass production and subdivided tasks, which facilitated the absorption of unskilled immigrants, and led to falling wages and increased hours" (64). Kosak notes that this mass production made garments like "cloaks and, later, shirtwaists, suits, skirts, kimonos, and dresses" available to the masses, adding that "within the ready-to-wear women's garment industry, cloak manufacture expanded more rapidly than any other branch" (64). Indeed, the cloak manufacturing industry becomes the vehicle for David Levinsky's assimilation and success in the United States, as he arrives in his new home at the opportune moment. Early in the novel, David remarks of this turn-of-the-century period, "When I learned the trade a cloak made of the cheapest satinette cost eighteen dollars. To-day nobody would wear it. One can now buy a whole suit made of all-wool material and silk-lined for fifteen dollars" (443). That this three-dollar difference would equate to sixty to seventy dollars today shows the impact that mass production and an influx of cheap labor had on American fashion and its accessibility between the 1880s and the early 1900s. One Carson Pirie Scott & Co. advertisement from 1899 boasts prices for quality cloaks as low as $6.50 (about $182 today). Manufacturers also provided a range of prices, styles, and qualities: lower-income women could participate in the fashion trend, while wealthier women could purchase the more luxurious styles and materials (the advertisement also lists cloaks at $150 and up—equivalent to over $4,200 in today's market).

During the late Victorian era, the United States saw the earliest department stores and mail-order houses, as well as the development of the garment industry. Cheaper materials were available thanks to the production of synthetics: by the late 1800s manufacturers relied on machine-made lace, and by the early 1900s textile manufacturers could cheaply replicate silk, velvet, and fur (Ewen and Ewen 117). Historians differ on which garments were mass-produced first. Some claim that ready-made fashions originated with cloak manufacturing. For example, Elizabeth and Stuart Ewen write, "It began with cloaks, modeled after those worn by European women of rank, emanating from factories and sweatshops in New York and Chicago." This trend, they add, was followed by mass-produced undergarments, then hats and dresses (131–32). The simplicity of cloak patterns (along with the fact that, unlike other garments, they did not require an exact fit) explains the garment's early mass production. However, other scholars claim that women's mass-produced fashion began first with the shirtwaist. The fashion historian Jessica Daves explains the origins of the "shirtwaist epidemic," observing that the popularity of "tailor-made suits" in the 1880s necessitated the purchase of blouses that could be paired with the suits' skirts and jackets: "From this fashion for the tailor-made suit came the need for the shirtwaist; then, worn with a separate skirt, without benefit of a jacket, it became almost the national feminine uniform" (29). By the early 1890s, shirtwaists were sold at Lord & Taylor for prices ranging from fifty cents to three dollars (Daves 30), a range equating to fifteen to eighty dollars in contemporary prices. Wealthy women could afford to purchase superior merchandise (better textiles, better and more exact fit, more expensive embellishments), but middle- and working-class women could participate in the fashion as well, albeit with less expensive, less individualized versions of the same pieces.[2]

In the previous chapter, I discussed characters in Edith Wharton novels who navigate within the upper echelons of New York society and set high standards for American fashion. In contrast, Cahan and Dreiser portray multiple class relationships to clothing: those working in the garment industry who cannot afford to buy the clothing they make; those members of a growing middle class who design, manufacture, or sell clothing; and those who have made money and can afford to buy and display the latest fashions. For Wharton, fashionable clothing belongs to a relatively fixed social elite; for Cahan and Dreiser, fashionable clothing is the trophy for individuals who have "made it," whether by scrupulous or questionable means. The American Dream ceases to mean simply freedom. It becomes instead the freedom to buy . . . or in the case of Carrie, amid her "dazzling" array of attractive options, the freedom to shop.

If American fashion parallels the American Dream at any moment in the twentieth century, then it comes as no surprise that the fashion industry would evolve to accommodate a heightened emphasis on consumerism in the United States. According to William Leach, author of *Land of Desire: Merchants, Power, and the Rise of a New American Culture* (1993), "From the 1890s on, American corporate business, in league with key institutions, began the transformation of American society into a society preoccupied with consumption, with comfort and bodily well-being, with luxury, spending, and acquisition, with more goods this year than last, more next year than this" (xiii). Leach marks this moment at the climax of the industrial era as a defining one in America's shifting ideology. As small, family-owned retail establishments gave way to huge department stores, as cities grew and more families became fragmented by urban migration and factory work, and as advertising and displays of goods increasingly connected American citizens with potential purchases, the ultimate goal of the average American citizen shifted. The very concept of the American Dream changed. This dream, loosely defined by the Declaration of Independence as "life, liberty, and the pursuit of happiness," ceased to represent merely the Protestant ideals of family, work, utilitarianism, and faith, and morphed into a more individualistic and materialistic ideal. The hallmarks of this "new dream," according to Leach, are "acquisition and consumption as the means of achieving happiness, the cult of the new; the democratization of desire; and monetary value as the predominant measure of all value in society" (3). This atmosphere of consumption delegitimized more spiritual and community-oriented ideals and promoted a "highly individualistic conception of democracy [that] emphasized self-pleasure and self-fulfillment" (Leach 6). In her widely regarded reading of *Sister Carrie* and consumerism, Blanche Gelfant draws a similar conclusion, likening Carrie's endless consumption to Abraham Maslow's hierarchy of needs, explaining that Maslow observed that women who have it all soon begin "asking for more. . . . After a period of happiness, excitement, and fulfillment comes the inevitable taking it all for granted, and becoming restless and discontented again for More!" (179). Certainly both David Levinsky and Carrie Meeber epitomize the American investment in the new dream as well as Maslow's hierarchy of needs; however, they implicitly challenge this new dream of materialist desire and fulfillment, for while both achieve it, neither finds happiness as a result.

David and Carrie exemplify the movement of outsiders (immigrants, migrants from rural areas, or people of color migrating from the South) into a U.S. city for economic opportunity and upward mobility, as well as more abstract ideals of personal freedom. Both Cahan and Dreiser juxtapose this mobility with a changing cityscape—a cityscape that hailed the earliest department stores, or "massive, imposing structures of consumption" (Ewen and Ewen 44). Ewen and Ewen suggest these stores carry a heavy symbolism: "The department store was more than a site for consumption, it was a *sight* of consumption; goods were graced in monumental splendor. . . . In the department store, industrial retailing created a place where the ideologies of progress and magic encountered the manifold needs of everyday life. From their beginnings, department stores were publicized as 'cathedrals' and 'palaces'" (45). Figure 6 features a nineteenth-century Tilly & Smeeton engraving of the new Grande Galerie Centrale department store in Paris. The high ceilings, grand staircases, stained glass ceilings, and elaborate draperies and wall sconces are typical of early department stores in both the United States and Europe, and contribute to the sense of awe and luxury these spaces often inspired.

Given these palatial interiors, it is perhaps no surprise that the clothing of this period tended to boast excessive detail and ornamentation. Ewen and Ewen draw a parallel between the evolution of department store design and the "ornamental" fashions of the late Victorian era. They explain that although the ready-to-wear industry made fashion accessible to more Americans, it maintained its class symbolism; fashionable clothing remained "an emblem of achievement" (143). The department store, they argue, "created an architectural environment that was palatial, a mimicry of space and style that was, by custom, a prerogative of opulence." This description of department stores echoes the imagery of the epigraph to this chapter, a vision of Carrie passing through "a showplace of dazzling interest" (21) and gazing at all the accessories she cannot afford. This passage conveys the hypnotic spectacle of the display, the association of purchasable goods with royalty and spirituality that Ewen and Ewen describe. Desire for these material things helped to shape and perpetuate a consumerist mentality. Americans who could afford such luxuries became addicted to buying and excess, to shopping as a leisure activity; Americans who could not afford them either went into debt or came to view shopping as an incentive for hard work. Material goods, and fashionable clothing in particular, became an end unto themselves.

In both *The Rise of David Levinsky* and *Sister Carrie,* the protagonists are

FIGURE 6. Tilly & Smeeton, engraving of Grande Galerie Centrale department store in Paris, nineteenth century. (Image courtesy of Art Resource, NY)

driven by just such a desire for *things* and what the characters believe these things will confer. Fashionable clothing initially inspires a sense of wonder (as characters are bewitched by displays of consumer goods) yet later confers a sense of achievement. In *From the Ghetto: The Fiction of Abraham Cahan* (1977), Jules Chametzky points to a similarity between Cahan's and Dreiser's narratives, for both embody the "archetypal rags-to-riches story." However, he distinguishes between the narratives by spotlighting David's moral struggle, how his early religious studies and sense of community make him constantly question "the individualistic American version of success" (141–42). I suggest that the macronarrative is the same in these novels: David and Carrie initially want something very basic (for David, freedom and food; for Carrie, an income), become caught up in the consumerist mentality of the American cityscape, become increasingly impressionable and opportunistic, achieve economic success, and ultimately still feel unfulfilled. The nuances that distinguish these texts and their commentaries on fashion, however, stem mainly from identity politics—from Carrie's gender and David's ethnic origins.

The Rise of David Levinsky

The Rise of David Levinsky serves as much as a fashion commentary as a commentary on American values beginning with the industrial era. Cahan, who ran and edited the *Jewish Daily Forward* from 1903 to 1946, dedicated much of his career to writing for the Jewish immigrant community in the United States; however, he was equally concerned with promoting socialist values and keeping his readers informed about contemporary issues. On the surface, *Levinsky,* his most popular novel, reads like Cahan's litany against American capitalism—a cautionary tale of a pious Jew who loses his soul through his absorption into the cutthroat world of American business. Certainly this reading of the novel has merit and places it squarely within a tradition of American immigrant literature as well as Jewish American literature.

Yet this reading neglects to account for the amount of detail and reflection devoted to the garment industry (aside from discussions of unionizing and labor relations), the increased affordability of women's fashion, or the relationship between clothing and courtship. Cahan's roots in journalistic writing render his attention to detail a part of his process, yet they do not explain his attention to fashion and spectacle. On the one hand, the clothes surface as yet another one of capitalism's excesses—unnecessary and expensive decoration. On the other hand, his attention to the democratization of fashion and the breaking down of fashion elitism neither furthers nor undermines a socialist agenda. In *The Rise of David Levinsky,* then, clothing offers a metaphorical distinction between art and its absence, between refinement and vulgarity, between restraint and excess. These demarcations reflect back on the moral character of the wearer. David plays the roles of wearer, producer, and observer. He uses the language of clothing to reflect upon the moral fiber or decay of the consumers he encounters, yet as he becomes more immersed in the consumer capitalist mentality, he grows less and less capable of reflecting on his own moral character.

The novel begins with the protagonist's birth in 1865 and traces David's life over the course of the next forty-five years, chronicling his immigration to the United States at the age of twenty, his rise in the garment industry, and his lonely bachelorhood as a middle-aged man. The novel begins and ends with David's disappointment, signaling both his rise from poverty and his dissatisfaction with success: "I feel a peculiar yearning for the very days when the doors of that restaurant were closed to me and when the Canal

Street merchant was a magnate of commerce in my estimation. . . . My sense of triumph is coupled with a brooding sense of emptiness and insignificance, of my lack of anything like a great, deep interest" (525–26). This progression from yearning to disillusionment, even a sense of soullessness, is crucial to Cahan's commentary on American fashion in the novel. *Levinsky* serves two functions in the context of American fashion history. First, as a work of realism, the novel depicts, accurately, Jewish immigrants' involvement in shaping the garment industry and their contribution to the democratization of fashion. Second, by portraying the moral decline of David Levinsky (a direct result of economic rise), Cahan offers a symbolic treatise on moral decay in America, as values shift from family, spirituality, and community to upward mobility and acquisition of material goods. While *Sister Carrie,* which I discuss in the next section, focuses more on the retail end of the garment industry, *Levinsky* focuses on production, manufacturing, and entrepreneurship, thereby fixing a lens on mass production rather than on individual designers or showrooms. This emphasis parallels a refocusing in American fashion from fashion as art to fashion as business—from a soulful to a soulless endeavor.

David's interest in succeeding as a cloak manufacturer is complicated by his past, his early life grounded in closeness to his mother and community, in the holy ecstasy of Talmudic study, and in the basic survival of abject poverty. David's life in Russia is characterized by love, devotion, and a deep sense of purpose. Cahan lingers on the spiritual beauty of this older life, rich with meaning and love, personified by David's mother and by his mentor/father figure Reb Sender. This spiritual essence permeates his sense of community and his strict observance of the Jewish Holiness Code, and it reveals itself most ecstatically in his Talmudic studies. Describing the Talmud, David explains, "To read these books, to drink deep of their sacred wisdom, is accounted one of the greatest 'good deeds' in the life of a Jew. It is, however, as much a source of intellectual interest as an act of piety" (27). The Talmud characterizes piety not merely as studying and showing respect but as exercising self-control and self-discipline. The professor of Jewish studies Shai Cherry explains that the God of the Torah surfaces as almighty, fearsome, and punitive, but the God of the Talmud is one of restraint, one who observes yet "is no longer intelligible or discernible" (319). This emphasis on restraint defines the piety of David's early life, making his later decadence seem misguided despite his success.

David's mother makes constant sacrifices to encourage her son's Talmudic study, and Reb Sender solidifies David's commitment to scholarship by taking him under his wing: "You are like a son to me, Davie. Be good, be genuinely pious; for my sake, if for nothing else. Above all, don't be double-faced; never say what you do not mean; do not utter words of flattery" (32). His mother's sacrifices, his mentor's encouragement, and the Talmud's wisdom shape David's moral core during his youth. Later, as he deviates from this core, he feels ever greater temptation to embrace the American values of assimilation and upward mobility, yet he retains an equally strong awareness that he is losing something valuable and intangible as a result.

The love for family and religion David feels as a child is juxtaposed with concerns of basic survival: violence, starvation, and cold. As a child David is bullied constantly and frequently suffers from a lack of food and adequate clothing. His mother even sacrifices her own meals to scrape together enough money for his education. His deprivations culminate in the loss of his mother, who is killed when she tries to protect him. The combination of this devastating loss and his time living with a wealthy, generous, yet less observant family reframes David's perspective and priorities. He has time to process his mother's loss. He falls in love with the young woman of the family, Matilda, who inspires an interest in secular learning, in romantic love, and in immigrating to America for a fresh start. For David, America becomes symbolic of a new life and the possibility for a richer spirituality, for pursuing his spiritual goals without the constant threat of pogroms and other forms of religious oppression. When David leaves for America, he hopes to make enough money to pursue higher learning. He has already begun to neglect his Talmudic studies, yet he believes his love for study and analysis will translate to secular education.

The earliest signs of David's deviance surface in his donning of clothes. While he is living with Matilda's family, she tucks back his sidelocks and dresses him in her brother's elegant Sunday uniform with its "glittering coat and cap" (75), making David view himself for the first time as handsome and well dressed. His donning of this uniform coincides with his first kiss with Matilda and his guarantee of passage money for America. David's "Americanization" and lust for women, therefore, become permanently linked to clothing. After his arrival in the United States, as he begins to accept American standards of dress and grooming, he symbolically erases his religious self, first by cutting his sidelocks and shaving his beard. Such gestures indicate a change in David's attitude about appearances, a shift from thinking of clothing as sinful ("dressing like a Gentile") to thinking of it as Americanizing—from "Gentile" to "genteel." David equates gentility and model American identity with tasteful men's clothing, with suits and ties, neatness, and subtlety: "I was forever watching and striving to imitate the dress and the ways of the well-bred American merchants with whom I was, or trying to be, thrown. All this, I felt, was an essential element in achieving business success; but the ambition to act and look like a gentleman grew in me quite apart from these motives" (180). A part of this self-imposed makeover involves learning not to gesticulate (327) and to "speak in a calm, low voice" (329). Unfortunately, David notes, performing in this way takes the passion and meaning out of what he is saying (329). This Americanization of David through appearance and demeanor helps bring about his involvement in the clothing trade and, later, the garment industry.

David is a good worker but does not have an art, and when he first arrives in America, his lack of a skill or trade renders him helpless—in contrast to his friend Gitelson, a skilled tailor. David perceives that the American garment industry offers more jobs for an ever-expanding work force, and it also extends fashionable clothing to the masses. As David works his way up from worker to entrepreneur to manager, the more talented and creative Gitelson stays an employed tailor. Cahan thereby suggests that the industry rewards the hustler, not the artisan or the intellectual. In the world of ready-made fashion, art suffers.

David's lack of passion for clothing design and production does not deter him from entering the business, first as a pushcart salesman, and later as a garment worker. Initially David enters the clothing trade to make enough money to pursue loftier goals. He sees his accumulation of wealth in the garment industry as a means to an end. Although David abandons his devotion to Talmudic study early in the novel, this form of intellectual stimulation is replaced by a more American goal: to further his studies in college and higher learning, to pursue a noble profession connected with intense intellectual study (he gives the example of a physician). He knows, and often affirms, that his heart and soul are not in any way invested in the garment industry, and he continually looks around for other forms of personal fulfillment even as he triumphs over his competitors. However, the competitive nature of the cloak manufacturing business becomes too intoxicating.

Cahan helps to contextualize David's rise in the garment industry, speaking through his narrator and offering a historical context for the expanding cloak and suit industry, an industry that flourished not only through design innovation but also through mass production and copying. One *Chicago Daily Tribune* article from 1889 approximates that $40–50 million worth of women's cloaks were being produced each year, with New York firms manufacturing about 75 percent of these cloaks ("About Women's Cloaks"). Eastern European Jewish immigrant labor played a primary role in this development. David explains that earlier waves of Jewish immigrants from Germany "were the pioneers of the industry" during the mid-nineteenth century. The industry expanded, however, through German-American ingenuity and a large labor force later in the century:

> Formerly, and as late as the '70's, women's cloaks and jackets were little known in the United States. Shawls were worn by the masses. What few cloaks were seen on women of means and fashion were imported from Germany. But the demand grew. So, gradually, some German-American merchants and an American shawl firm bethought themselves of manufacturing these garments at home. The industry progressed, the new-born great Russian immigration—a child of the massacres of 1881 and 1882—bringing the needed army of tailors for it. There was big money in the cloak business, and it would have been unnatural if some of these tailors had not, sooner or later, begun to think of going into business on their own hook. (139)

David makes these observations when he begins in the industry, as a laborer responsible for binding seams. The observations help to contextualize his rise, for as he builds his own business, he appeals to prospective buyers as a Russian Jew to steal business away from established German Jewish competitors.

The 1860s and 1870s, according to Kosak, marked a shift in the division of labor for clothing production. Before the rise of ready-made clothing, women's suits were relegated to outside tailors for skilled labor; these tailors would enlist the help of family members for finishing (65). The period when David enters the garment industry saw the development of the "team system of production" in garment manufacturing. Unskilled workers were hired to execute different stages of the garment, and the tailor's role was minimized (Kosak 65), as reflected in the fate of David's friend Gitelson, who initially finds tailoring work but later struggles to make a living. Kosak explains how the division of labor reflected an emerging social order, with "the industry's top echelons represent[ing] German Jewish entrepreneurs" (67). David, as a Russian Jewish immigrant, seeks to undermine and outsell his predecessors.

David appropriates the narrative of Jewish contribution to his advantage, for example during his meeting with buyer Henry Gans, when he remarks that Russian manufacturers like him have lower expenses: "I explained . . . that the German-American cloak manufacturer was primarily a merchant, not a tailor; that he was compelled to leave things to his designer and a foreman, whereas his Russian competitor was a tailor or cloak-operator himself, and was, therefore, able to economize in ways that never occurred to the heads of the old houses" (337). David's remarks to Gans are deceptive, for he implies that he himself is a tailor and understands the business inside and out, when in fact he uses his Russian Jewish status to hire nonunion workers for lower wages. Within the garment business, David's gift lies not in designing beautiful clothing but in economizing, making fine clothes accessible for less money, reducing costs and maximizing profits for retail establishments and manufacturers. During the same meeting with Gans, David points to one of the suits in the store—"a brown cheviot trimmed with velvet"—and proclaims, "It's really a beautiful garment. I haven't the least idea how much you pay for it, of course, but I do know that I could make you the identical coat for a much smaller price" (223). His meeting with Gans showcases yet another one of David's talents: his ability to finesse, to outbid, and to embellish the truth in order to make a sale.

As David hones these skills and increases his business, his practices grow more corrupt, his business methods more cutthroat. He abandons his Talmudic studies as well as his American goals of higher learning, he exploits his landsmen workers as he gets greedy, and he becomes sexually and romantically unethical, often viewing women as objects to win (whether sexually or as a way of asserting superiority over their husbands). He finds justification for his actions, not in the Talmud or any other religious scripture, but in the theories of Herbert Spencer and Charles Darwin, reflecting, "A working man, and every one else who was poor, was an object of contempt to me—a misfit, a weakling, a failure, one of the ruck" (283). Later David admits, "I looked upon poor people with more contempt than ever. I still called them 'misfits,' in a Darwinian sense" (347). As David grows more distant from the poor financially, he distances himself emotionally, deliberately forgetting that he once identified with them, and that several incidents of dumb luck, combined with the pity of near strangers and his own unsavory business practices, saved him from being permanently among their ranks. Worse yet, David conducts his business in a self-serving, exploitative manner under the guise of philanthropy and concern for his fellow Jew: for example, he forms the Levinsky Antomir Benefit Society to avoid workers unionizing or striking, keeping wages low (378), and he manages to pay his workers less for more work by giving them time off on the Sabbath. As his career progresses, he begins pirating designs, deceiving buyers, and growing gluttonous—feeling his fortune of "more than one hundred thousand dollars [about $2.7 million today] . . . was not climbing rapidly enough" (347).

Such turns in David's character mirror similar turns in American social values. Cahan juxtaposes David's transformation with the changing landscape of American business and industry, as well as the changing values of the American people. As David begins to accumulate more and more wealth, he indulges in excesses, paralleling a national and cultural decadence that he has criticized and equated with moral decay. We see the relationship between morality and fashion most prominently in two passages: David's reunion with Matilda in the United States, and his visit to the Catskills. In the first incident, when David hears of a socialist meeting where he expects to meet his former love, he prepares himself by donning his most expensive and luxurious clothing—including a fur coat. Recalling how Matilda once fussed over his appearance and even dressed him in her brother's school uniform, David assumes she will be impressed by his wealth and his genteel appearance. When he approaches Matilda, he is harshly rebuffed: "'Of course I know you,' she snapped, taking stock of my mink overcoat. 'And I have heard about you, too. You have a lot of money, haven't you? I see you are wearing a costly fur coat.' And she brutally turned to speak to somebody else" (269). Until this point in the narrative, David has sought and earned the respect and admiration of others with words, with knowledge, and through finding a common ground. He assumes his expensive coat will impress the woman who once dressed him in her brother's clothing and admired his figure. He fails to take into account, however, her socialist loyalties, as well as the inappropriateness of wearing a luxurious garment to a meeting about the poor.

The choice of the mink coat seems even more hypocritical because David often equates trends in women's fashion with licentiousness and vulgarity, perhaps a vestige of his old Talmudic studies. In 1905 he notes how women begin wearing makeup as part of their daily attire. As the epigraph to this chapter shows, David connects such showiness with American prosperity yet also with harlotry. In the Catskills scene, David observes a microcosm of American culture in which newly wealthy Jewish men (many of whom have, like David, worked their way up in the garment industry) and their families show off their success: "The crowd was ablaze with diamonds, painted cheeks, and bright-colored silks. It was a babel of blatant self-consciousness, a miniature of the parvenu smugness that had spread like wild-fire over the country after a period of need and low spirits" (404). Many of these peacocking residents, David suggests, are single and interested in ensnaring attractive and promising husbands or wives.

All around him, David observes women clad in revealing clothing, women with excessive ornamentation, men ostentatiously boasting of their earnings, and young men and women dancing and touching provocatively in public view. He describes the resident "two weekers," women with "a large supply of dresses and shirt-waists of the latest style, and altogether the two weeks' vacation ate up, in many cases, the savings of months" (404); he observes "a large number of handsome, well-groomed women in expensive dresses and diamonds, and some of these were being kissed by puny, but successful-looking, men. 'They married them for their money,' I said to myself" (418). Finally, during dinner, he notes that the women constantly watch and compare their attire to the women around them, and he likens these women to "so many chorus-girls tripping before a theater audience, or like a procession of model-girls at a style-display in a big department store" (421). David learns from his dinner companion that the women "kept tab on" each other's clothing to see when and if they duplicated outfits.

Strangely, as David observes this smorgasbord of consumerist excess, he sees himself as an outsider, one choosing not to participate. He arrives in the Catskills with every intention of leaving quickly, of traveling farther to meet his fiancée, Fanny, a woman from an observant Jewish family who seemingly fulfills David's desire for a proper wife. Yet Cahan makes it clear that David has become part of this consumption-driven community. He behaves without scruples in his romantic pursuits: he fails to meet his fiancée when he finds a more desirable prospect among the Catskills residents; he flirts with and stalks his women shamelessly; and he makes sure to air his own success and wealth with as little subtlety as possible.

The culmination of the Catskills display of fashion and wealth occurs in the dining room, where Cahan clearly conflates the American Dream with an age of materialist consumption. David sits in the loud, rowdy dining room, observing the diners around him, until the band begins to play the "Star-Spangled Banner":

> It was an interesting scene. Men and women were offering thanksgiving to the flag under which they were eating this good dinner, wearing these expensive clothes. There was the jingle of newly-acquired dollars in our applause. But there was something else in it as well. Many of those who were now paying tribute to the Stars and Stripes were listening to the tune with grave, solemn mien. It was as if they were saying: "We are not persecuted under this flag. At last we have found a home." (424)

The scene marks the only moment David does not seem to pass moral judgment on his fellow residents. He reads into their silence a gratitude for their freedom from persecution. Yet the juxtaposition of their silent respect with their "expensive clothes" and "newly-acquired dollars" suggests that these residents, like David, are animated by a different America—not the land of the free, where they arrived as beggars, but the land of wealth and upward mobility, the land that has allowed them to forget their old selves, clinging to a vague semblance of community as they strive for more things, more clothes, more jewels, more money; wealthy husbands for their daughters, monetary success and social status for their sons.

David's time living among these residents reinforces his desire for a wife, yet not the woman he has already chosen, for Fanny's desirability fades in comparison to the single women he encounters in the Catskills. The business mogul and fierce competitor in David sees a wife as the final piece of his puzzle, and when he meets a fair prospect, he maneuvers to win her as he would a desirable business deal—and then loses interest in the prospect when a more attractive one comes along. But the serious Talmudic student, the loving son and pupil in David, detects a void in his life of luxury and competition. He wants to fill this void and believes he needs either a wife or a reconnection with his Jewish past. When David initially gets engaged to Fanny, before his visit to the Catskills, he reflects, "The vision of working for my wife and children somehow induced a yearning for altruism in a broader sense. While free from any vestige of religion, in the ordinary meaning of the word, I was tingling with a religious ecstasy that was based on a sense of duty" (399). Unfortunately for Fanny, David senses that she fulfills this sense of duty, but not the passionate longing for companionship that overwhelms any nobler aspirations for family.

David comes to believe he can fulfill both of these voids—a need for companionship and a reconnection with his spiritual path—by marrying Anna Tevkin, a young socialist and the daughter of a famous Yiddish poet. What is most revealing in David's obsessive pursuit of Anna is not his feelings for her—feelings that appear superficial and based more on her disinterest than his interest—but his attempts to win over Anna's father. David enjoys profound spiritual discussions with Tevkin, in which they weigh the values of America and Russia. Through these conversations, Cahan reveals the deeper connection between the world of show, the garment industry and its materialist trappings, and what has been lost by those who embrace the American Dream.

After reading David one of his poems, Tevkin explains that America has imprisoned his soul, and that Russia is "a freer country . . . for the spirit, at least." He continues: "The Russian people are really a warm-hearted people. Besides, one enjoys life in Russia better than here. . . . There is too much materialism here, too much hurry and too much prose, and—yes, too much machinery" (459). The rapid industrialization and booming garment industry have contributed to a whirlwind society in which acquisition and the beautiful image have become top priorities. For Tevkin, the loss lies not in the existence of such a country, but in watching his fellow immigrants come to embrace its values, initially out of an instinct for survival but ultimately because they come to accept such consumerist values as their own. They forget their past, they view their new clothing and possessions as trophies for overcoming their personal and collective struggles, and they forget the spiritual core that once propelled them.

Cahan uses the increasingly consumerist urban atmosphere and evolving American fashion industry as fitting backdrops for David's cultural disillusionment and loneliness. This atmosphere of excess and desire, of competition and deception, promotes values that contradict the cherished ethos of David's youth. Late in the novel he senses his mistake, his misdirected ambitions. After years of materialist pursuits and "Spencerian-agnosticism" (388), David repeats to his audience more and more that he is "lonely" and unhappy (526). Unable to find a wife or to immerse himself in the Jewish community, David turns to his lost intellectual ambitions, envying the immigrants who "have distinguished themselves in science, music, or art"

(529). He muses, "The day when that accident turned my mind from college to business seems to be the most unfortunate day in my life. I think that I should be much happier as a scientist or writer, perhaps. I should then be in my natural element, and if I were doomed to loneliness I should have comforts to which I am now a stranger" (529). David laments his abandoned pursuit of scholarship as the one thing that could have eased his loneliness and brought him fulfillment, yet he makes no move to change his life's path. This complacence, this unwillingness to change his course—this acceptance of his lonely yet easy life—is ultimately the hallmark of the New American Dream.

Chametzky connects Cahan's gloomy ending with the fate of the American Jewish community: "So ends *The Rise of David Levinsky*—a haunting, suggestive, and I think finally, prophetic book. Two generations from Levinsky, many thoughtful people in the Jewish community speak of a spiritual *malaise* that seems to be present in its more or less affluent American existence" (143–44). Certainly David's fate can be interpreted as a cautionary tale for younger Jews of the time, or for newly arrived immigrants reading Cahan's work. Yet the last lines of the novel feel specific to the burgeoning garment and fashion industry of the United States even as they recall David's Jewish roots: "I can never forget the days of my misery. I cannot escape from my old self. My past and my present do not comport well. David, the poor lad swinging over a Talmud volume at the Preacher's Synagogue, seems to have more in common with my inner identity than David Levinsky, the well-known cloak-manufacturer" (530). Cahan ends the novel with the words "well-known cloak-manufacturer," a title that fails to make David feel any pride or self-worth. He earned this title by distancing himself from everything he once aspired to and loved, by embracing materialist values. As a result, as David surveys his wealth, his accomplishments, his enormous profits from clothing the masses, he feels empty, alone, and unfulfilled.

Sister Carrie

Abraham Cahan's novel offers a cynical vision of industrial capitalism: a vision of women as advertisements for their husband's wealth, daughters decorated and displayed to ensnare future husbands, men verbally sparring and boasting to compete for attention, and all in the language of clothing, money, possessions, and business acumen. David Levinsky's journey may have begun with a desire for both survival and wisdom, yet the consumerist culture of industrial America eroded his values over the years, propelling him into a field and a persona he fails to escape. Both he and the reader recognize that he has grown into a very different sort of person by the end of the story—as he observes, the "inner identity" he connects with his past and the professional identity of his present "do not comport well" (530). In contrast, Carrie Meeber of *Sister Carrie* stays much the same throughout her journey: her desires multiply, but her essential nature goes through no dramatic transformation. Dreiser offers a vague sense of Carrie's innocence and family life in the novel's opening, as she fearfully leaves behind Columbia City, yet from these first pages when she sizes up the jazzily dressed Drouet, Dreiser alludes to Carrie's ability to read people and situations to her advantage. If David looks upon women presenting themselves as prospective possessions, Carrie crafts herself into such a beautiful possession.

To situate Carrie's physical transformation and survivalism, Dreiser provides a detailed account of the world she enters: the late nineteenth-century American city—first Chicago, then New York. Many of the novel's critics, including Paula E. Geyh, have highlighted the importance of the city settings of the novel in shaping Carrie's desires and directing them toward commodities: "Dreiser's turn-of-the-century Chicago and New York are carefully mapped assemblages of department stores (the novel mentions five by name) and assorted showplaces (streets, theaters, restaurants, hotels) where the subjectivities of his protagonists are established through their purchases and public displays of consumer goods" (415). Once Carrie has entered the space of the cityscape, she cannot escape a constant bombardment of clothing, accessories, and other commodities for purchase. She directs her free will toward navigating to a social and economic position in which she will best be able to purchase such commodities and to participate in the spectacle.

Dreiser takes great care to sketch the changing cityscape in terms of its streets, shops, theaters, parks, and neighborhoods, frequently stepping into the narrative to comment on how it has changed over the course of the nineteenth century. The city's evolution into its current consumer-driven state mirrors changes in American fashion during the period. In her discussion of "visual economies and commodity culture" in the novel, Bärbel Tischleder relates the expanding industrialization of the city to the expansion of visual media (advertising, fashion journalism, films, billboards): "Accentuating the look rather than the character of both people and things, these media promoted a new orientation toward the visual. . . . An unprecedented quantity, variety, and, most notably, visibility of material goods manifested not only new modes of commerce and circulation, but also changed the face of American cities" (59–60). She likens Carrie to *The House of Mirth*'s Lily Bart, noting that both "are presented as self-conscious 'actors,' who are quite aware of the theatrical forms of social interaction" (60). Her analysis speaks to Carrie's aptitude for acting, a career that eventually secures her wealth; however, her acting underlines a larger reality about the period and setting: the cityscape allows anonymity, and thereby creates the opportunity for Carrie's literal refashioning—in her dress, her style, and her socioeconomic position.

From the beginning of the novel, Dreiser depicts Carrie as a woman who notices clothing and cares about her appearance.[3] She is poor and cannot afford nice clothes, yet she attempts to dress neatly and in a way to flatter her figure: "She dressed herself in a worn shirtwaist of dotted blue percale, a skirt of light-brown serge rather faded, and a small straw hat which she had worn all summer at Columbia City. Her shoes were old, and her necktie was in that crumpled, flattened state which time and much wearing impart" (32). Even coming from a small town, Carrie knows enough to feel self-conscious about her shabby appearance, but she also knows how to make use of the few pieces she owns to appear as fashionable as possible in her limited circumstances. Carrie's awareness of her surroundings, her ability to read others' appearances and demeanors and to contrast them with her own, gives her an advantage in an unsympathetic and bustling metropolis that propels her, if not toward happiness, then at least toward comfort and leisure.

While Cahan characterizes David Levinsky as a hustler, a man who succeeds because of his ability to read people and think on his feet, Carrie surfaces as more patient and cerebral. She is, as many scholars have argued, a creature of desire, operating within a context of "biological determinism" (Gelfant 179); as Gelfant notes, Dreiser tends to liken "human beings to insects and animals, all subject to ineluctable drives that characters experience as desire" (179). Nevertheless, Dreiser gives the reader insight into Carrie's observations and her strategizing when faced with choices in relationships and career. Her choices are not always instinctual, but studied and deliberate: she observes, interprets, and makes choices accordingly. Many critics have noted her first meeting with Drouet on the train, characterizing it as a meeting of two sets of clothing. Rather than giving a general description of Drouet's dress and appearance, Dreiser describes the man meticulously, from textiles to shirt buttons:

> His suit was of a striped and crossed pattern of brown wool, new at that time, but since become familiar as a business suit. The low crotch of the vest revealed a stiff shirt bosom of white and pink stripes. From his coat sleeves protruded a pair of linen cuffs of the same pattern, fastened with large, gold-plate buttons, set with the common yellow agates known as 'cat's-eyes.' His fingers bore several rings—one, the ever-enduring heavy seal—and from his vest dangled a neat gold watch chain, from which was suspended the secret insignia of the Order of Elks. The whole suit was rather tight-fitting, and was finished off with heavy-soled tan shoes, highly polished, and the gray fedora hat. (3–4)

Having only seen the dress of her small hometown, Carrie is impressed with Drouet's appearance, which Dreiser characterizes with words like "polished," "gold," and "new." She senses his wealth, yet the reader, following Dreiser's cues, suspects something ostentatious in Drouet's attire—a deliberate attempt to exhibit and attract. Men's fashion columns of the day (ca. 1889–90) cautioned against showiness, especially when it came to wearing jewelry. One *Washington Post* piece from 1890 cautions (citing a *Sun* reporter): "Men of any pretensions to fashion do not now wear watch chains. . . . The severity of fashion regarding jewelry is undoubtedly due to the abuse of the ring craze five or six years ago. . . . a gentleman is now distinguished by an entire absence of jewelry of every kind" ("Cheap Jewelry"). Columns of the time target men wearing watch chains and rings as especially out of fashion; it is likely that Dreiser specifically selected these details for Drouet to mark him as wealthy but lacking in taste and refinement.

Once Carrie has lived in the city for a while and had an opportunity to study its fashions, she is able to recognize the subtler yet classier dress of Hurstwood, whose clothes are characterized as "rich": "The coat lapels stood out with that medium stiffness which excellent cloth possesses. The vest was of a rich Scotch plaid, set with a double row of round mother-of-pearl buttons. His cravat was a shiny combination of silken threads, not loud, not inconspicuous." Having established the subtlety of Hurstwood's attire, Carrie goes on to compare his clothing with Drouet's: "What he wore did not strike the eye so forcibly as that which Drouet had on, but Carrie could see the elegance of the material. Hurstwood's shoes were of soft, black calf, polished only to a dull shine. Drouet wore patent leather, but Carrie could not help feeling that there was a distinction in favor of the soft leather, where all else was so rich. *She noticed these things almost unconsciously*" (95–96, emphasis mine). Dreiser's wording here suggests Carrie has evolved into a savvier interpreter of appearances—she instinctually recognizes taste and its absence, and just as instinctually, her romantic interests shift from the exuberant Drouet to the dignified Hurstwood, a man who can give her the position and distinction Drouet has failed to provide.

Carrie's reading of men's fashion is only one of many abilities she adopts through her city living. Drouet merely initiates her into a life of commodities and consumption—as his mistress, in fact, Carrie herself has become a commodity. Her requests for marriage have nothing to do with love, or even a sense of moral righteousness; instead, she senses that being a wife (as opposed to a mistress) will raise her social position and, therefore, her "value." Carrie thinks not in moral but in survivalist terms: she understands her own points of weakness first, and then attempts to use her assets to better her position.[4] Many critics of the novel—and of Carrie—insist she is singularly materialistic; however, I argue that she's only as materialistic as everyone else, for she has been interpellated by the same urban capitalist culture. Carrie is not distinct because of her desires, but because of her ability to play with surfaces to achieve what she desires while maintaining a feminine and passive persona. In his reading of Carrie's interactions with the inventor Bob Ames, whom she meets later in the novel, David T. Humphries comments on this specific ability of Carrie's: "Despite her limited use of language, she is able to read and respond to the meaning in the appearances and gestures at hand and to perceive possibilities for herself and others in the 'tawdry' show. In other words, Carrie develops by acting in and observing the scene; she identifies the role that each person plays and then considers how to respond by adjusting her own role" (43). While Humphries's analysis here is specific to Carrie's dinner in a New York dining room, her adaptation applies to nearly every major scene in the novel: she adjusts to her surroundings, thereby continually bettering her position. Dreiser contrasts her adaptability with Hurstwood's inability to evolve, which for him translates literally to an inability to survive.

Both Dreiser and Cahan present protagonists whose desires and self-perceptions are manipulated first by the need to survive, but later by competition and consumerism. If David is fueled by the competitive nature of the cloak manufacturing business, Carrie is fueled by the beautiful display—that is, while David loses himself in the obsessive desire to maximize profits by creating garments when the industry is thriving, Carrie acts on her desire to purchase and to emulate, for she believes the promise of the merchandise and the advertisers: that owning these pieces will ensure her happiness. Such happiness was, implicitly, what the clothes—placed in the context of magazines, department storewindows, and advertisements—promised.

As the nineteenth century came to a close, fashion had become far more consumer oriented (making shopping a popular pastime), and it had become more democratic—that is, more pieces were available at affordable prices, blurring the lines between various social classes. In addition, fashionable clothing expanded to include more separates, allowing women to create outfits and, to some extent, create a personal style. In his assessment of Carrie's "cuteness" and its role in the novel, Charles Harmon notes, "Knowing that in the city her clothes go far to fix her identity, Carrie defers making shopping decisions in favor of mentally trying on the range of personalities that are for sale" (126). Harmon illustrates how the fashion world of this historical moment was moving toward an emphasis on self-definition through clothing. Her early shopping excursions represent what he calls her "middle state," "when she *considers yet refuses to commit herself* to the subtle yet discrete identities that are promised by the purchase of each separate commodity. . . . Such an attitude transforms each bit of finery (as long as it remains unbought) into a symbol of her own idealized capacities to embody an infinite range of personalities" (127). Harmon's description spotlights the importance of display and of the parade of clothing through public spaces in the city. Every time Carrie enters a retail space or sees a shopwindow, Dreiser carefully depicts the influence of the presentation, the arts of advertisers and visual merchandisers who know the power of well-displayed clothing over the average consumer. In one example, early during her stay in Chicago when she is still living in poverty with her sister, Carrie goes out to shop for a new coat she desperately needs, intending to use money Drouet has provided. Yet on seeing the garments, rather than thinking in terms of economy and practicality, she thinks in terms of aesthetics and the social value of merchandise: "When she entered the store, she already had her heart fixed upon the peculiar little tan jacket with large mother-of-pearl buttons which was all the rage that fall" (67). In the short move from chilly outdoors to lush, warm boutique, and the quick shift from being penniless to holding Drouet's money in her purse, Carrie has already ceased to think of clothing as a necessity and instead views it as a commodity that can connote status.

Dreiser augments the implicit power of the garment with the even more potent influence of its surroundings—department stores. He speaks of them as a recent development, as something that may be a passing trend in retail: "The nature of these vast retail combinations, should they ever permanently disappear, will form an interesting chapter in the commercial history of our nation. . . . They were handsome, bustling, successful affairs, with a host of clerks and a swarm of patrons" (21). In his nearly two-page description, Dreiser conveys the constant activity and crowds, the well-dressed sales clerks, and the "showplace of dazzling interest and attraction" that each counter presents. He also briefly alludes to the organization and management of these enterprises, suggesting their pertinence to the contemporary cityscape and lifestyle. Dreiser, as well as the novel's critics, implies that the department store is a commercial and educational enterprise: it educates women on the different lives available to them through its showcases, and its merchandise represents the necessary items for purchase that can help them achieve those lives. Tischleder likens the department store to the museum, which became popularized as an institution around the same time. While museums display "ethnographic artifacts" to instruct patrons about the lives and cultures of different people or eras, "the department store displays goods as essential props of modern living. And as the ethnological object is seen to convey information about its provenance—the way of living of its makers and users—, the commodity suggests a desirable lifestyle—the tastes and glamour of its (potential) buyers" (66). Even today, department store windows and mannequins help patrons visualize one piece of merchandise as part of something greater—a look, a persona, a lifestyle.[5] Catalogs, advertisements, and fashion magazines supplemented the displays of the department stores, teaching readers/viewers what to buy as well as what kinds of lives they should be envisioning, where they could wear these pieces, and what such pieces would confer.

The displays were enshrined in the magnificent arrangement and architecture of the department store buildings—enormous spaces meant to overwhelm and elevate patrons. Earlier in the chapter I noted how Ewen and Ewen compare these buildings to both "cathedrals" and "palaces," suggesting that patrons could experience awe and elegant luxury upon entering such a space. The authors describe the rotunda design of Lord & Taylor, one of the establishments Carrie visits in New York: "The rotunda design created a spectacle of air, space, and light that provided a symbolic retreat from the terms of an increasingly congested city life. Such innovations of structure and display provided a seductive and promising context for the retailing of industrial wares" (144). Indeed, the spaces and arrangement of merchandise were designed to seduce; even today, men and women often use the language of temptation when discussing the pull of the department store. Geyh observes this same phenomenon in *Sister Carrie,* for as Carrie shops, she imagines that she hears the merchandise enticing her: "The fetishistic seductiveness—'Ah, such little feet . . . how effectively I cover them'—of the shoes' discourse is also remarkable for what it suggests about the transformation that the city has wrought in Carrie" (423). In this last clause, Geyh indicates how the seductive interior of the store has an amnesiac property—even for those women who have participated in producing the very merchandise they peruse.

When Carrie first visits a department store, she does so while looking for work, tempted by each item yet unable to purchase anything. In this space she also becomes aware of her appearance and her position: "Not only did Carrie feel the drag of desire for all which was new and pleasing in apparel for women, but she noticed too, with a touch at the heart, the fine ladies who elbowed and ignored her, brushing past in utter disregard of her presence, themselves eagerly enlisted in the materials which the store contained" (22). Carrie becomes analytical in this moment, connecting her clothing and economic need with the way other women view her and treat her. Yet she only feels this despair when comparing herself with the other women. When she turns her attention to the merchandise, she becomes more wistful, even hopeful. Harmon contrasts Carrie's experience shopping with her brief experience working in the Chicago shoe factory: "If Carrie's sense of self expands into a realm of infinite potential while shopping, while at work it contracts to a narrow space that is equally abstract—the counter sublime of the body in pain" (128). The contrast between these two experiences—the "narrow and dull" work of "running a machine that punches holes in the upper of a man's shoe" (Harmon 128) and the wonder of perusing endless beautiful women's apparel, each piece of which contains its own promise of beauty and position—eliminates any moral concern or deliberation from

Carrie's future decisions. Her choice to become Drouet's mistress, and later Hurstwood's, may be justified by the language of pragmatism or romance, yet Carrie has experienced a life of deprivation in a heartless city, and her choices are motivated by increasing the distance between herself and this earlier state. Beautiful clothing becomes a kind of armor: it helps her feel with greater certainty that she has guarded herself against poverty and debasement.

Dreiser maps Carrie's increased knowledge of clothing and style, her awareness of the proper way to wear different pieces and to create a look that maximizes their power to make her appear pretty and to elevate her class in the eyes of observers. Both Drouet and Hurstwood notice these changes in her, and their desire for her intensifies: "At two Carrie came tripping along the walk. . . . She had just recently donned a sailor hat for the season with a band of pretty white-dotted blue silk. Her skirt was of a rich blue material, and her shirtwaist matched it, with a thin stripe of blue upon a snow-white ground. . . . Her brown shoes peeped occasionally from beneath her skirt" (143). Dreiser describes Carrie's ensemble through Hurstwood's eyes, and rather than simply describing the clothes as static, independent pieces, he emphasizes their dynamism by delineating Carrie's motions. She comes "tripping along" because the clothes compel her to do so. She allows her "brown shoes" to "peep" flirtatiously. She holds "her gloves in her hand," suggesting she does not plan to wear them but wants to display them nonetheless. Dreiser's language illustrates Carrie's adeptness with clothing and presentation. A woman does not become fashionable, he implies, merely by having enough money to purchase the right pieces and then putting them on. Rather, a woman becomes fashionable when she knows what to wear, how to wear it, and how to move in symbiosis with the garments and accessories.

Though Carrie's clothing has steadily improved, her constant contact with better-dressed consumers fuels her desire for better, more expensive pieces. This desire becomes most apparent after she has moved with Hurstwood to New York, where the public parade of clothing on Broadway, in the theater, and in fancy dining rooms makes Carrie more conscious of her own appearance and her desire to exhibit it. In addition, fluctuating trends ensure she will never have all the clothes she needs, for new styles continue to emerge, keeping the mechanism of the department store and the fashion industry at large profitable. Carrie's yearning for clothes has shifted from partial necessity (earlier she wants a jacket both because she is cold and because she admires its appearance) to sheer consumer desire; we see evidence of this shift in her admiration of Mrs. Vance, whom she describes as "stunningly arrayed in a dark-blue walking dress, with a nobby hat to match. Carrie had gotten herself up charmingly enough, but this woman pained her by contrast. She seemed to have so many dainty little things which Carrie had not. There were trinkets of gold, an elegant green leather purse set with her initials, a fancy handkerchief, exceedingly rich in design, and the like" (297). Though Carrie envies her friend's pretty looks, her jealousy is tempered by Mrs. Vance's kindly suggestions and mentoring. Mrs. Vance indulges Carrie's desire to look prettier and to appear more in public. She offers polite suggestions for new purchases: "Have you seen the new gloves with the oval pearl buttons? . . . The next time you get a pair of shoes, dearie . . . get button, with thick soles and patent-leather tips. They're all the rage this fall" (303). Dreiser contextualizes Mrs. Vance's suggestions within the rising popularity of department stores among the upper classes: "Oh, dear, have you seen the new shirtwaists at Altman's? They have some of the loveliest patterns" (303); "'Why don't you get yourself one of those nice serge skirts they're selling at Lord & Taylor's?' she said one day. 'They're the circular style, and they're going to be worn from now on. A dark blue one would look so nice on you'" (304). Carrie is grateful for, rather than offended by, Mrs. Vance's suggestions. As Gelfant suggests, Mrs. Vance personifies the type of clothing advertisement to which Carrie is so susceptible "by associating commodities with satisfaction and social class and creating . . . enviable images for a shopper's avid eye to see" (181). Carrie envisions her friend as a kind of fashion mentor: she recognizes Mrs. Vance's social superiority, and her sense of pragmatism and understanding overrules any pretensions to vanity—yet another reason Carrie can rise above her station.

Through Mrs. Vance, Carrie learns the importance of public exposure in New York, the women and men parading their finery on Broadway and Fifth Avenue while getting in and out of a spectacular array of carriages (307). It is because of her contact with the Vances and exposure to this finery—not because of his neglect or his idleness—that Carrie grows resentful and distant toward Hurstwood: "In the whole time she had been in New York Hurstwood's modified state had not permitted his bringing her to such a place. There was an almost indescribable atmosphere about it which convinced the newcomer that this was the proper thing. Here was the place where the matter of expense limited the patrons to the moneyed or pleasure-loving class" (307). In this context, Carrie also meets Ames, who helps her see that she has focused too many efforts on achieving surface goals: in contrast to his more contemplative observations about her persona and her acting, Drouet and Hurstwood appear shallow and overly concerned with superficial desires.[6] Carrie's ultimate decision to leave Hurstwood, then, is twofold: first, he can no longer provide her with the material things (fine clothing, social position) that helped entice her from Drouet in the first place—in fact, he prevents her from securing these luxuries for herself; second, Ames has made her aware of another, nonmaterial dimension of her desire that neither Hurstwood nor Drouet has cultivated. He has alluded to a sense of meaning and purpose beyond superficial pleasures.

Carrie is in a much better position to pursue her desires after leaving Hurstwood than when she first set out on her own. Having the social graces, confidence, and sense of style she gained through her contact with first Drouet, then Hurstwood, and then Mrs. Vance, Carrie has an easier time with finding employment in New York. Dreiser contrasts her early, hopeless search for employment in Chicago with her far more successful search in New York. She feels bolder and, with a full awareness of her past struggles, understands the consequences of not finding a place. In addition, she has managed and accentuated her figure, no longer the slight, pale woman who approached firms during a Chicago winter. At the Casino she encounters a manager who "judged women as another would horseflesh" (366), and Carrie's pleasing appearance earns her a part in the chorus. Her employment success only deepens her frustration with Hurstwood's idleness, and Dreiser steps in to Hurstwood's defense: "She forgot her youth and beauty. The handicap of age she did not, in her enthusiasm, perceive" (368). The changes to women's fashion—the relative affordability, the emphasis on style and taste—combined with Carrie's attractiveness, place her at an advantage professionally and economically.

Unlike David Levinsky, Carrie finds herself in a career that she actually wants, and one in which she can potentially excel. Humphries cites Paul A. Orlov's reading of the novel, noting that acting "can lead to a sympathy towards others and a more authentic sense of identity" (43). Carrie's ability to act parallels her understanding of clothing: as an analytical observer, she has years of training in donning a costume (her apparel), adapting her behavior to suit her situation, and charming her audience. Her charm, like her clothing, is understated, pleasing, and never showy. And as her observance of others, like Mrs. Vance, has helped her improve her appearance, she also absorbs their feelings and behaviors, channeling them into her various acting roles: "her unique ability is that in observing the appearance of others she takes account of their possibilities and relates these possibilities to her own process of becoming. For Carrie, emulation is a process of transformation" (Humphries 43). As a reader of surfaces, Carrie can re-create the appearance of an emotion without having to experience the emotion herself.

Unfortunately, as we have seen in the case of David Levinsky, the new American Dream can foster a sense of complacency. After achieving success as a comic actress, comfortably situated in a lush New York hotel room with a salary of $150 per week (equal to about $4,000 per week today), Carrie grows disillusioned with fortune: "With her one hundred and fifty in hand, Carrie could think of nothing particularly to do. In itself, as a tangible, apparent thing which she could touch and look upon, it was a diverting thing for a few days, but this soon passed. Her hotel bill did not require its use. Her clothes had for some time been wholly satisfactory. Another day or two and she would receive another hundred and fifty" (441). Despite Carrie's realization that her material comforts and salary will not secure her happiness or affection, she stagnates rather than looking inward.

Dreiser hints at Carrie's potential for happiness during a later meeting with Ames when he shows his disappointment that she has stuck with comedic acting and inspires her to do a more serious play. He tries to explain what Carrie has to offer in the field of drama, and "she got the idea that her look was something which represented the world's longing" (469). Ames explains, "That puts a burden of duty on you. It so happens that you have this thing. It is no credit to you—that is, I mean, you might not have had it. You paid nothing to get it. But now that you have it, you must do something with it. . . . [T]urn to the dramatic field. You have so much sympathy and such a melodious voice. Make them valuable to others. It will make your powers endure" (469). Ames cautions Carrie that eventually her looks and her gift will disappear; she has only a brief chance at immortality. As with Mrs. Vance, Carrie is not offended by the advice—in fact, it makes her feel important and less lonely. Yet while earlier in the novel, before she has earned her fortune, she might have made the change, at this stage she has reached the plateau of material wealth and complacency: "Still, she did nothing—grieving. It was a long way to this better thing—or seemed so—and comfort was about her; hence the inactivity and longing" (470). The accumulation of such a vast fortunate engenders a kind of inertia. Like David Levinsky, Carrie has a sense of what could give her the fulfillment and human connection that she currently lacks, yet she fails to act or change her situation, for she suspects that once she takes a step, "on and on beyond that, if accomplished, would lie others for her. It was forever to be the pursuit of that radiance of delight which tints the distinct hilltops of the world" (486). After years of working and striving to achieve her desires, Carrie despairs that no effort can bring her to a place of happiness. At this stage in her life, therefore, she prioritizes comfort and security over risk and the potential for human connection.

In the final passages of the novel, Dreiser characterizes Carrie's wealth as what "seemed life's object," and he acknowledges her cache of possessions—"her gowns and carriages, her furniture and bank account" and circle of sycophantic friends, whom "she had once craved" (484). After describing her many blessings, he adds, "and yet she was lonely. In her rocking chair she sat, when not otherwise engaged—singing and dreaming." Dreiser uses words like "dreams" and "beauty" in these pages yet juxtaposes them with "loneliness," "blind," "longings," "heartache." Her rocking in her rocking chair symbolizes this vacillation between her sense of hope as she pursues a desire—believing it will bring her happiness—and her sense of disillusionment and alienation when these dreams fail to deliver. In her rocking chair, Carrie moves back and forth—without really moving.

Carrie's fate is an apt allegory for the promise of American fashion, the mechanism that first drives her away from her family and into Drouet's care—and the same mechanism that, at least in part, drives her to abandon Hurstwood. In her book *Fashion Zeitgeist* (2005), Barbara Vinken offers the following description of fashion: "Glittering and blinding, fashion draws attention away from the substance of things. It is the very personification of the individual alienated in the rush of consumption, of the self lost in the brilliant world of commodities" (3). Upon her first entry into a department store, Carrie is entranced by the display of goods, and her identity becomes molded by these decorations: first, in the pursuit of a position that will allow her to purchase whatever she desires, and second, in her ability to read people based on their display of these commodities. Her life becomes an alienated and lonely one, with no connection to family, no sense of loyalty, and no ability to achieve genuine fulfillment. Again, Dreiser does not fault

Carrie for her persona, but characterizes it as a natural product of an increasingly industrialized, increasingly consumer-driven environment.

For the American fashion industry to thrive, clothing designers and manufacturers, retailers, advertisers, journalists, and anyone else who stood to profit from its expansion had to change the way Americans thought about clothing. Americans couldn't merely purchase a new item when an old one wore out: consumers had to constantly want to buy more garments and accessories. Cahan's and Dreiser's novels, taken together, help illustrate the social, cultural, and economic forces that acted on the individual's psyche to change him or her from a creature of survival, one who seeks both physical comfort and basic human connection (e.g., Carrie initially gravitates toward Drouet in part because he is kind to her in an otherwise indifferent environment), to a creature of materialist desire. Walter Benn Michaels has argued that "Carrie's economy of desire" exposes and even sanctions "the unrestrained capitalism of the late nineteenth and early twentieth centuries." He continues: "The power of *Sister Carrie,* then, . . . derives not from its scathing 'picture' of capitalist 'conditions' but from its unabashed and extraordinarily literal acceptance of the economy that produced those conditions" (376–77). For both Carrie and David, the economic forces contributing to such "unrestrained capitalism" include public displays of fashion by people of various social classes (not just the wealthiest elite), constant bombardment with merchandise displays and advertisements, the burgeoning garment industry, the thriving field of fashion journalism, and the increasing prevalence of the department store.

The change in American mentality and goal orientation to one of acquisition, or material desires, shaped the American economy and understanding of wealth. This historical moment, the convergence of industrialism, fashion, and nationalist ideology, would change the U.S. citizenry into a culture with a tendency toward excess. Consumer capitalism and its ideology reinforced a rags to riches myth, but both Cahan and Dreiser challenge this myth in two important ways. First, their protagonists, while savvy and eager to rise, are helped along their ladders of success by random strokes of luck. David pinpoints a series of chance encounters and accidents as crucial moments in his climb to economic success, while Carrie has the fortune of her beauty and charm—a less attractive woman in her position would face a different set of challenges in her struggle to survive. For women, rags to riches stories of this period tended to take on a Cinderella narrative of being valued for one's looks and then rescued by a wealthy man. Many of the stories penned by Anzia Yezierska, which I discuss in the next chapter, take on a similar narrative.

The second challenge these authors present to the new American Dream is the resulting loneliness and alienation, a modern malaise that seems a side effect of embracing the consumer capitalist mentality. When the motive for achieving material wealth is superficial, they suggest, the feelings that follow its achievement will be equally unfulfilling.

three

The Immigrant in the Era of Simplicity

I want that beautiful plainness
that only the rich wear. A dress
that looks simple enough for the
poor only that it's different.
—Anzia Yezierska,
Salome of the Tenements

On January 1, 1972, my great-great-uncle Paul Orange celebrated his hundredth birthday among his family, friends, and a group of news reporters. Orange was an immigrant success story and an inspiration to the Jewish community in New York. He was ten years old when he immigrated from Romania with his parents and twelve siblings. His father, Michael, was trained as a tailor, and he continued his trade in New York. When Paul and his brothers were old enough, they joined the trade, establishing a costume company called Orange Brothers.

Paul and his brothers rose quickly in the design industry. They expanded their company, designing for Broadway productions and movie stars. They grew from a costume company to a clothing company, and soon they were presenting gowns to elite clients on Fifth Avenue and in the prestigious Place Vendôme in Paris. They had an illustrious clientele that included the Astors, Vanderbilts, and Whitneys—and even First Lady Edith Wilson, whose ball gown was displayed at the Smithsonian until recently. Despite their success in designing couture, the Orange Manufacturing Corporation did not limit their clientele to the elite. They also made clothing for middle- and working-class Americans, under the label Orange Frocks.

Like Abraham Cahan's character David Levinsky, who eventually "develop[ed] [his] whole business along the lines of popular prices" (522), my ancestors saw the economic potential for designing clothes for the masses; however, unlike Levinsky, whose clothes never reached high-end status, they achieved and retained their luxury label and status. Their ability to compete on a design level with Parisian couturiers for elite clients while simultaneously designing ready-made clothing for the larger American population parallels the growth of other labels during the early twentieth century. Levinsky epitomizes the American immigrant with a good business sense, but the Oranges represented immigrants with business sense and design talent.

Catering to both high-end and lower-class clients would have been difficult only a decade or two earlier. The first ready-made garments were of poor quality, and department stores did not offer the comprehensive sizing that would ensure a proper fit. Yet the quality of ready-made or "ready-to-wear" (as we now call them) clothes would improve by the 1920s, when, according to the fashion historian Bonnie English, "three preconditions were met: a competitive pricing system, advanced manufacturing technologies which produced goods that were well made and designed, and an effective distribution network" (32). Beginning with Charles Frederick Worth in the early 1900s, haute couture designers began producing "similar, less expensive lines for the middle class American Market" (2). English also notes that 1920s designers, especially Gabrielle "Coco" Chanel, began to use more affordable materials, started creating ready-to-wear or prêt-à-porter clothing under their own labels—Chanel was one of the first to do so in the late 1920s (37)—and used simpler silhouettes with fewer trimmings, thereby making the clothing easier to copy with affordable materials. The combination of these factors brought fashionable clothing more permanently into the realm of even the working class, including the immigrant workforce who helped manufacture the garments.

Immigrant narratives do not tend to celebrate being able to purchase poorer quality American-style clothes. However, they do celebrate acquiring beautiful, higher quality clothing, which tends to carry a heavy symbolism in these stories of self-transformation and upward mobility. The increasingly simple designs of the 1910s and 1920s, as well as the increasingly utilitarian and functional inspirations for high fashion, helped to collapse class barriers in the realm of fashion and style. The more opulent styles of Victorian and Edwardian haute couture were not designed for working women, or even mobile women (e.g., women who rode bicycles, played active sports, or drove cars).[1] However, early modern fashion—with the exception of some Poiret designs like the hobble skirt—favored working conditions and mobility, and therefore a broader range of lifestyles. Even before the famous drop-waist, slim gowns of the Roaring Twenties, fashionable clothing was maintaining the functionality of the war years as it embraced new trimmings and embellishments.

Writers of immigrant fiction and memoirs during the early twentieth century tended to incorporate modern ready-to-wear fashion into their narratives in at least one of three ways. First, and most commonly, clothing—and the clothing factory—surfaced as a symbol of both hope and oppression. Millions of immigrants arriving in the United States from 1880 to 1924 ended up working in the garment industry, usually in sweatshops, and therefore the conditions of the shops, their impact on the worker, and the feeling of distance the workers felt from the garments they helped to create became common themes in literature of the period. Sometimes, as in the case of Cahan's "A Sweat-Shop Romance," the shop is merely a setting in the background that helps facilitate relationships among the characters. Or, as in *The Rise of David Levinsky,* it serves as a stepping-stone to a more illustrious career. In other instances, descriptions of the dehumanizing conditions of the clothing factories further the author's socialist agenda, or at least the author's call for better conditions and treatment of immigrant laborers, as in Michael Gold's *Jews without Money* (1930): "Once my Aunt Lena lay sick in our bedroom. There had been a rush season in the shop, and she had worked too hard. The sweatshops were run on piece-work then, a system of Egyptian slavery under which the strongest crumpled, as though it were the bubonic plague" (chap. 11, sec. 8). Although Cahan, Gold, and other Jewish immigrant writers like Emma Goldman and Anzia Yezierska often used their writing to further socialist agendas and expose the harsh conditions of clothing factories, in addition to advocating reforms, these narratives helped make an American-born audience aware of the many obstacles facing immigrants wishing to assimilate into the American mainstream. Accounts of the long hours, low pay, unsanitary conditions, and physical strain of the work helped readers comprehend the work ethic of immigrant laborers as well as the difficulty of achieving success in the United States. Many immigrant narratives show protagonists working all day in a factory and still attending classes in the evenings, in the hope of getting an education and speaking English fluently.

A second way clothing surfaces in these narratives is to highlight the assimilation process as immigrants begin to adopt American dress. In chapter 2 I discussed this process in the context of *The Rise of David Levinsky:* David sees the purchase of fine clothing as marking his elevation in status and his symbolic assimilation into American culture. Willa Cather illustrates a similar phenomenon in her novel *My Ántonia* (1918), except that her immigrant characters erase not only their ethnic difference but also the roughness associated with their rural upbringing. In this novel, the aspiring dressmaker Lena Lingard learns how to sew and to copy original gowns, and she teaches the other girls, including Ántonia: "When she was not going to a dance, [Ántonia] sewed until midnight. . . . Under Lena's direction she copied Mrs. Gardener's new party dress and Mrs. Smith's street costume so ingeniously in cheap materials that those ladies were greatly annoyed, and Mrs. Cutter, who was jealous of them, was secretly pleased" (214). Copying higher-end dresses would become increasingly popular as more members of the middle and working class wished to dress elegantly, or at least fashionably.

Lena's interest in dressing like an American overlaps with the third, less frequent, way immigrant narratives feature clothing: some characters display an awareness of and fascination with fashion, often shown by their studying Parisian books of clothing or longing wistfully for a beautiful gown. In Anzia Yezierska's 1925 novel *Bread Givers,* for example, the narrator's sister Mashah Smolinsky takes care, even in the face of abject poverty, to embrace the latest American fashions: "'Give a look only on these roses for my hat,' cried Mashah, running over to the looking glass over the sink. . . . 'Like a lady from Fifth Avenue I look, and for only ten cents, from a pushcart on Hester Street. . . . these pink roses on my hat to match out my pink calico will make me look just like the picture on the magazine cover'" (2–3). Mashah's references to Fifth Avenue and "the magazine cover" suggest that she does not merely strive for a neat appearance but for a stylish and beautiful one.

Mashah's insistence on fashion and beauty in a life fraught with poverty recalls the ethos of the January 11, 1912, Bread and Roses strike at a textile factory in Lawrence, Massachusetts—a strike led by Polish immigrant women. The strike began when workers' wages were cut an amount equivalent to two weeks' worth of bread (Ross 59). It received its famous name because of the workers' signs reading "We want bread and roses too!," a reference to a James Oppenheim poem (Ross 59–60, 61). The phrase refers to a human need not only for basics, like food, but also for beauty and art. Yezierska echoes this sentiment in each of her major works, most literally in her novel *Salome of the Tenements* (1923) when the protagonist, Sonya Vrumsky, buys a beautiful bouquet of red roses and gives one to a poor little girl in whom she sees "the need for beauty, the famine for bright color" (72). In each of her major fictional works, Yezierska underlines the sentiment of the Bread and Roses strike: basic survival is not enough; human beings need more to feel content. As Oppenheim puts it, "Hearts starve as well as bodies; give us bread, give us roses!" For Yezierska's heroines, the human need for beauty surfaces in the form of romance, poetry, flowers, an attractive home, and pretty clothes.

Since many early immigrant narratives tend to focus on basic survival, or the initial disillusionment faced by hopeful arrivals in the United States, the attention to luxury items like fashionable gowns and elegant suits seems surprising. While most immigrant narratives discuss high-end fashion only briefly, and in relation to an individual gaining success as a designer or manufacturer (as in *Levinsky* and *My Ántonia*), Anzia Yezierska discusses it extensively in her work, especially in *Salome of the Tenements.* Since she's writing a few years later than Cahan and Cather, about a period later than Michael Gold's work, it makes sense that Yezierska would make higher-end clothing a part of her narrative. Unlike the other writers, her stories focus more on romance, often with fairy-tale elements (Yezierska herself was known as the "Sweat-Shop Cinderella"). In addition, as a woman with socialist leanings, she often juxtaposes life in the tenements with life in wealthier parts of New York. Finally, she was writing after World War I, when fashion was moving toward simpler and more utilitarian styles—styles that could be emulated, that were more affordable, and that emphasized restraint. Because Yezierska's work incorporates all three uses of clothing mentioned above (clothing as labor, clothing as an Americanizing agent, and clothing as art), I focus on her body of literature in this chapter.

Yezierska's works exhibit a widespread belief among immigrants that clothing and style held the keys to achieving their dreams—whether they dreamed of wealth, husbands, careers, or merely becoming real Americans. The increasing accessibility of ready-made clothing intensified the poorer classes' desire for fashion and style. With this rising accessibility, immigrants who worked their lives away in the garment industry but could not afford the clothing themselves suddenly saw their dreams within their reach (Ewen and Ewen 70). In *Channels of Desire,* Elizabeth and Stuart Ewen explain, "For hardworking, ill-housed immigrants, despised by the middle-class 'natives,' clothing offered one of the few avenues by which people could assume a sense of belonging. . . . The abundance of cheap ready-to-wear was one of the first acquisitions of the urban poor" (156). Although stylish clothing was considered by many—especially older generations of immigrants—to be a luxury rather than a necessity, younger generations of immigrants recognized clothes as the key visible signifier that could make the difference between a job and unemployment, between marriage and spinsterhood, between acceptance into the American mainstream and rejection as an outsider.

Immigrants like Yezierska therefore looked at clothing and style as one means by which they could transcend their social, ethnic, and economic castes. In her fiction Yezierska maps out the concrete details of material acquisition and physical transformation necessary for assimilating into an American ideal. These codes of behavior and representation include maintaining personal hygiene and cleanliness, wearing tasteful and simple tailored clothing, consuming American cuisine, learning to speak and write standard English, refraining from shouting or gesticulating during conversation, establishing clean and plain living accommodations, achieving independence from family and community, and dating (eventually marrying) an American. Yezierska foregrounds dress and taste as the biggest clues to an individual's assimilability.

Yezierska believed that beauty and taste in clothing resided in the quality of materials, the way the cut or silhouette could flatter a woman's figure, and the way the color and style enhanced a woman's natural beauty rather than distracting from her natural assets. In many ways, her ethos of fashion echoes that of Coco Chanel, who famously remarked, "Dress shabbily and they remember the dress; dress impeccably and they remember the woman." Anyone from the wealthiest socialite to the poorest factory worker could learn the fundamentals of style and dress, just as any woman, regardless of class, could mistake cost for elegance. In her autobiography *Red Ribbon on a White Horse,* Yezierska acknowledges, "The poorest shopgirl with her mind on style managed to look as smart as other shopgirls" (56). Her statement, written nearly a quarter of a century after most of her fiction was published, speaks to her faith in American democratic fashion: she believed stylish clothing was not limited to the wealthiest women, that women could find clothing that suited their individual figures, tastes, and lifestyles. The problem, for Yezierska, was twofold: (1) poorer classes and immigrants lacked instruction, and therefore knowledge, about fashion and style; and (2) earlier ready-made clothing, which was all most poorer immigrant women could afford, was mass-produced and therefore not tailored to suit individual women's bodies. In her writing Yezierska both critiqued and instructed, praising the contemporary mode of simplicity chic and denigrating gaudy and cheaply made clothing as well as the traditional garb in which most working-class women were attired.

Yezierska's emphasis on cleanliness, simplicity, and tailoring (or sometimes draping) in clothing speaks to the mode of the era. The association of Anglo-American style with simplicity was not a long-standing one, but began during World War I. Out of necessity, fashion in the United States during the war took a radical shift from the opulence of the Edwardian period, a period marked by excessive ornamentation and an emphasis on the decorative rather than the functional. In *Vogue History of 20th Century Fashion,* Jane Mulvagh writes of the restrictive nature of this clothing, which "hampered movement," noting of Edwardian women, "Their lives were almost exclusively domestic, and social life was private, time-consuming and precisely ordered, in terms of both etiquette and dress. Having little else to do, women were preoccupied with the minutiae of clothing and its upkeep. The ability to be fashionable was a sign of social status" (2). She notes that upper-class women of the Edwardian era would not only change clothing throughout the day but also visit Paris "twice a year to order the season's wardrobe" (3). Even before the war, however, this mode of excess and expense showed signs of change. Paul Poiret rose to prominence in Paris around 1908, gaining recognition with his Empire line (5), a narrower silhouette and simpler look than typical Edwardian style, which tended to favor a curvier, more mature figure. An October 15, 1913, *Vogue* feature quotes him as saying, "If the design is simple, the gown will be beautiful" (Poiret). His gowns, like the silk evening dress featured in figure 7 (ca. 1912–14), show a drastic departure from the layered, voluminous skirts of the Victorian and Edwardian eras. Instead, the gown has a narrower, column-like silhouette and a more natural overall shape.

In *As Seen in Vogue,* Daniel Delis Hill explains the changes in style begin-

FIGURE 7. Paul Poiret evening dress, 1912–14. (Brooklyn Museum Costume Collection at the Metropolitan Museum of Art, gift of the Brooklyn Museum, 2009; gift of Mrs. Andrew J. Love, 1962, 2009.300.2503; metmuseum.org, OASC/public domain)

ning in 1914 that "reflected women's everyday needs rather than the glamour or mystique of fashion" (29).[2] He articulates the increasingly democratic styles of the period that emerged from these needs: "Clothes that provided comfort and freedom of movement were necessary for a great number of women who had to undertake all sorts of activities for the war effort, from volunteer work with emergency agencies to full-time employment filling vacancies for men away in the military" (29). The clothing of this period fit women more loosely: rather than the restraints of whalebone corsets, women had more flexibility, though clothing could still have structure and tailoring. In addition, women's clothes featured raised hemlines, more inexpensive fabrics, and quieter colors; at times resembled menswear in their "shapeless and simple" style; and often drew from "military motifs" (29).

The privations of World War I, particularly in Europe, called for more moderate fashions and a move away from opulence. Many American women were leaving the home to join the workforce, and this activity called for more comfort and ease of movement. The innovations in materials, corsetry, skirt lengths, and volume during the late 1910s and early 1920s reflected this shift.[3]

This atmosphere of refinement and necessity catalyzed innovation and ingenuity in design, with a momentum that would continue until the Great Depression.[4] After the war Poiret continued to design his narrower silhouettes, but as more female designers emerged, so did the trend of "comfort chic" embodied by Coco Chanel, Madeleine Vionnet, and Edward Molyneux (Hill 36). Designers incorporated more knitwear and began to design gowns without the structure of corsets in mind, and this emphasis on comfort would make Poiret's designs less relevant to the mode. Chanel represented and continues to represent simple elegance and comfort in women's dress.[5] Her signature look championed simplicity, both because turbulent economic times required it and because simple elegance showcased a woman's natural beauty rather than eclipsing it with ornamentation. Mulvagh notes of Chanel's emergence as a designer, "Eager to set herself apart from the 'cocotte' and enjoy the same physical freedom as the men she accompanied, she dressed in comfortable, masculine-inspired sports clothing. . . . She turned elegance on its head, she made the over-decorated appear ridiculous by highlighting the charm of the tomboy" (10). Chanel set the bar for comfort chic, and despite fluctuations in trends and modes over the decades, her brand has adhered to her initial principles of style and fashion. Some writers suggest that Chanel's success derived from her ability to mix unusual or unexpected textiles;[6] others point to her ability make women look more youthful, largely owing to the effortless appearance of her ensembles. One April 15, 1923, *Vogue* article describes her as "staunch supporter of youthful chic" (Hillis, "A Seat" 49). This ability to make women appear younger through construction and styling became both admirable and necessary during a period that valorized slenderness, simplicity, and youth.

While the simpler gowns of the 1920s might seem more affordable to the masses, the simplicity of the garments—whether a tailored suit or a draped silk dress—still required a fit appropriate to an individual woman's physique. In her study of clothing in Yezierska's fiction, Katherine Stubbs relates the prominence of ready-made clothing in the United States, as well as the rise of haute couture in Paris, to Yezierska's exploration of class and ethnic divisions: "Materially, the mass production of clothing in standardized styles meant that many members of even the lowest classes of society in urban centers could afford to purchase new clothing. Ideologically, the ready-made garment seemed to make possible a form of egalitarianism, an equal access to attractive commodities" (160). The simultaneous haute couture movement was "in a sense an answer to the threat of the ready-made—a way to redraw rapidly dissolving boundaries between the elite and the common, the exclusive and the vulgar" (162). As ready-made clothing began to dissolve the distinctions in dress between American and immigrant, upper and working class, the continued elevation of haute couture designers reestablished those distinctions. Yet the rising popularity of ready-to-wear clothing and improvements in its production, as illustrated by Yezierska and Abraham Cahan, helped to characterize the era as one in which hierarchical boundaries were constantly blurred.

Stylish clothing and romance, for Yezierska, were the best ways to transcend one's otherness, and thus her Russian-Jewish immigrant heroines strive for both. These heroines, characterized by emotional outbursts and rebellion against both their poverty and the patriarchal traditions of the Old World, fall in love with seemingly unattainable Anglo-American Prince Charmings—teachers, sociologists, or philanthropists. Her male characters are conflated with America while the heroines aspire to be American; the male is deified while the heroine deems herself "unworthy"; and the contrast between male and female serves to reveal the ethnic markers that characterize Russian Jewish immigrants as cultural outsiders. Although Yezierska critiques the emotional restraint and puritanical manners of the dominant culture, this critique is muted by her characters' near-worship of American men, American customs, and American fashion.

The Prince Charming to Yezierska's "Sweat-Shop Cinderella" heroine serves as the catalyst for her physical transformation into an assimilated American woman. Scholars have alternately connected the male character in these works to John Dewey, with whom Yezierska had a romantic attachment when she was twenty-three years old, and to James Graham Phelps Stokes, a philanthropist whose marriage to Yezierska's friend Rose was ultimately doomed owing to their insurmountable cultural and sociological differences.[7] In her autobiographical work *Red Ribbon on a White Horse* (1950), Yezierska describes her torrid romance with Dewey (granted the alias "John Morrow"), lingering on the details of his wife's "natural poise and elegance"

(110) and his brutal rejection of Yezierska. After expressing his love in letters and in a passionate kiss by the Williamsburg Bridge, Morrow withdraws from Yezierska and treats her with coldness. When pressed for an explanation for his change in demeanor, he thunders back at her: "You're an emotional, hysterical girl, and you have exaggerated my friendly interest" (116). This contrast between the cold, restrained philanthropist and the "emotional, hysterical" immigrant became, for Yezierska, a central symbol in her works and an opportunity to reflect on the emotional and physical changes necessary for immigrants to gain acceptance and security in the United States. She used fashion, particularly women's dress, to exemplify the immigrant plight: according to Yezierska, the younger generation of immigrant women had a passionate desire to adopt American practices, yet their endeavors were limited by a lack of both worthwhile Americanizing agencies and fiscal means. Her literature became simultaneously a message to nativist Americans that Eastern European immigrants wanted to assimilate (and *were* assimilable) and a form of instruction to unassimilated immigrant women on how to adopt American traits, values, and appearances with limited means.

Hungry Hearts and Other Stories

Writing during a time of intense nativist discourse, just a few years before the government would legislate strict quotas on immigration from eastern and southern Europe, Yezierska, in her first major work of fiction, helped to humanize immigrant women by highlighting their eagerness to embrace American customs. In her 1920 collection *Hungry Hearts and Other Stories,* Yezierska offers vignettes of the lives of Russian Jewish immigrants living in crowded tenements and longing for comfort, love, success, and American acceptance. The first two stories of the collection, "Wings" and "Hunger," portray a Jewish immigrant woman's pursuit of an Anglo-American man, a sociologist named John Barnes who has moved to the Lower East Side to study Russian immigrants. Like the other "Dewey figures," John is as a divine figure in the eyes of Yezierska's heroine, Shenah Pessah, who exclaims to herself, "But he was not a man! He was God Himself!" (36), and who repeatedly refers to his "white radiance." Her deification of John only intensifies when he takes it upon himself to assist in Americanizing her by giving her advice and later by offering to take her to a library. Even after John has rejected her, Shenah Pessah takes the rejection as an impetus to "build herself up"—in other words, his godlike presence is responsible for compelling her to assimilate into the dominant culture and to educate herself. While Yezierska's later texts indicate her interest in subverting the stigmatization of immigrants, in "Wings" and "Hunger" her character fails to critique the supercilious, hypocritical, and puritanical qualities of John Barnes. The aim of these short stories seems less about subverting stereotypes and more about impelling immigrant women to conform to standards of American dress and behavior. These stories, coming before the Johnson-Reed Act of 1924, could be read as a kind of call to action. Yezierska recognized the sociopolitical tide rising against immigration and the danger of ending the flow of immigrants from Europe.

In "Wings," as in Yezierska's 1923 novel *Salome of the Tenements,* the Anglo-American male's physical appearance and dress instantly appeal to Yezierska's heroine. The heroine reads his clean, tailored clothing as evidence of his "Americanness," his confidence, and his financial success. She also characterizes him as "white" (a reference to his immaculate appearance, though implicitly his race as well), associating his whiteness with a kind of divine light or heavenly glow. In addition, she describes her love interest with specific attention to age, for the heroine typically views the man as either a figurative or literal teacher.[8] John Manning in *Salome of the Tenements* embodies these last two traits: "The premature greyness of his hair was to her a nimbus—a cloud of white light, adding the final touch of divinity to the luminous features" (8). This description marks Manning as distinguished and mature, but like John Barnes, he is deified by the heroine's idealized vision of him.

Yezierska's heroines also tend to contrast their love interests with men from their own community, both in temperament and in appearance—the pushy fish peddler widower with a passel of children, the starving but romantic poet, or, in the case of "Hunger," the immigrant with bad teeth who remains loyal to his roots. Once she has begun working in a sweatshop, Shenah befriends Sam Arkin, an immigrant more settled than she because of his supervisory position at the factory, his bank account, and his ability to sign his name. Shenah contrasts him with John, lingering on Sam's physical appearance: "As Shenah Pessah listened, unconsciously she compared Sam Arkin, glowing with the frank conceit of the self-made man, his neglected teeth, thick, red lips, with that of the Other One—made ever more beautiful with longings and dreams" (58). Her reaction reveals Yezierska's emphasis on hygiene, even as she codifies Arkin's appearance (e.g., his "thick, red lips") as ethno-racially "other." Arkin is financially secure, and his adoration of and friendship with Shenah imply that he does not perpetuate the patriarchal values of the Old World, yet his security and affection are not enough to convince her to marry him. Ultimately, she rejects Arkin because of his unwillingness to cut off ties to Old World ways, his emphasis on material acquisition over higher learning, and his physical appearance—especially his facial features and his clothing—that highlight his ethno-racial difference.

As Shenah reads John Barnes's appearance and clothing, Yezierska offers a brief glimpse of his own thoughts as he reads Shenah's appearance with the patronizing attitude of the social reformers. Upon encountering Shenah for the first time and viewing her ragged appearance, John "congratulated himself at his good fortune in encountering such a splendid type for his research" (5). He does not take a personal interest in Shenah as an individual with longings and romantic fantasies; instead, he sees her as a prototype with the potential for facilitating his research. John does not seek to get to know Shenah intimately, but instead, in a manner typical of contemporary pseudoscientific inquiry, merely looks for affirmations of his assumptions about the nature of immigrants. In Shenah, John sees "[t]he whole gamut of the Russian Jew—the pendulum swinging from abject servility to boldest aggressiveness" (10). He reads Shenah's shabby clothing, gesticulations, excited speech, and desperation as endemic to her "race." In later works and in her autobiography, Yezierska would challenge this view, indicating that these are cultural traits that can be adopted or altered as needed. However, in this early work, she implies that this eagerness and enthusiasm are unique to the Russian Jewish immigrant, and that these traits can enrich an increasingly cold, materialistic American dominant culture.

When John begins to pay attention to Shenah, she perceives it as romantic—a way to bring her, intellectually, to his level. Therefore, she sees it as her task to transform herself physically, to appear worthy of him. Shenah associates beauty with vibrant color; therefore, to attract John, she assumes that her appearance needs to be exuberant and colorful. Her desire to dress in a manner worthy of John's attention drives her to sell her most precious possessions to a greedy pawnbroker. She then takes her meager sum with the intention of spending the full amount on a new suit of clothing.

Shenah goes shopping among the brightly colored ready-made clothes, looking for an ensemble that matches her emotional intensity: "At last she espied a shining straw with cherries so red, so luscious, that they cried out to her, 'Bite me!' . . . The magic of those cherries on her hat brought back to her the green fields and orchards of her native Russia. Yes, a green dress was what she craved. And she picked out the greenest, crispest organdie" (16–17). Even when Shenah attempts to attract the more somber, conservative sociologist through clothing, she lets her emotions rule her decisions by selecting a dress for its brightness and the nostalgia it evokes rather than with calculated strategy. When Shenah meets John later that evening, they visit the library, where she comments upon how "quiet" the librarians appear: "'Yes,' he replied, with a tell-tale glance at her. 'I too like to see a woman's face above her clothes'" (21). Shenah immediately realizes her mistake, sensing that her clothes, which had charmed her with their bright color, are garish and cheap looking. Instead of appearing more American, Shenah physically expresses the emotional intensity that characterizes her as a Russian immigrant.[9] John, like the librarian, embodies the mode of the era—simple lines and subdued colors, which Yezierska's heroines read as refinement. The dialogue between Shenah and John also reveals the intended effect of the simplicity trend: its restraint serves to showcase the individual's beauty.

The scene feels instructional in its differentiation between gaudy and simple clothing. Shenah, in her eagerness for beauty and her desire to look more American for John, assumes that any new clothing available in the shops will make her appear more American. She lacks the trained eye of the stylish woman and selects bright clothing rather than clothing that will showcase her brightest features. Mulvagh notes how the upper classes would view this tendency among poorer classes with derision: "The immigrants' desire for fine clothing was the object of ridicule and moralizing by the middle class. Unable to appreciate the meaning of clothes to those who were denied nearly all else, they would refer to these fashionable poor, walking up the avenue, as a 'Monkey's Parade'" (157). Shenah dons her colorful dress and adorned hat with confidence, yet on recognizing her mistake feels the humiliation of one who has tried to transcend her caste and failed. Through this scene, Yezierska both characterizes the contemporary mode of simplicity, thereby instructing her immigrant reader on signifiers of American appearance, and cautions against the impulsive purchase of gaudy ready-made clothing.

Salome of the Tenements

Unlike Shenah Pessah of "Wings" and "Hunger," Sonya Vrumsky, the heroine of *Salome of the Tenements,* exhibits more knowledge about American fashion in her attempt to woo her philanthropist Prince Charming, John Manning. *Salome* is semiautobiographical: the romance between Sonya Vrumsky and John Manning echoes the relationship with John Dewey (aka John Morrow) that Yezierska describes in *Red Ribbon on a White Horse.* However, in her introduction to the novel, Gay Wilentz likens the Sonya–John Manning union to the relationship between Yezierska's friend Rose Pastor and the philanthropist and political activist James Graham Phelps Stokes. Wilentz notes how the Pastor-Stokes union represented, at the time, a collapse of socioeconomic and ethnic boundaries: "[T]he Stokeses worked with the socialists and tried to overcome class and ethnic differences to make their marriage and its democratic aims work" (xvi). Their marriage, according to Wilentz, ended because of Rose's support of the Communist Party. She left her husband in 1923: "She had realized the unsuitability of his liberal ideology for accepting true social change and of his desire to maintain his privileged, elite lifestyle" (xvi). While Yezierska's relationship with Dewey informs the physical attraction between Sonya and John Manning, the Pastor-Stokes union helps explain the disillusionment, born from Sonya's perception of Manning's ideological hypocrisy and his repression of emotion, that contributes to the dissolution of the union.[10]

The novel opens with Sonya's first meeting with Manning and thus echoes the structure of "Wings": "His low voice of cultured restraint thrilled through the girl like music. Even his formal manner—his unconscious air of superiority—roused in her the fire of worship" (1). Again we see the immigrant heroine's idolization of an older, Anglo-Saxon character depicted with formality and emotional repression. Yet this description also connotes a more sexualized interaction. Sonya's sexuality proves a central theme (as suggested by the book's title) and a departure from *Hungry Hearts.* Stubbs suggests that Sonya's sexualization derives not from her attraction to men but from the way she wears clothing and presents herself, as well as her response to the clothing style of her love interest: "Yezierska depicts a Jewish clothing worker who indulges in an intensely personal and erotic relation to clothing; in that novel, clothing is used as a vehicle to engage in a fascinating attempt to transgress and transcend forms of economic and social hierarchy" (157). Sonya's understanding of good taste and style allows her to seduce more than one male character into giving her what she wants and to win the heart of John Manning. Stubbs asserts that such an ability to seduce through clothing and physical appearance fed Anglo-American fears that working-class women could alter their appearance through clothing, secure the attentions of wealthy men, and collapse cherished class boundaries.[11] Indeed, Yezierska openly conflates the "emotional" and "hysterical" labels with a kind of primitive sexual vitality, suggesting that what Americans condemn in immigrant women actually strengthens the lifeblood and passion of American culture.

Sonya confirms dominant culture fears of immigrant aspirations. To win Manning, she takes great pains to erase all traces of poverty from her appearance, room, and apartment building. Her success in attracting Manning stems not only from these changes but also from her knowledge of the dominant culture aesthetic—the austerity of dress and decor that communicates class and breeding. What Manning perceives as the Russian immigrant's ability to mimic American style on a minimal budget actually results from Sonya toiling for weeks to transform herself and to charm, manipulate, or blackmail different men into giving her things for free.

Sonya's understanding of simple fashions derives from both observation and instinct. She recognizes her own assets as well as the potential for fashion to showcase those assets. Her fellow immigrants associate elegance with excessive finery or bright colors. Her landlady Mrs. Pelz, for example, arrives at Manning's home later in the novel "decked in the gaudiest finery of Essex Street" (123), including a "silk waist" and "diamond earrings." Sonya, however, knows that elegance comes from the quality of a garment and its ability to highlight a woman's best features, making her appear more beautiful.

Yezierska first reveals Sonya's understanding of fashion in a scene where she shops for an ensemble to wear for Manning. When she visits a ready-made clothing store on the Lower East Side, she remarks upon the cheapness and garishness of its wares. When a salesperson shows her a sailor hat—a vestige of Edwardian fashion—Sonya remarks, "Something simple I want—yes, but soft and formed on the lines of the head" (15). Her description calls to mind early models of the cloche hat, invented by the Parisian milliner Caroline Reboux in 1909 but popularized during the 1920s. This early moment in the novel exposes Sonya's knowledge of contemporary style, suggesting that one does not have to be able to afford the latest fashions to recognize style and taste. Rejecting the recycled ready-mades, Sonya goes straight to Fifth Avenue, having heard about a Paris-educated designer named Jacques Hollins. Sonya is drawn to Hollins not only because of his reputation as a prominent designer but also because of his Jewish background (he has changed his name from Jaky Solomon) and his reputation for creating simple clothing that transforms women. Hollins highlights women's most beautiful features while concealing their imperfections,[12] as "Sadie of Trimmings" from an Essex Street shop explains: "Rich women with no worries on their heads but how to catch on to men, they don't care what price they lay down for a dress so long it'll make them shine out different. . . . he studies their faces and their shapes and the color of their hair and the shade of their skin" (15–16). Hollins's name is known around town for his transformative talent and the care with which he designs for the individual client. Yezierska captures, through Hollins, the ideal of the designer: one who relies not on excess to make a woman stand out but on finding her individual beauty and creating, in the design, a stage to showcase that beauty.

While Hollins's wealthy clients need his design skills to transform their figures, Sonya enters his shop as an ideal client (aside from her inability to pay him). Her body needs no padding or cinching. Her youth and beauty allow Hollins to draw on his artistic inclinations and create clothing for the perfect model rather than use his pragmatic knowledge of how to present women as more attractive than they are. For Sonya, the project is not to transform but to reveal—to "make [her] look like [her]self" (16). Sonya appeals to Hollins with her seductive power, with her reference to their common Jewish roots, and especially through their shared artistic vision. She knows Hollins appreciates her "hunger for beauty," thinking "This was the god of clothes! In every fiber of her being she felt a kinship with him—a divine understanding of beauty!" (22). During their first meeting, she exclaims, "[O]nly you can know that the hunger for bread is not half as maddening as the hunger for beautiful clothes. Why, day after day, for years and years, I used to go from store to store, looking for a hat, a dress that will express me—myself" (23). Sonya rails against "the blood poison of ugliness" (23) and "hideous ready-make stuff" (22). Her diction expresses exhaustion with the rags of poverty, the ill fit of cheap clothing, and the anonymity of poor-quality ready-made fashion. Hollins is moved by Sonya's appeals as well as by her physical beauty, and after seeing her in his creations, he declares, "Dressing you has been art" (31).

Through the novel's interactions between Sonya and Hollins, Yezierska instructs her audience in style and taste, speaking to a contemporary emphasis on personal style—a crucial element of democratic fashion. Women of the 1920s could express their individual tastes and embrace more flexibility in their garment selection because of contemporary designers' emphasis on comfort and simplicity, as well as the range of experimental trends during this period—for example, sports clothing as everyday wear, Egyptian and Turkish ornamentation, and Persian and Chinese motifs (Hill 50, 44, 36). One of the most common critiques of American fashion, according to *Vogue,* was women's tendency to latch onto a trend without knowing how to incorporate it into an already established, individualized look. During the early 1920s, *Vogue* articles and advertisements challenged American readers to embrace the concept of personal style, which meant putting together ensembles that best suited a person's individual appearance and expressed his or her personality and lifestyle. One 1922 Printz-Biederman advertisement, for example, defines "personalized style" as "the art of choosing lines that best become your figure." The advertisement cautions that though a garment "may have beauty and richness and may observe the newest features of the mode, real Style it cannot have unless it suits the individual figure" ("Advertisement: Printzess"). The versatility of clothing, the less constricting foundation garments, and the prominence of draping, slim silhouettes, shorter hemlines, and tailored suits during the 1920s made understanding one's own proportions and style far more important.

Sonya and Hollins comprehend these elements of fashion and personal style. After their consultation, in the chapter "The Democracy of Beauty," Hollins designs a gray draped gown for Sonya, paired with a turban-style hat and accompanied by luxury undergarments, including silk stockings. He explains to her, "With your color and verve there must be nothing but simple lines. That's why I wanted this nun-like grey with a touch of sheer batiste against the whiteness of your throat" (26). As Sonya reacts to seeing herself and experiencing the feel of luxury garments, Yezierska conveys how her donning of the new ensemble is a religious experience for both Sonya and Hollins. Sonya feels "a triumphant sense of spiritual superiority" (28) once she puts on Hollins's design, and she declares, "I feel like a radiant being" (29); meanwhile, Hollins remarks, "I always dreamed of designing clothes that would express and reveal the human soul, but it was only bodies that came to me for gowns" (29). The spiritual language raises the clothing commentary of the novel from being merely a reflection on the accessibility of clothing and style to a statement on the elevation of the designer to a kind of mythical, godlike status. The designer, for Sonya, has the power to make women feel younger, richer, more comfortable, more radiant, and more beautiful. Implicitly, he or she helps the woman acquire the things in life (a job, a husband, etc.) that she most desires.

Ultimately, the deified Hollins/designer replaces the deified Manning/philanthropist as Sonya's romantic ideal. It is Hollins who first helps Sonya perceive the cracks in Manning's benevolent façade. He tries to caution Sonya about the hypocritical and patronizing nature of philanthropists like Manning: "'You mean . . . he is one of those philanthropists who come with a gilded cane to tap ash-cans and garbage heaps? I suppose,' he added cynically, 'playing with poverty is more exciting than knocking golf balls'" (30). Sonya discovers Manning's paternalistic manner too late: after they have married, she realizes that his ideas for the settlement house are completely impractical and dehumanizing; his idealistic notions about democracy derive from his privileged existence and lack of real contact with the immigrants; and his attraction to Sonya is primarily sexual—a response to her "primitive" and "oriental" nature (both descriptors are used repeatedly)—rather than his faith in her ability to teach him about uplifting the poor. Moreover, she perceives as early as their wedding reception that although she can pass as an Anglo-American through her impeccable taste and new clothing, passing also requires a suppression of her emotions, particularly the enthusiastic nature that bewitched both Manning and Hollins.

At the wedding reception, one of Manning's wealthy guests appraises Sonya, thinking, "Astonishingly well-dressed. . . . Her gesticulating hands show her origin" (121). The moment is surprising, for Sonya has illustrated a hyperawareness of the various physical signifiers of difference she can control. While working at the settlement house for Manning, for example, she looks to the image of the *Mona Lisa* hanging in his office as her inspiration, musing "How much more alluring to men is what she keeps hidden about herself—her mystery of restraint, than our Russian madness to tell everything—to strip our souls naked in the untamed wildness of our desire!" (84–85). These moments illuminate Sonya's inner conflict: she admires the restrained beauty of Anglo-American style and recognizes its elegance, yet she also finds beauty in the emotional expression of her Russian origins. In marrying Manning after the torrid beginning of their love, Sonya hopes he will encourage her to embody the elegance of the dominant culture while allowing her the freedom of expression to which she is accustomed. She establishes this desire for balance early in the novel, after she first dons Hollins's design: "You made me look like Fifth Avenue-born. Only—I don't want to have the tied-up manners of a lady" (26).

Once Sonya realizes she cannot strike this desired balance between refinement and passion in her relationship with Manning, she loses her attachment to him, and the plot points that spell the demise of their marriage seem less significant than her shift in feeling. Having witnessed the hypocrisy of a well-meaning Anglo-Saxon philanthropist and the haughty puritanism of bourgeois society, Sonya longs for the vivaciousness of her ethnic community, yet she has grown accustomed to privilege, and her community no longer accepts her as one of them. At the end of her marriage to Manning, Sonya recognizes him for who he really is: "At last the curtain was down. There was no revelation, no flame—only the pale flicker of a burnt-out star, only the winter coldness of a sterile race" (146). While Sonya's observation may characterize Manning and Anglo-Saxons as cold and "burnt-out," Sonya herself seems to lose some of her ethnic vitality by the end of the novel. Although she initially believes in Manning's philanthropy, her love for him has been fueled by passion and romance; her interest in Hollins, though they share an artistic vision and passion, is far more calm, calculated, and pragmatic. Before rushing to Hollins in the unstable days after her marriage, Sonya chooses to build herself up as a designer.

When she finally has a chance to design a dress, Sonya declares, "I want that beautiful plainness that only the rich wear. A dress that looks simple enough for the poor only that it's different" (169). Her phrasing foreshadows the language used to describe Chanel's little black dress, though it would not appear until several years later. In 1926 *Vogue* referred to this model as "The Chanel 'Ford'—the frock that all the world will wear" ("Fashion: The Debut" 69). Most likely, Yezierska was already influenced by Chanel's aesthetic and design goals, which Chanel expressed on multiple occasions even early in her career. Yezierska continues: "What she wanted was a costume, plain enough for everybody but distinctive enough to make it effective for any occasion. She wanted the wearer to have the joy of a dress that could be slipped on in a moment, and yet give the luxurious sense of a fitted gown. A supple, clinging thing in everyday serge, veiling yet revealing the lovely curves of a woman's body" (169). Yezierska's description of the simple, everyday dress is reminiscent of Chanel's early dress designs (like the one featured in fig. 8), which rose to popularity during the early 1920s and often featured simple lines, seams that flattered the body, and subtle colors. Mulvagh observes of this post–World War I period, "The most popular expression of liberated clothing was the tailored suit. . . . With simple changes of accessories, the suit could be worn from nine in the morning until six in the evening, a godsend for the woman of limited income and busy lifestyle" (50). Sonya designs with her own experience in mind, the need for one look to suit many occasions—the very opposite of the Edwardian mode. Though Sonya aims to find the right cut and style to suit a range of women, she also recognizes "that she must keep within the prevailing fashion, in order that her creation might be a commercial success" (169), thus despite her disdain for trimmings she uses braid to keep the garment in the mode (the wool dress in fig. 8 also reflects this trend). Harrison-Kahan explains that the success of this work, dubbed the "Sonya Model," lies in "its many contradictions": "Sonya makes her name by bringing seemingly contradictory elements together, much like Chanel, who was known for promoting a feminine look inspired by the masculine" (321–22). Harrison-Kahan draws attention to the "hybridity" of Sonya's dress, a technique that echoes Chanel; however, the dress carries additional symbolic value. Like Chanel, Sonya draws from her experience as a member of the working class as well as her more recent experience with high society to design a dress with the elegant simplicity of the elite, yet in a style suitable for a more versatile clientele. Her instinctual knowledge of construction and the female form makes her a huge success and allows Hollins to find her.

Sonya's understanding of fashion, despite her humble origins, challenges notions that only upper-class women can distinguish tasteful clothing from gaudy clothing. In fact, Hollins's clients lack her refinement. Sonya resists a ready-made industry that caters to the lowest common denominator of taste, one that throws cheap, flashy pieces at the poor instead of simpler, more tasteful pieces that can be instructive in how to dress stylishly. Instead, she and Hollins endeavor to embark on a new business venture: a store on the Lower East Side specializing in designing beautiful and stylish ready-made clothing at affordable prices.

Sonya views this business venture as a way to honor her past—both as a poor immigrant worker and as Manning's emotionally repressed wife: "Going into a new experience, she knew, could bring her no forgetfulness of the

FIGURE 8. Gabrielle "Coco" Chanel wool dress, ca. 1924. (Metropolitan Museum of Art; purchase, Irene Lewisohn Bequest, 1975, 1975.7; image courtesy of Art Resource, NY)

past, nor the closeness of spiritual identification which she had found at the moment of parting with this man of a different race" (183). Sonya does not seem to regret the loss of her emotional vitality, nor does she seek to rediscover it. Instead, this new venture offers the possibility of nurturing her artistic talent through design, her romantic inclinations through a partnership with Hollins, and her loss of community through providing beautiful clothing and stylistic guidance at affordable prices.

In her analysis of Sonya's new business, Stubbs notes that "to bring Fifth Avenue to the Lower East Side would be to eliminate the class differential upon which the distinction between couture and ready-made was historically based" (168); thus Sonya has seemingly resolved the tension between her sense of duty and her desire to maintain her comfortable middle-class lifestyle. Yet Stubbs notes the irony of Sonya's plan: "These copies of couture will simply be attractive ready-made gowns—and their attractiveness will itself be in question, for these copies will not meet Sonya's primary criterion for beauty, a garment's correspondence with the unique body and personality of the consumer." While Sonya's dresses in this new venture will be ready-to-wear, it is important to differentiate between these ready-to-wear garments and those she encounters on Essex Street. The Essex Street ready-made clothes are gaudy and embellished with cheap trimmings, designed to attract women who want to stand out but know little about style. They have little connection with the simple styles of the early 1920s. Sonya and Hollins's shop, in contrast, reflects the ambitions of my ancestors when they began the Orange Frocks label. Sonya and Hollins maintain a store on Fifth Avenue and one on the Lower East Side; the Oranges had their stores on Fifth Avenue and in the garment district on Seventh Avenue. In both cases, the designs still originate with the artist but, thanks to comprehensive sizing, would be ready-to-wear for women shopping on a budget. To collapse these two types of ready-made garments would be like suggesting a $3,000 Versace gown sold at Neiman Marcus is of the same quality as the $199 Versace for H&M dress distributed by the retail chain, and that this dress is of the same quality as a dress purchased at a budget chain like Walmart. This is not to suggest that all three stores cannot produce fashionable clothing, only that consumers expect different levels of quality depending on where they make their purchases.

The key values of affordability, fit, and style permeate the clothing of Yezierska's heroines in their assimilated, Americanized incarnations. Women can only achieve stylistic sophistication, she suggests, through a combination of resourcefulness and study. Sonya in *Salome of the Tenements* and Mashah in *Bread Givers* have a natural knack for style and beauty, but Yezierska also suggests this knowledge can be acquired over time. In *Bread Givers,* the narrator, Sara Smolinsky, initially makes the mistake of impetuously purchasing bright-colored hat trimmings and makeup. When Sara applies her dearly bought purchases, she feels exposed and humiliated: "I felt shamed and confused with my false face. It was as though the rouge had turned into a mask, and I could not breathe through the cover. . . . When I got to the laundry I hurried into the cloakroom to tear the roses off my hat and wash the paint off my face" (183). After this initial mistake, Sara spends years focusing on her studies, meanwhile observing the way her much-younger peers in college dress: "I had seen cheap, fancy style, Five- and Ten-Cent Store finery. But never had I seen such plain beautifulness. The simple skirts and sweaters, the stockings and shoes to match. The neat finished quietness of their tailored suits. There was no show-off in their clothes, and yet how much more pulling to the eyes and all the senses than the Grand Street richness I knew" (212). The women she observes, like the librarian Shenah encounters in "Wings," are not wearing couture, but tailored clothing that suits their figures and shows taste and restraint.

After saving her money and observing the refined taste of her dominant-culture peers, Sara selects a suit: "Finally, I decided on a dark blue. Plain serge only! Yes. But more style in its plainness than the richest velvet" (239). Sara waits while the saleslady tailors the suit to fit her perfectly, and her new suit becomes her most prized possession (she even refuses to rend her garments in the Jewish tradition when her mother dies). This progression in Sara's style embodies Yezierska's ethos of assimilation: initially working, studying, and saving; then, while still saving, observing the style and taste of the day (by observing shoppers on Fifth Avenue or studying magazines, like Sara's sister Mashah); and finally, purchasing a practical, versatile, and simple garment that showcases a woman's individual shape and personality in its refined elegance.

In a May 1, 1922, *Vogue* piece titled "Fashions from the New York Point of View," the author describes the fashionable New York woman as follows:

> The New York woman, consciously or unconsciously, appreciates the dramatic background of Fifth Avenue. . . . Seen through the analyzing eye of an artist, the fashionable woman of New York has grown more subtle, more reserved, and has learned to choose her clothes with the independence of an aristocrat. Her life to-day, embracing a wider activity than that of the past, calls on her to face the problem of dressing appropriately, picturesquely and practically; but above everything, she has attained perfection in the art of wearing her clothes. (37)

The post–World War I era of fashion opened up previously unseen opportunities for women wishing to appear fashionable and to transcend class boundaries. Meanwhile, the era placed a greater burden of responsibility on the consumer, not in the expense of the garments, but in the ability to develop a personal style and to exercise restraint so her clothes and accessories do not overwhelm her person. The early 1920s, therefore, ushered in a new era in which women would push the boundaries of freedom in dress: freedom to reveal their natural shapes, freedom to move with comfort and ease, freedom to blend inexpensive, ready-made garments with pricier, tailor-made pieces.

If Poiret helped to introduce simplicity and a narrower silhouette into women's fashion, Chanel and Vionnet helped to introduce comfort and movement. Their innovations would help catalyze a wave of experimentation during the mid- to late 1920s, when designers would look to non-Western cultures, architecture, and even machinery for inspiration. As the 1920s progressed, hemlines would become shorter and women of fashion would have more options to choose from if they wished to embrace the mode—menswear-inspired looks, African- or Asian-inspired gowns, knitwear and tailored suits, dresses with fringe or sequins to create the illusion of motion, among others. Fashion became more easily conflated with art but, more importantly, with personal expression and experimentation as it entered the era of high modernism.

four

The Modern Woman and the Slim Silhouette

The niece spun slowly and slimly on one high heel: the sweet young curve of her shanks straight and brittle as the legs of a bird and ending in the twin inky splashes of her slippers, entranced him. Her hat was a small brilliant bell about her face, and she wore her clothing with a casual rakishness, as though she had opened her wardrobe and said, Let's go downtown.

—William Faulkner, *Mosquitoes*

The look of the modern woman was arguably the first fashion industry profile engineered by women. While women had dominated the dressmaking industry since the 1600s, male designers had controlled the face of high fashion since the dawn of haute couture (Steele 11). Nevertheless, by the 1920s, Paris had seen the rise of female couturiers, including Coco Chanel, Madeleine Vionnet, Mme. Grés, Nina Ricci, Jeanne Lanvin, and Sonia Delaunay (ibid.). Many fashion historians have theorized that female designers best understood the needs of modern women—women who were more active in sports, women who rode bicycles and drove cars, women who worked outside the home, women who traveled and socialized more than their forebears, and women who expressed their sexuality more freely.

Many of the aesthetic elements traditionally associated with femininity (an ample bust, curvy hips, long hair, demure clothing, an hourglass figure) were repudiated by 1920s fashion. Instead, models' figures were straight and slender, elongated and surreal in fashion sketches and illustrations. Women bobbed their hair and hid much of it beneath bell-shaped cloche hats. Fashion magazines teemed with ads for hair removal, fad diets, methods for preventing or camouflaging wrinkles, and undergarments that flattened breasts and stomachs to streamline the body. Clothing styles and makeup distorted women's natural shapes and features even further, as women layered their faces with theatrical makeup, designers dropped waistlines far below women's natural waists, undergarments bound women's breasts, chemise dresses hung loosely on women's frames, obscuring natural curves, and Americans helped to launch masculine-style knit sportswear as a mode at home and in Paris.

While Vionnet introduced the elegant and comfortable bias-cut gown, and Jeanne Lanvin was known for designing for women of all ages, Gabrielle "Coco" Chanel is the designer most often credited with crafting the iconic 1920s mode. In her comparison between fashion and art, Jo Ann C. Stabb explains the role of Chanel in promoting this new, slim, somewhat standardized aesthetic, noting how Chanel likened clothing to "the assembly-line, industrially produced Model T Fords."[1] Stabb also points to Chanel's habit of "wearing her boyfriend's clothing for its practical comfort and rebellious symbolism, resulting in abstracted and flattened curves of the female figure echoing the geometry of cubism." These elements of Chanel's aesthetic—appropriating tailored menswear for women, simplifying the look of women's wear, and prioritizing comfort and mobility—would dictate the look of the modern woman. Chanel thereby departed from fashion modes not only by simplifying dress and making it more comfortable but also by disrupting heteronormative modes of dress, traditional gender norms, and standards of beauty.

The unconventional clothing of the modernist period took on a different, symbolic role in both American culture and American literature. The literary modes of realism and naturalism, discussed in the previous three chapters, integrate fashion and clothing into literature in a documentary style. The clothes are part of the landscape; they help delineate social class, location, and time period. However, in modernist literature, clothing functions more symbolically. Fashion is more stylized and exaggerated. While a particular fashion choice may carry symbolic meaning in any of these movements or literary works, in works of literary modernism a more concise description or small detail (a man's felt hat, a pink suit, a mention of bare legs or shoulders) carries a heavy connotation. As the move toward democratic fashion continued into the mid-1920s, therefore, writers became more reflective about the women such stylistic shifts created.

In a scene in William Faulkner's early novel *Mosquitoes* (1927), several writers and artists are sitting on the deck of a yacht and discussing women. Dawson Fairchild, a writer, complains to several of his male acquaintances, "We, you and I, grew up expecting something beneath a woman's dress. Something satisfying in the way of breasts and hips and such. But now . . . Now, on the street, what do you see? Creatures with the uncomplex awkwardness of calves or colts, with two little knobs for breasts and indicated buttocks that, except for their soft look, might well belong to a boy of fifteen." Fairchild's friend Julius Kaufmann agrees, calling the modern women "shrill and stupid." He asks, "Who was the fool who said that our clothing, our custom in dress, does not affect the shape of our bodies and our behavior?" (240). Kaufman's question characterizes the fashion industry in an interesting way: societal change does not initiate new fashion trends; new fashion trends initiate societal change.

In the context of the novel, this dialogue between Fairchild and Kaufmann carries a note of irony. During their time on the yacht, the *Nausikaa,* these men have ignored the older, shapelier women on the yacht and paid attention only to the young, slim flappers—those who seem the least interested in their attention. These men thus recognize what their society deems attractive and stylish, and they are instinctually drawn to it. However, they seem nostalgic for an older model of femininity and beauty.

Julius Kaufmann's implication that "our custom in dress" *does,* in fact, "affect the shape of our bodies and our behavior" constructs the persona of the modern woman as seen through the male gaze. Canonical, male modernist writers F. Scott Fitzgerald, William Faulkner, and Ernest Hemingway draw from the feminine ideal and style mode of the mid-1920s to sculpt modern female characters in their novels. For Fitzgerald, the professional woman golfer Jordan Baker surfaces as the modern woman in *The Great Gatsby* (1925); for Faulkner, Patricia ("Pat") Robyn of his early novel *Mosquitoes* (1927) embodies the boyish physique and defiant attitude of the 1920s mode; for Hemingway, Catherine Bourne of his posthumously published novel *The Garden of Eden* (1986), set during the late 1920s, experiments with cross-dressing and a sexual relationship with another woman. Hemingway's heroine Brett Ashley of *The Sun Also Rises* (1926), whom I discuss briefly in this chapter, epitomizes the modern woman's sexual liberation and bohemian persona.

The dress and defiant attitude of these characters seem to embrace the ideals of democratic fashion: the clothes have increased comfort and allow for greater ease of movement; the women take liberties with gender norms of the time and place, liberties often symbolized by their clothing choices; the women attempt to transcend boundaries of class and, at times, even gender, sexuality, and race; and the women express themselves through their clothing and style choices. We might read hope and promise into their style and their "jaunty" attitudes—the possibility of additional freedoms granted to women, or the possibility for women to break permanently with traditional gender expectations. However, rather than representing, ultimately, the aesthetic and artistic promise of the "Lost Generation," these women—translated through the male gaze of the authors—surface as antiheroines. Their "female masculinity,"[2] as written by canonical male writers, is not a fully realized transcendence of gender binaries but an attempt to appropriate power perceived as endemic to being a man. With their men's clothes, short haircuts, and boyish bodies, they come to embody the modernist themes of paralysis and sterility, forcing the other characters—male and female—to look back on older modes of femininity with nostalgia.

Before delving into these novels, however, I want to offer a fuller sociohistorical and fashion-related context for the modern woman—both as she emerged in the 1920s and as she was rendered by prominent male artists. This modern woman is bohemian, slender, haughty, and slightly androgynous. While the modern woman may be a social construct or an artistic archetype, her persona is grounded in reality, inspired by socioeconomic changes after World War I. Writing about changing fashions as depicted in *Vogue,* Jane Mulvagh describes a postwar suspicion of the "*nouveaux riches,* the wives of the war profiteers" (48). She notes, "Partly in reaction to this new element in society, it became smart to assume poverty, or at least a Bohemian lifestyle. Women cultivated alternatives to preoccupation with dress—literature, politics and, in some cases, careers. Fashion responded to this social evolution" (49). History offers us prototypes of these bohemian women: for example, the writer and art connoisseur Gertrude Stein, modernist poets like Marianne Moore and H.D., the eclectic performer Josephine Baker, and the actress and dancer Louise Brooks. Fashionable women of the time wore slim, chemise-style dresses or slim-tailored menswear looks. One *Vogue* editorial from November 15, 1923, quipped, "We all remember the era of the Gibson Girl. . . . Still more remarkable is the influence of the mode for the slender, not to say diaphanous, figure, which has flourished since the war and which shows not the slightest decline in popularity. Every woman apparently can taper from the shoulders now if she wants to hard enough" (Hillis, "Fitting" 44). The combination of the slender styles of the 1920s with women's increased involvement in public life (culture, literature, politics, athletics) helped to generate the familiar image of a seemingly aloof, effortlessly fashionable, and slightly arrogant modern woman.

In addition to cultivating a deeper interest in politics, careers, and the arts, women of the 1920s broke with traditional gender roles in other ways. More women became actively involved in sports, especially golf and tennis; the 1920s saw the rise of female professional athletes like the tennis champion Helen Wills and the golfer Edith Cummings. It became socially acceptable for women to drive cars and legal for them to vote. More women used birth control, held athletic records, spoke openly about sexuality, bobbed their hair, smoked cigarettes, wore makeup, and donned more masculine-style clothing (Hill 41). In issues of *Vogue* from this period, many car ads were still directed at men, but new ads began to target women drivers. The increased social acceptance of women driving cars had a symbolic dimension: it meant women were increasingly mobile and farther from the home, increasingly modern and technologically savvy, and increasingly independent—able to meet friends, visit the golf course, or drive into or out of the city without being chaperoned by a man.

The modern woman asserted her independence in other ways as well, most of which challenged longstanding definitions of gender boundaries. Other advertisements from the early 1920s help highlight some of these changes, particularly the numerous ads and photographs featuring women in sporting attire, often carrying golf clubs or leading horses (fig. 9). Words like "clever," "smart," "rakish," "gay," and "jaunty" were used to describe women of fashion, rather than the traditional "elegant" or "feminine." While the sociopolitical changes in American culture may have fueled many of these changes, the fashion, as it adapted, only encouraged the blurring of gender boundaries. *Vogue* columns commented on the masculine styles of clothing and the boyish body type, as in one 1922 piece which observed, "Men and women are becoming every year more indistinguishable" (qtd. in Hill 50). Though Chanel became famous for donning her boyfriend's clothing and setting a trend of menswear for women, even her earlier designs appropriated the attitude and style of "the dandy," according to Barbara Vinken: "That the dandy is the reference becomes apparent, not because of the kind of clothing appropriated, but rather because of the manner in which this fashion is worn. The *désinvolture,* the nonchalance, . . . in short, the carefully cultivated appearance of not having invested any thought into the clothes that one wears—all this belongs to the credo of the perfect dandy" (23). The fashion plate image of the haughty, aloof flapper who wears her gown with an effortless grace exemplifies this style and attitude, and it became the recognizable, stylized image of the 1920s woman, replicated in fashion illustrations, in film, in literature, and in historical memory.

For the next decade American popular culture would reflect this challenging of traditional gender roles and expectations for women's style, as epitomized by the popularity of sportswear, menswear-inspired fashions, the promotion of an elongated, boyish silhouette for clothing, and gender-bending or homosocial advertisements, often depicting multiple women in lingerie reclining on couches or beds together or admiring one another's figures. Illustrations from *Vogue* in the 1920s featured elongated, stylized, often androgynous figures that appeared neither sexual nor feminine. Yet these patterns of challenging traditional concepts of gender and sexuality in behavior and in dress were reciprocal. In his book *Fashion as Communication,* Malcolm Barnard explains that "fashion and clothing are more instrumental in the process of socialization into sexual and gender roles; they help shape people's ideas of how men and women should look" (111). Barnard points to the way the fashion industry might draw inspiration from its target market, as well as the way it can guide the behavior of that market. In the case of the early to mid-1920s, perhaps, as Mulvagh suggests, the fashion industry was simply responding to the way women were embracing new roles or the way they adopted hobbies and behaviors typically associated with men. Or perhaps the process worked both ways: the behavior of a few, reflected in advertisements and new styles of couture, became the behavior of a generation of women; innovations in design by artists like Chanel made women aware of new possibilities in dressing for style and comfort.

More important, though, were the ways this fashion challenged accepted notions of gender, sexuality, and even sex, long accepted as a biological

FIGURE 9. Abercrombie & Fitch advertisement, 1922. *Vogue,* April 1, 1922, p. 9. (Image courtesy of Condé Nast)

rather than socially constructed classification. By repeatedly using the word "sexless" in his description of the modern woman, Faulkner queers expectations of gender and sex, for his modern woman is both celebrated as a paragon of female beauty and simultaneously denied her classification as female. Because the modern woman herself was often complicit in subverting those aspects of her physical appearance which would signify her as female (by wearing flattening undergarments, cutting her hair short, binding her breasts, or dieting to hide her curves),[3] she queered constructs of gender and sex. This queering surfaced in the clothing designs of the period, in the advertisements and models that set standards of beauty for the period, and in the female characters of modernist literature.

Fitzgerald, Faulkner, and Hemingway explore this relationship between the modern woman as fashion plate and the modern woman as character in *The Great Gatsby, Mosquitoes,* and *The Garden of Eden.* Each of these novels takes place (at least in part) in a relatively isolated setting, distant from the city life with which one might normally associate these fashionable, modern characters. In *The Great Gatsby,* investor Nick Carraway narrates the lost romance between the self-made, new money Jay Gatsby and the old money, married socialite Daisy Buchanan. The narrative is set in fictional East and West Egg. These towns (which echo the social scene and appearance of the Hamptons) are separated from New York City by a "valley of ashes," and with Gatsby's over-the-top galas, take on a dreamlike, fantasy quality. Faulkner's *Mosquitoes* portrays a "ship of fools" plot, based on his experience during a yachting expedition in 1925 on which he was joined by a group of artists and writers (including the author Sherwood Anderson).[4] Although the novel opens in New Orleans's French Quarter, most of the narrative takes place on a yacht (the *Nausikaa*) stranded on Lake Pontchartrain, on what was supposed to be an brief cruise of artists and writers organized by a wealthy patroness, Mrs. Maurier, and the sexually frustrated dandy, Mr. Talliaferro. The yacht ends up stranded in the lake for several days, and its guests begin to annoy each other more and more with each passing hour.

Like *Mosquitoes, The Garden of Eden* features relatively few major characters, isolated from their usual surroundings. The novel focuses on a writer, David, and his new wife's experimentation with appearance and sex during their honeymoon on the Côte d'Azur. Hemingway supposedly based the novel in part on his honeymoon with Pauline Pfeiffer, his second wife, and the sexual games he played with her and with Mary, his third wife.[5] As in the other works, the isolation of the characters adds to the experimental feel of the novel, as though it provides opportunity for the modernist heroine/antiheroine to test boundaries and rebel against traditional roles. Hemingway, though, was further removed from the era of his novel (having written most of it during the 1950s), and therefore he may have taken artistic liberties with his narrative that he might not have taken had he written *The Garden of Eden* in its historical moment.

In these novels, the modern women appear fashionable, popular, and desirable, but the authors do not create flattering portraits of these women: Jordan is deceptive and cold, Pat is reckless and immature, and Catherine is volatile and manipulative—at least, so they seem through the eyes of the male characters, and to some extent the authors themselves. Their presence tends to herald anxiety and destruction. These three renderings of modern women therefore complicate the very freedoms they represent through their attitudes, behavior, and clothing.

The Great Gatsby: Jordan Baker

The Great Gatsby has become so synonymous with 1920s fashion that numerous fashion spreads inspired by flapper styles have been themed around the novel. The costume designers of this novel's most famous film adaptations have relied on high-end fashion houses—Ralph Lauren for the 1974 adaptation, and Prada and Tiffany for the 2013 version—to complete their visions. The historian Deirdre Clemente argues that in *The Great Gatsby* Fitzgerald uses clothing for several purposes: as a way "to set the mood," "as a sort of backdrop to his story," and "as character development," to reveal boundaries of gender and socioeconomic class (Interview). Surprisingly, though, the novel does not feature many actual descriptions of women's clothing. In fact, much of the clothing described is worn by either Jay Gatsby, usually in the form of expensive but flashy suits, or Myrtle Wilson, whose figure and style do not comport with the 1920s slim standard. In contrast, Nick describes the clothes worn by Jordan and Daisy (regarded as the most stylish women in the novel) only in brief or vague terms: for example, he might mention their flowing white dresses or Jordan's golfing attire without a detailed description.

This vagueness in itself characterizes their fashion as modern, for it hints at the garments' simplicity. By depicting the attitude of Jordan and Daisy, as well as their activities, style of speaking, and wealth, Fitzgerald has given the

FIGURE 10. *Vogue* cover, September 1, 1922. (Helen Dryden, *Vogue;* image courtesy of Condé Nast)

context clues needed for their style. His contemporary readers would recognize the reclining, bored, slender, stylized, and wealthy woman lazily smoking her cigarette from hundreds of print media images, much like the *Vogue* cover pictured in figure 10: a lounging, elongated figure wearing a modish turban, drop wasted gown, and string of long beads. Daisy's clothing casts her as Fitzgerald's woman caught in between—modern and old-fashioned, pragmatic and romantic. Jordan, on the other hand, is his modern woman.

Jordan Baker, given a man's name like Pat Robyn and *The Sun Also Rises*'s Brett Ashley, is not the heroine of *The Great Gatsby,* but instead serves as a friend to both Daisy Buchanan and Jay Gatsby, and a potential romantic interest for Nick. Unable to perceive her importance to the novel, readers often question her role in the narrative or simply ignore her in critical readings. If we read Jordan as a modern woman viewed through the male gaze, however, her role seems clearer. She surfaces as a contrast to both Myrtle and Daisy in her rejection of traditional femininity as well as her symbolic rejection of a traditional female narrative; unlike the other two women, she has no tragic tale of romance in the story—her parting with Nick barely fazes her. Fitzgerald's treatment of Jordan is subtler than Faulkner's treatment of Pat Robyn, or Hemingway's treatment of Catherine Bourne: Jordan represents the passing of the romantic and heralds the reign of the modern—the purely functional and the purely pragmatic.

Through Nick's eyes, Jordan appears modern in her defiance of gender norms, her detached attitude, and her comfort with both technology and athletics. Clemente notes, "Jordan Baker wears very flapper-esque clothing and her body is very strong, she's a professional athlete. So her clothes say, 'Hey, I'm the modern woman.' They're very sportswear-oriented; in the 1920s sportswear was just becoming socially acceptable for clothes. And she's the most modern woman that Fitzgerald really ever writes, in my opinion." Indeed, Jordan is a paragon of modernity: she is a professional golfer (allegedly based on the famous golfer Edith Cummings), and she recklessly drives automobiles throughout the novel—in fact, she is named after two top-selling automobiles of the era, the Jordan Motor Car and the Baker Motor Vehicle (MacPhee 208). Her body defies the expectations of softness and curves for the female form; instead she appears "slender" and "small-breasted," and she stands "like a young cadet" (Fitzgerald 15). Nick also describes her appearance as "charming" yet "discontented." Several critics have interpreted Jordan's masculine body and dress as an indication of her homosexuality[6]—in fact, Truman Capote originally wrote Jordan's character as a lesbian in his screenplay for what became the 1974 film adaptation. I suggest, however, that Jordan's clothing, body type, profession, and even homosocial behavior with Daisy serve to position her as the embodiment of modernity.[7]

In contrast to Jordan, Jay Gatsby and Myrtle Wilson, Tom Buchanan's mistress, surface as the novel's romantics and aesthetes: for Myrtle and Gatsby, beauty doesn't have to be functional, emotions do not have to be carefully controlled, and romance doesn't have to be practical. In her discussion of Tom's blue coupé and its symbolic role in the novel, Lauraleigh O'Meara argues that the blue car helps to draw these distinctions among the key characters: "Fitzgerald defines the personas of Gatsby and Myrtle through the aesthetic attributes of marketplace commodities, while the shortcomings in Jordan's personality are developed through images of automobiles functioning as technology" (75). O'Meara points out, as evidence, Myrtle's insistence on a pretty lavender cab during her encounter with Tom and Nick (since the cab's pleasing appearance has nothing to do with its function), and the descriptive language used to convey the sensuous luxury of Gatsby's vehicle (74). Her analysis helps underline Jordan's unique characterization in the novel: her detachment and pragmatism are the qualities that, for Fitzgerald, ensure her physical and psychological survival.

O'Meara's reading of Jordan and Tom, which portrays them as prioritizing function over appearance, is consistent with their characterizations as modern and upper class. When designing costumes for the 2013 adaptation of *The Great Gatsby,* Catherine Martin was puzzled by Tom's coming to dinner after playing polo without changing his clothing. On consulting with a fashion historian (most likely Deirdre Clemente), she learned, "It was part of 'upper-class casualization.' . . . The '20s . . . marked the advent of casual prep, the polo shirt, the chino. Tom's clothes signaled the new modernity of sportswear, a rejection of the stuffiness of Europe. And at the same time, polo clothes at dinner 'showed you were of the better classes, that you had enough money to participate in sport'" (Bullock). Tom's class and wealth are so beyond question that he wears both effortlessly, his sports clothing a reflection of his leisure and his confidence. Fitzgerald again gives the reader numerous context clues about the extent of Tom's massive fortune and security—the $350,000 pearl necklace he gives Daisy as a wedding gift in 1919, for example, would equate to about $4.7 million today.

In contrast to Tom, Gatsby is overly conscious of his clothing. The sheer volume of his wardrobe speaks to a man desperate to show off, not one assured of his social class. Clemente draws attention to the brightness of Gatsby's clothes (at various moments in the novel he is dressed in a silver suit or a pink suit),[8] noting his clothing is "super well tailored, over-the-top, put-together—that says, 'I need to care about my appearance because I haven't been educated, because I'm not really from the class I'm pretending to be from'" (Interview). Gatsby is so showy about his clothing, in fact, that he literally throws his luxurious wardrobe in Daisy's face in a display of excess that he hopes will convey his elevated class status (97).

Like Gatsby, Myrtle emerges as an aesthete and, despite her seemingly crass persona, as a romantic. Her clothing conveys her desperation to escape her current situation and become Tom's wife, as well as her naïveté in believing such a thing will come to pass. While some critics view Myrtle as pragmatic rather than romantic (using sex to escape her class), Fitzgerald suggests that she perceives Tom as her rescuer or white knight—in other words, she projects a romantic cliché onto their affair. Her clothing and how she wears it also give context clues as to how readers should interpret this character in relation to Daisy and Jordan. Clemente has noted the duality in this character's wardrobe, suggesting Fitzgerald "uses fabric to signify [her] socioeconomic transition from garage owner's wife to Manhattan mistress" ("My Big Idea"). She cites the "elaborate afternoon dress of cream-colored chiffon, which gave out a continual rustle as she swept about the room" (35). Clemente explains that Myrtle changes into this dress at the New York apartment, seemingly to dress the part of Tom's companion.

What is most striking about Myrtle, however, is not this deliberate costuming or even her complicity in displaying Tom's wealth, but the way the reader sees her clothing through Nick's eyes. During his encounters with Myrtle, Nick details her clothes because of the way they fit her body. When he first sees her, he observes, "Her face, above a spotted dress of dark blue crêpe-de-chine, contained no facet or gleam of beauty but there was an immediately perceptible vitality about her as if the nerves of her body were continually smouldering" (29–30). Myrtle and Daisy both seem constantly struggling to contain emotion (evident in the shaky sound of Daisy's voice), but Myrtle's "vitality" surges through her entire body and makes itself evident in her clothes' inability to contain her. Later Nick notes: "She had changed her dress to a brown figured muslin which stretched tight over her rather wide hips as Tom helped her to the platform in New York" (31). Through Nick's description the reader gleans that unlike the straight, slim figures of Jordan and Daisy, Myrtle has a curvaceous body that refuses to fit properly into modern clothes—that almost seems to resent being forced into them. Tom's preference for Myrtle as a sexual companion, as compared to his preference for the more fashionable Daisy as his social companion and part of his public persona, implies a discrepancy between the beauty ideal dictated in the context of a particular era and the beauty ideals to which men are naturally drawn.

As the woman in between, Daisy translates as a former romantic, caught between her former romantic self as Daisy Fay, Gatsby's love, and her current disillusioned pragmatism, with all its trappings: her superficial marriage to Tom, her deceptively perfect home, her performance as a loving mother, her desire for position and respectability. Daisy first appears wearing a white dress, in a room of fluttering curtains (12)—this image proves one of the most memorable of Daisy's attire, aside from the "three-cornered lavender hat" (90) she wears to tea at Nick's house. Clemente explains, "Daisy wears laces and whites because she's Southern and she's feminine and she's always been taken care of by a man. They also have her in lavender—she does wear a lot of whites and lavenders, but feminine clothing" ("My Big Idea"). Clemente characterizes Daisy as "feminine," not a quality associated with modernity—her association with lavender in fact recalls Myrtle's preference for the lavender cab.

The mention of her white clothing, however, offers a different reading of Daisy. If lavender represents femininity in the novel, and green (as in the green light at the end of the Buchanan's dock) represents hope, white implies a false purity.[9] Daisy's white clothing and reference to her "white girlhood" are not meant to suggest real innocence, but to indicate the façade of girlish innocence she presents to the world—a façade that deceives Gatsby and, at least initially, Nick. The white clothing points to a common feature in Daisy and Jordan (who also wears white in her first scene). Both characters rely on façades to maintain an emotional distance from the world. In their first scene, Nick observes, "Sometimes she and Miss Baker talked at once, unobtrusively and with a bantering inconsequence that was never quite chatter, that was as cool as their white dresses and their impersonal eyes in the absence of all desire" (16–17). Daisy's "impersonal eyes" and clothing similar to Jordan's—in another scene they both wear "small tight hats of metallic cloth" (127)—show that she has more in common with this modern character than with the more emotional and naive Myrtle.

This distant and impersonal demeanor proves the defining personality trait of the modern woman in Fitzgerald's eyes, and he thus dresses his most modern female character in cool white or metallic fabrics and masculine golfing attire. He uses adverbs, not adjectives, to depict Jordan by how she does things rather than by what she looks like: she "responded absently" (47), "held my hand impersonally" (47), "repeated abstractly" (57), "yawned gracefully in my face" (57). Such descriptions are meant to show Jordan's deliberate distancing. She is often described as looking like a photograph or "a good illustration" (185), or as observing others rather than participating in the action: "It's a great advantage not to drink among hard-drinking people. You can hold your tongue, and moreover, you can time any little irregularity of your own so that everybody else is so blind that they don't see or care" (82). Nick also notes that Jordan "instinctively avoided clever, shrewd men" (63). All her deliberate aloofness, her posing, and her simple attire exude an image of control and calm, of absolute rationality.

Jordan's modernity shields her from the psychological and physical trauma faced by the other characters. She escapes her rejection by Nick unscathed despite her claim that he "did throw [her] over," for it causes her only a minor inconvenience: "I felt a little dizzy for a while" (186). Fitzgerald contrasts Jordan's minor dizziness with the tragic fates of the far more emotional Myrtle and Gatsby. After she's hit by Gatsby's car, Myrtle's body is described in gruesome detail: "[W]hen they had torn open her shirtwaist still damp with perspiration they saw that her left breast was swinging loose like a flap and there was no need to listen for the heart beneath. The mouth was wide open and ripped at the corners as though she had choked a little in giving up the tremendous vitality she had stored so long" (145). The wording used here—especially the emphasis on the female-coded "breast" and "heart"—speaks to loss of vitality, a triumph of function and modernity over the aesthetic and the feminine. In this moment, as well as the moment Gatsby is shot in his pool, Fitzgerald predicts the triumph of the modern and the death of the romantic. He predicts, with a note of gloom and resignation, that women will become like Jordan, embracing the coldness, distance, and rationality necessary for their emotional and physical survival. Myrtle's violent end is far more gruesome, however, since Fitzgerald conflates her romanticism with her sex: her breast is literally torn off (by Daisy, no less), leaving her a "sexless" creature.

Mosquitoes: Pat Robyn

William Faulkner, like Fitzgerald, often engages the themes of the passage of time and the trauma of entering the modern world in his novels. In *The Great Gatsby,* Fitzgerald narrates a physically violent end to those who cannot break with the past and desensitize themselves; in Faulkner's most famous novels (among them *The Sound and the Fury* and *Absalom Absalom*), the damage tends to be more psychological. On the surface, Faulkner's novel *Mosquitoes* deviates from his thematic focus, for it feels humorous and satirical, more focused on the artists and writers he parodies. However, through his underlying narrative of fashion and aesthetic standards, Faulkner hints at the same contrast between the romantic and the modern.

Though Faulkner does not provide many details about Pat Robyn's clothing in *Mosquitoes,* he does provide details about her boyish, slim body—as well as what she has opted *not* to wear. Her figure, her youth, and her sparsely accessorized style contrast sharply with her aunt, Mrs. Maurier, patroness of the artists' cruise on Lake Pontchartrain. Through these characters, Faulkner offers a more humorous version of the Jordan/Myrtle contrast in *The Great Gatsby,* yet this humor unveils a deeper and more scathing criticism of the modern woman. For Fitzgerald, the modern woman is simply and practically attired to convey her pragmatism and coldness, as compared with the more flamboyantly attired romantic woman who emanates her emotional persona and love for the aesthetic through her clothing. Yet for Faulkner, the modern woman—while dressed in similar slim, simple clothing—projects her immaturity and volatility through her appearance. She acts in a vain attempt to violate the status quo and to experiment for the sake of experimenting. The older, more traditional and feminine woman acts to keep up appearances. Neither figure presents a very flattering female portrait, although Faulkner ultimately hints at a preference for the romantic.

Unlike Fitzgerald, Faulkner does not filter the modern woman through a single male gaze but through multiple male perspectives: his own; the women's clothing buyer Ernest Talliaferro; the self-important writers and artists Dawson Fairchild, Julius Kaufmann, and Mark Frost; and the brooding yet talented sculptor Gordon. When the novel first opens we see both Mrs. Maurier and Pat through Mr. Talliaferro's eyes: "She was under full sail and accompanied by a slimmer one when she saw him, but she tacked at once and came about in a hushed swishing of silk and an expensive clashing of impediments—handbag and chains and beads. Her hand bloomed fatly through bracelets, ringed and manicured, and her hothouse face wore an expression of infantile trusting astonishment" (16). Mrs. Maurier's style, then, is characterized by excessive ornamentation. Such ornamentation, according to the art theorist Lewellyn Negrin, would have been considered old-fashioned: "During the period of modernism, ornament was much maligned as inessential, superficial, deceptive, and irrational. Thanks to the doctrine of functionalism, which was the central platform of modernist design philosophy, all that did not contribute to or enhance the practical utility of an object was regarded as an unnecessary excrescence" (117). Negrin adds that ornamentation was also associated with femininity, "sensuousness," and "irrationality." Each of these traits is consistent with Faulkner's characterization of Mrs. Maurier as old-fashioned, irrational, and somewhat silly.

If Mrs. Maurier seems overdressed and over-the-top, Pat seems underdressed and aloof. Like Jordan Baker, Pat defies norms of feminine appearance and behavior, and she wears her clothes "with a casual rakishness" (19). Her style seems modern, but her youth (or appearance of youth) also marks Pat as Faulkner's version of the modern woman. Talliaferro's perception of Pat helps highlight her contrast with her aunt: "Mr. Talliaferro was conscious of the clean young odor of her, like that of young trees; and when they passed beneath lights he could see her slim shape and the impersonal revelation of her legs and her bare sexless knees" (21). Faulkner makes multiple references to Pat's boyish figure, though he also shows through his male characters that her body represents an ideal for the novel's time period. He based Pat partly on Helen Baird, a woman he courted in New Orleans and to whom he dedicated the novel.[10] In a 1925 poem entitled "To Helen, Swimming," Faulkner writes, "Silver reluctant hands of water lose / Her boy's breast and the plain flanks of a boy." His wording closely echoes the description of Pat when Gordon swings her out of the water: "Sunset was in his eyes: a glory he could not see; and her taut simple body, almost breastless and with the fleeting hips of a boy, was an ecstasy in golden marble, and in her face the passionate ecstasy of a child" (82). Recognized as one of few talented artists on the boat, the sculptor Gordon admires Pat's physique: "Gordon examined with growing interest her flat breast and belly, her boy's body which the poise of it and the thinness of her arms belied" (24). Although Faulkner repeatedly characterizes Pat as "sexless" (21, 24) and as having a masculine physique, she surfaces as a beauty ideal.

Early in the novel, Gordon unveils a marble sculpture of his "ideal woman" to Mrs. Maurier and Pat, as well as Mr. Talliaferro: "motionless and passionately eternal—the virginal breastless torso of a girl, headless, armless, legless, in marble temporarily caught and hushed yet passionate still for escape, passionate and simple and eternal in the equivocal derisive darkness of the world" (11). When Pat encounters the marble sculpture, she sees in it her own likeness: "Her jaw in profile was heavy: there was something masculine about it. But in full face it was not heavy, only quiet. Her mouth was full and colorless, unpainted, and her eyes were opaque as smoke" (23–24). Faulkner lingers on the likeness between Pat's body and the sculpture, but also Pat's face and profile, elements missing from the sculpture. Like Jordan Baker, Pat's eyes are gray and appear emotionless, even cold. Watching her expression, Gordon asks if she likes it: "'I don't know,' she answered slowly. Then: 'It's like me'" (24). This sculpture, which Gordon has described as ideal, becomes significant, since early in the novel it sets a standard of beauty associated with youth and a slender, boyish figure.

Though Faulkner does not, as I have noted, describe much of Pat's wardrobe, he characterizes her by the clothing she takes off or by the way her style deviates from what the others wear. On the yacht most of the guests dress in appropriate southern attire with an artistic flair "in their colored clothing . . . dressed for deep water in batik and flowing ties and open collars, informal and colorful" (54). Pat shocks her aunt by wearing a dress with "neither shoes nor stockings" (59). When she goes swimming, she appears "clad in a suit of her brother's underwear—a knitted sleeveless jersey and short narrow trunks" (81). Faulkner's attention to these details is at once revelatory about Pat's character and indicative of the fashion mode. Women were just beginning to show more skin in their ensembles by wearing shorter skirts, and they had begun wearing thin silk stockings that served an aesthetic function (to accentuate their legs) rather than a practical one (to keep them warm). Pat, however, forgoes the stockings, drawing even more attention to her bare legs. Women's swimwear wasn't introduced until 1920, after Carl Jantzen engineered the light knitwear used for swimsuits (Hill 161), and therefore a woman donning swimwear and jumping in the water with men was still a novelty. By wearing her brother's underwear, Pat's ensemble also speaks to the trend of jersey knits and women wearing menswear.

Pat's exposed skin also serves as a motif in the novel, for it draws attention to her naked form—the very form Gordon has captured in his sculpture. In several scenes, Faulkner describes Pat's naked torso as a "white bathing suit": "She had dragged her dress up about her shoulders, revealing her startling white bathing suit between her knickers and the satin band binding her breasts" (179–80). His details in describing her nudity recall Gordon's sculpted creation—a flat-chested torso carved from marble—yet they also speak to contemporary fashion in the 1920s. First, he shows how undergarments at the time were meant to flatten the figure, making it less curvy and more boyish, though since Pat has few curves she only binds her breasts. Second, he shows the trend of tanning that coincided with the development of women's swimwear.[11] This trend of exposing skin and binding breasts parallels—perhaps even motivates—Pat's behavior, the way she follows her brother and wears his clothes, the way she breaks social conventions seemingly out of boredom, and the way she toys with sexual boundaries. As the character Julius Kaufmann suggests, the revolution in fashion conventions facilitates radical changes in social behavior.

Pat's sexual behavior, judged by her aunt as inappropriate, surfaces through the male gaze less as a form of rebelliousness and more as an immature attempt at experimentation. Faulkner offers some justification for Pat's behavior—the superficial provincialism of her aunt irritates her; she sees phony and self-promoting behavior among the guests on the yacht; and she feels resentful about the restrictions placed on her choices based on her class and gender. For example, Pat constantly follows her brother around, even hoping to follow him to Yale (114), and later she seeks to escape the monotony of the *Nausikaa* by running off with David, the ship's steward. Hearing of David's travels, she jealously remarks, "Gee . . . I wish I were a man, like that. I bet it's all right, going around wherever you want to" (123).[12] After asking more about his adventures, she continues "with hushed young longing": "'And that's what you get for being a woman. I guess I'll have to get married and have a bunch of kids.' She watched him with her grave opaque eyes. 'No, I'm not, either,' she said fiercely" (124). Such scenes offer a glimpse of Pat's frustration with gender norms and expectations, and she sees no desirable models for alternatives among the women on the *Nausikaa*.

Pat further illustrates her desire to escape boundaries of class and gender through her interactions with Jenny, a girl of lower social class whom she befriends and invites on the cruise. Their relationship takes on a homoerotic tone as Pat observes and critiques Jenny's body as she undresses, and Jenny lies in bed naked with Pat (137–39). Faulkner also details the underwear keeping Jenny's figure tightly bound: "Her undergarment was quite pink, enveloping her from shoulder to knee with ribbons and furbelows. She loosened a few of these and stepped sweetly and rosily out of it, casting it also under the table. . . . She stripped off her stockings and laid them on the dressing table" (138). Because of Jenny's more curvaceous body (when she tries on Pat's dress and looks in the mirror she sees her body "bulging it divinely" [203]), it may seem as though Faulkner provides two alternative models of beauty in these two young characters—the women who garner the most male attention in the novel. However, Faulkner suggests that Jenny hides her curves and appears similar to Pat when dressed; when Mrs. Wiseman catches Jenny trying on Pat's dress, she is startled: "I had no idea there was that much difference between them, [she] thought. It's far more exciting than a bathing suit. . . . 'Jenny,' she said, 'I think—really, I—Darling, you simply must not go where men can see you, like that'" (203). Her reaction suggests that even the older women on the ship—those excluded from the men's notice—believe that the men will act on primal sexual instincts when confronted with a curvaceous woman's body.

Pat's experimentation with Jenny may carry homoerotic overtones and can be read as yet another way she queers conventional understandings of the body, gender, and sexuality. However, their behavior also serves to characterize Pat as a living embodiment of fashion images one might see in contemporary issues of *Vogue.* Pat's appraisal and conversation with Jenny echo the appearance of a host of 1920s advertisements for women's corsetry and lingerie. Several Franklin Simon & Co. advertisements, as well as similar ads for Kenlastic, depict women in their negligees admiring one another or lying together. In a P.N. ad, from a May 1, 1922, issue of *Vogue* (fig. 11), one woman looks at herself in the mirror in a corset while another woman, fully clothed, sits and watches. This image is contrasted with one of a woman (clothed) wearing the old-fashioned corset with stays, accompanied not by another woman but by a man. The caption reads "In the days of irksome stays." This juxtaposition implies that not only the corset but also the ensemble and the mode of courtship are old-fashioned and out of mode. Instead, the images represent a homoeroticism that excludes men, as well as a representation of the female—rather than the male—gaze. While these ads do not necessarily openly invite women to experiment sexually, they posit such intimate play among women as more comfortable physically and emotionally than the behavior and dress required for courtship with men. They reposition binding undergarments as sexual, flirtatious, and physically comfortable, unlike earlier advertisements that underlined the stiffness of corsetry.

The sheer number of these homoerotic images in lingerie ads further reinforces Pat as a fashion plate for the 1920s. When Pat tells Jenny, watching her undress, "You've got a funny figure" (139), her remark is not simply a sexual appraisal: she acknowledges that Jenny's curves, previously obscured by her lingerie, mark her as outside the fashion norm of the period. When Jenny replies, "It's no funnier than yours," she unconsciously indicates the absurdity of projecting a single norm for women's bodies—and, implicitly, sexuality.

Despite providing some justification for Pat's rebellious sexual behavior, Faulkner ultimately characterizes her efforts as rash and usually fruitless. Her attempts to follow her brother are thwarted, and her adventure with David turns into a debacle when they get lost on shore and are attacked by mosquitoes. Even her haughty, saucy behavior with Gordon proves disastrous when he reacts by holding her over his lap and spanking her, and then cradling her afterward like he would a small child. Faulkner thereby attempts to

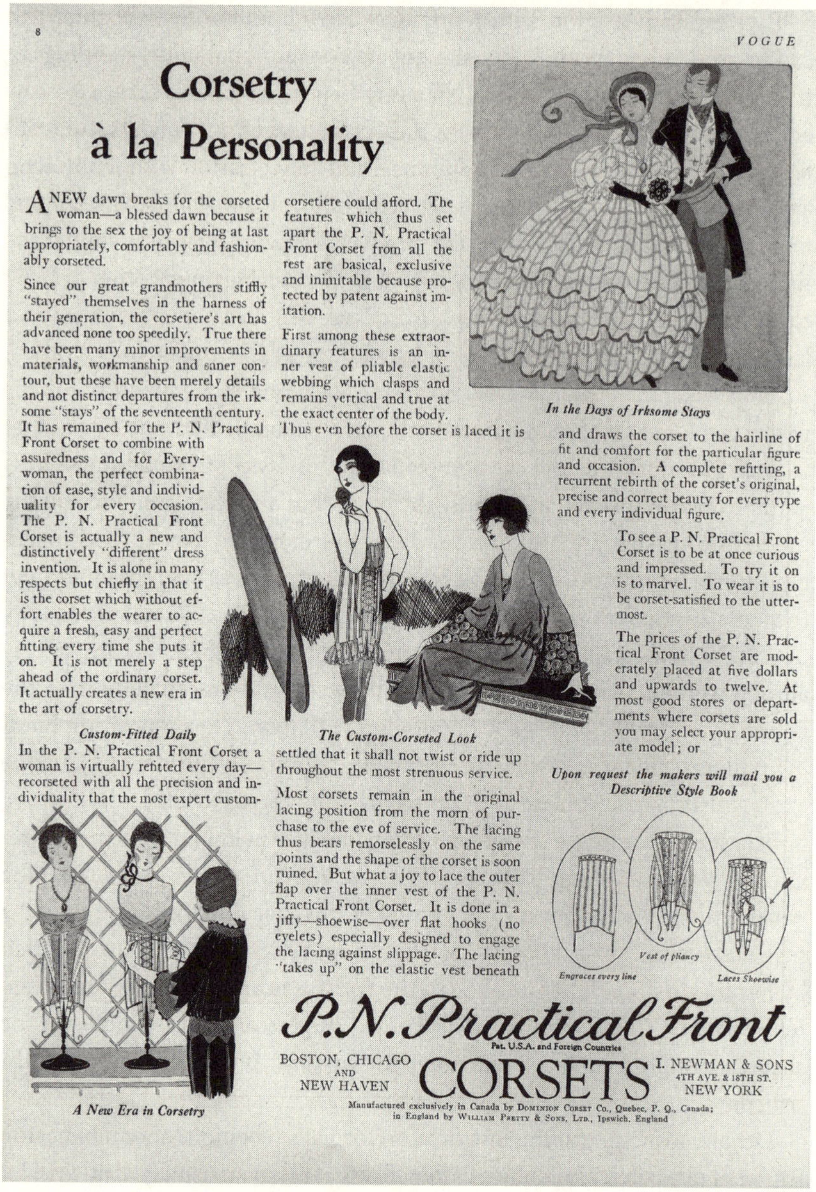

FIGURE 11. Advertisement for P.N. (Dominion) corsets, 1922. *Vogue,* May 1, 1922, p. 8. (Image courtesy of Condé Nast)

reinscribe patriarchal binaries of gender behavior as the men and the older women seemingly conspire to push back against Pat's queer behavior.

Pat represents a standard of beauty based on youth, slenderness, and subtle masculine traits that the other women envy, and that some attempt to replicate in their own appearances. She inspires both admiration and jealousy. In a state of frustration, the artist character Dorothy Jameson compares herself to Jenny and Pat: "Two women who had no interest whatever in the arts, yet who without effort drew to themselves men, artistic men. Opposites, antitheses" (104). Dorothy laments that Pat and Jenny receive so much male attention so easily solely because of their lithe figures and visible youthfulness, while she, the more sophisticated, intelligent, and curvaceous woman, must maneuver and compete to attract a man's attention.

Faulkner resists attributing any fault to men for this restrictive mode and hints that the slim silhouette is not a product of male desire. Toward the end of *Mosquitoes,* Fairchild reads a poem about Hermaphroditus to his colleagues, remarking that modern verse, like the subject of the poem, has become a "perversion." He adds, "Kind of like men nowadays are not masculine and lusty enough to tamper with something that borders so close to the unnatural. A kind of sterile race: women too masculine to conceive, men too feminine to beget" (252). His conversation with Julius Kaufmann and Mark Frost shows that though they have watched and lusted after the young women, they do not understand their own attraction.

Even Gordon reconsiders his aesthetic standards by the end of the novel. For much of *Mosquitoes,* he is infatuated with Pat, viewing her as a paragon of beauty. Yet in a surprising moment alone with the aging, fleshy Mrs. Maurier, Gordon clutches the older woman's face and stares at her, remarking, "'There's something in your face, something behind all this silliness,' . . . His hand pinched the loose sag of flesh around her mouth, slid along the fading line of her cheek and jaw. 'I suppose you've had what you call your sorrows, too, haven't you?'" (154). Though his strange behavior upsets Mrs. Maurier, we later find that Gordon glimpsed something beautiful in her features. After the yacht's return to New Orleans, Gordon shocks his friends Fairchild and Kauffman by revealing his newest work, a clay sculpture in the likeness of Mrs. Maurier's face:

> It was clay, yet damp, and from out its dull, dead grayness Mrs. Maurier looked at them. Her chins, harshly, and her flaccid jaw muscles with savage

> verisimilitude. Her eyes were caverns thumbed with two motions into the dead familiar astonishment of her face; and yet, behind them, somewhere within those empty sockets, behind all her familiar surprise, there was something else—something that exposed her face for the mask it was, and still more, a mask unaware. "Well, I'm damned," Fairchild said slowly, staring at it. "I've known her for a year, and Gordon comes along after four days . . . Well, I'll be damned," he said again. (322)

Gordon recognizes a beauty in Mrs. Maurier, but he also guides the others to that beauty and complexity through his art. His sculpture gives Mrs. Maurier a depth she has not had throughout the novel, yet it reflects most favorably on Gordon for seeing what the others did not see. In his discussion of *Mosquitoes* as Faulkner's artistic self-portrait, John Earl Bassett explains that Pat "threatens [Gordon's] art while entrancing him" (53), since she physically embodies his ideal. By sculpting Mrs. Maurier's face in clay, Gordon has created a work of art "more substantial and meaningful than the real model on which it was based, leaving it uncertain as to whether the real Mrs. Maurier does indeed have such complexity" (53–54). Whether Mrs. Maurier has such complexity matters less, in this context, than Gordon's believing she does. The true artist has turned his attention away from the young but immature modern woman to the aging romantic, thereby implying that her flesh, her age, and her efforts to reinvent herself as patroness of the arts mask a deeper, buried beauty that is ultimately more fertile for the artist than her niece's youth and simplicity. Perceiving Pat as a threat to his art thus implies more about Gordon's attitude toward modernity than about any romantic feelings he may have harbored. In abandoning his torso sculpture, Gordon chooses not to anchor his art in the present or future mode, but in an excavation and reexamination of the past.

The Garden of Eden: Catherine Bourne

Faulkner's modern woman is superficial and rash, while Fitzgerald's is haughty and aloof. Hemingway's modern woman, in contrast, is sexually magnetic and extremely destructive.

When readers think of a modern woman in a Hemingway novel, many tend to think of Brett Ashley rather than Catherine Bourne. Brett, in fact, serves as a kind of precursor to Catherine as Hemingway's "New Woman," for both are independent, wear their hair short, have athletic bodies, and attract the sexual interest of other women (Rohy 68)—Jake Barnes, the narrator of *The Sun Also Rises,* even claims, "She started all that" (*Sun* 30). Brett is first introduced (in the published version) as "damned good looking," and through Jake's eyes she appears attractive, slightly masculine, and modern: "She wore a slipover jersey sweater and a tweed skirt, and her hair was brushed back like a boy's. . . . She was built with curves like the hull of a racing yacht, and you missed none of it with that wool jersey" (29–30). With these concise details about Brett's appearance, Hemingway immediately characterizes her as a modern woman: she wears jersey, she has a boyish haircut, and she is slender. Though Brett has curves, they are "like the hull of a racing yacht"—that is, she appears streamlined, functional, and hard like a fast piece of machinery. Every main character in the novel is attracted to Brett, though some—like her fiancé Mike and the bullfighter Pedro Romero—attempt to make her more feminine to suit their own vanity: Mike asks her to wear a different hat when he sees her in a "man's felt hat" (35), and Pedro asks her to grow her hair long (246).

Though Jake loves Brett Ashley and finds her beautiful, his disillusionment with her intensifies as the novel progresses. He has a mysterious war injury to his genitals that has rendered a real union between them impossible, and therefore Jake abides Brett by believing that they would be together if not for his wound—at least, he does for most of the narrative. Over time, Jake sees the anxiety and tension she evokes in his group of friends, he has to fight against his own misery whenever he is with her, and he witnesses the way she destroys the bonds between men in the group. He watches her somewhat passively until she falls in love with Pedro Romero, a Spanish bullfighter Jake idolizes for his style and his masculinity. Jake repeatedly characterizes Pedro's bullfighting style as having "purity" (171), and he recognizes the man's uniqueness: "This was a real one. There had not been a real one for a long time" (168). When Brett falls for Pedro, Jake attempts to intervene for the first time, telling her "Don't do it" and "You oughtn't to do it" (187). Indeed, she refuses to listen, and her relationship leads to one of her rejected lovers nearly beating Pedro to death.

Jake's bitterness toward Brett at the end of *The Sun Also Rises* offers a clearer sense of Hemingway's attitude toward the modern woman. Such women are lively and beautiful, and especially appealing because they seemingly represent a perfect fusion of ideal feminine and masculine traits. Brett wears the latest styles—for example, the sleeveless black dress characteristic of Chanel and the "wool jersey" (also Chanel inspired)—and looks sexy and elegant wearing them. Yet she is also tough (she doesn't look away during the bullfight), she gets drunk in public, and she speaks openly about her sexual appetite. By the end of the novel, though, Jake has chronicled Brett's destruction of several people (Robert Cohn, Pedro Romero) and relationships (Jake's bond with the hotel owner Montoya). As Brett once again laments that she and Jake "could have had such a damned good time together," he bitterly remarks, "Yes, isn't it pretty to think so?" (251).

Brett has more complex development than Jordan Baker and Pat Robyn, and she therefore appears less stylized and more grounded in reality. Like Catherine, however, she is more exaggerated in her actions and personality, as well as in her ability to destroy the men around her. These women are not simply functioning as fashion standards in their respective models. Instead, they set the trends for others, and through these characters, Hemingway establishes the root of the mode rather than showing yet another of its followers.

In *The Garden of Eden,* Catherine Bourne adopts signifiers of masculinity as though donning a new ensemble. She takes masculine dress to an extreme, well beyond Jordan Baker's contemporary sportswear: she cuts her hair "as short as a boy's. . . . cut with no compromises" (14) and dresses in men's clothing—slacks, shorts, striped fishermen's shirts and suits. When sleeping with her husband, Catherine demands to "be the boy": she insists he call her "Peter" while she calls him "Catherine," and she sodomizes him (17). In this novel Hemingway takes the masculine mode beyond the boyish figure of a character like Pat or the lifestyle (golfing, driving, remaining single) of a character like Jordan: Catherine and David switch gender roles in bed, and she actually alters her appearance to be more androgynous.

Much of the scholarship on the modern woman, or the New Woman, conflates the trend of women donning men's clothing with both women's political activism and women's experimentation with different sexual orientations and gender identities. Valerie Rohy's discussion of the New Woman suggests that the 1920s represent a second phase of this figure in American culture. She sees the first phase as women's participation "in the suffrage movement and other reforms" and the expansion of "the 'woman's sphere' into the masculine public realm" (69). The second phase, however, she associates with women's desire to start careers, experiment sexually, and dress or behave like men. As this figure developed in the 1920s, she continues, "the New Woman crystallized cultural anxieties about female gender roles and earned widespread criticism in American popular culture and medical discourse; by the 1920s the public imagination had identified the New Woman as a masculinized figure whose manner and dress, if not her erotic cathexes, evoked lesbianism" (69). Her description of this second generation of the New Woman mirrors Hemingway's characterization of Catherine: he conveys her evolution from a feminine and seemingly compliant wife and partner to a highly modern, masculinized, experimental, and destructive woman. One premise of lesbian critical theory is that lesbian relations can be a separatist political statement, casting heterosexuality as a patriarchal political institution. By rebelling against sexual normativity, then, Catherine rejects the patriarchy that has confined her to a secondary role as housewife and companion to her writer husband. But while her sexual behavior could easily be confined to the bedroom, a secret between David and herself, the changes to Catherine's physical appearance serve as a means of advertising her rejection of that secondary role, of displaying the shift in their gender roles to the public.

Catherine exhibits her modernity most apparently through her clothing choices, her obsessive tanning, and her sexual experimentation. Her odd behavior and style, rather than shocking or alienating observers, instead inspires admiration and, in some cases, even emulation. After cutting her hair short, Catherine receives compliments on the unconventional style; when she purchases a fisherman's shirt and later tailored pants she predicts, rightly, that "[e]verybody will [wear them] next year" (79); her new friend Marita imitates her haircut, tanning habits, and style of dressing, as does David. The pattern of emulation serves as a clue that rather than casting Catherine as a social pariah, Hemingway characterizes her as an object of desire, even envy.

Catherine's relationship with Marita is explicitly erotic. We can read her homoerotic behavior as a desire to experiment with boundaries—a desire less concerned with sexual orientation and more concerned with defying traditional gender and sexual norms, exploring freedoms in small, intimate social interactions that might lead to larger imagined freedoms. When Catherine and her husband role-play in bed, she asks him, "Do you like me as a girl?" When he replies, "Yes," she remarks, "That's good . . . I'm glad someone likes it because it's a god damned bore" (70). It may be tempting to read Catherine as a repressed homosexual, whose acts of restlessness stem from the strain of repression and an obligation to fulfill the role of a traditional wife. However, such a reading would reinforce a sexual binary that the text resists. Instead, as with Pat and Jordan, Catherine surfaces as an experimental character who covets the experience of masculinity because of the freedom she believes it entails. After cutting her hair, she proclaims to her husband, "I'm a girl. But now I'm a boy too and I can do anything and anything" (15). Her role-playing offers a kind of escapism, not from the repression of living as a heterosexual woman, but from the transition to living as "a housewife" (24). Carl P. Eby argues in *Hemingway's Fetishism* (1999): "Catherine's fetishistic games soon dominate her life, and she repeatedly insists that they are not a matter of choice. She *has* to do these things and is powerless to do otherwise" (16). Aside from her destruction of David's manuscript toward the end of the novel, most of Catherine's actions seem compulsive, not premeditated.

This characterization of Catherine as a repressed woman living out escapist fantasies is underlined by the race transformation implications of Catherine's obsessive tanning. Initially she claims to tan in order to further isolate herself and David from other people: "I can because I'm lion color and they can go dark. But I want every part of me dark and it's getting that way and you'll be darker than an Indian and that takes us further away from other people" (30). Her desire to be "dark" also mirrors the primitivist fantasies of modernist writers and performers. Early in the manuscript, in a segment of dialogue left out of the edited novel, Catherine declares, "I don't want to be a white girl anymore and I'm half-caste already and I think I can be darker and it still be good" (qtd. in Eby, "'Come Back'" 102). She tells David, "White women will always bore you" (ibid. 101). Considering all Catherine's changes, she represents not merely the modern woman, but modernism: she symbolically challenges previously accepted Western norms and assumptions about gender, about sexuality, and about whiteness.

It is not so surprising, then, that the character of Catherine elicits so much more anxiety than Jordan, Pat, or even Brett. Early in the novel, Catherine declares to David, "I'm the destructive type. . . . And I'm going to destroy you" (5). She fulfills her own prophecy when she burns David's entire manuscript, claiming his stories were "worthless" (222). The moment is arguably the novel's climax: Catherine's resentment toward David, his writing, and his clippings has escalated over the course of the novel, and she embodies his and the readers' fears when she burns his manuscript. The published version of the novel, edited by Tom Jenks, resolves this anxiety, since the ending is hopeful and even romantic. Catherine leaves after her confrontation with David, and David and Catherine's lover Marita remains with him as he re-creates his entire manuscript (even better than the first version). Marita thus surfaces as a more supportive and submissive partner for David, a catalyst for his creative productivity.

Hemingway's original manuscript, however, features a "provisional ending," in which Catherine and David talk on a beach sometime in the future, contemplating a double suicide (Eby, *Hemingway's Fetishism* 113). The provisional ending feels unresolved, with both parties unable to act: David does not complete the manuscript, the more feminine woman is absent from the scene, and both David and his modern woman consider completing the cycle of destruction by ending their lives.

The link between Catherine's changing appearance and her increasing volatility and resentment offers an interesting lens for revisiting the role of fashion in this novel. Given that Catherine was based largely on Pauline Pfeiffer (even though Hemingway's other wives influenced the character), Catherine's style choices may reflect some of Pauline's own interests in the fashion world. Pauline Pfeiffer had worked for American *Vogue* for several years before meeting Hemingway, and by the time they met, in 1925, she was working for the editor of French *Vogue* (Hawkins 1). In one particular piece from January 1, 1922, entitled "Madame in Search of Her Youth," Pfeiffer's slightly bitter tone is unmistakable as she bemusedly proclaims her interpellation by the beauty industry. At the end of her experience visiting salons for numerous, often painful treatments, she concludes:

> To-day, I am a new woman. I have, I am honest about it, new responsibilities, too. I don't have the time to do as much reading as I formerly did, and I have had practically to dispense with the theatre—except matinees—and the opera. But, I can not neglect the night-treatments. And then I have my appointments during the day, and there are the nail shapers to keep on my fingers several hours a week, and the mud packs when I want to look especially well, and the milk-bath, and the herb pack after undue exposure, and the eggs. (90)

Though Pauline writes for a fashion magazine and willingly participates in these treatments, her tone betrays her resistance. The obsession with beauty and youth, she implies, distracts from her intellectual pursuits. We see this same thinly veiled resentment in Daisy Buchanan, Jordan Baker, Pat Robyn, and Catherine Bourne.

Pfeiffer's resentful tone spotlights several new concerns in the evolution of democratic fashion—an issue that becomes even more apparent when perusing the 1920s *Vogue* advertisements for antiaging formulas and fad diets (like soaking in a series of perfumed baths or wearing rubber garments to lose weight). Looking at Pfeiffer's editorial combined with these advertisements, the female characters' resentment is easier to comprehend than the male characters' anxiety about the New Woman. Both the authors and the women of the 1920s recognized that any fashion that moves in the direction of utility, affordability, comfort, versatility, and individual expression tends to coincide with a lifting of gender and class barriers in American culture. At the same time, the slim silhouette demands that heavier women reduce, curvier women bind their breasts, and aging women pay for expensive beauty treatments. As centuries of strict class boundaries in the fashion world were collapsing, they exposed the complexity of patriarchy. As a result, more and more American women would write themselves into traditionally male-dominated spheres—including the fashion industry, the art world, and the literary canon.

During this period in fashion, the advertisements, the slender fashion models, and the fashions themselves destabilized binary constructions of the gendered body (male/female), gender norms (masculine/feminine), and sexuality (straight/lesbian). As New Women, Jordan, Pat, Brett, and Catherine participate in that queering. Though Fitzgerald, Faulkner, and Hemingway, in their own ways, attempt to reinscribe the feminine mode within their texts (or to reject the modern), the texts themselves—like the fashions—resist such reconstruction. During the same decade, authors would begin to deconstruct other oppressive binaries through the lens of fashion, including constructions of racial identity.

five

The Black Middle Class and the Primitive

> Not only were ear-rings bought, long ones brightly enameled, but glittering shoe-buckles and two great bracelets. Helga's sleeves being long, she escaped the bracelets. . . . The ear-rings, however, and the buckles came into immediate use and Helga felt like a veritable savage as they made their leisurely way across the pavement from the shop to the waiting motor.
>
> —Nella Larsen, *Quicksand*

In his description of a "night in Paris" in the June 1, 1927, issue of *Vogue,* John McMullin narrates his first encounter with the performer Josephine Baker, lingering on the interplay of her ornate clothing and the contours of "her graceful body" (51). Through this interplay, McMullin characterizes Baker as glamorous yet savage and animalistic. His narrative of the evening is supplemented by a Carl Erickson illustration depicting the nightclub scene (fig. 12). The central focus of the illustration is Baker's exposed back, forming a provocative S-shape with the swishing fabric of her gown and the curve of her neck.

Later in his *Vogue* piece, McMullin describes Baker's clothing, skin tone, and body in a sexualized and orientalist fashion:

FIGURE 12. Illustration of Josephine Baker, 1927. *Vogue,* June 1, 1927, p. 51. (Carl Erickson, *Vogue;* image courtesy of Condé Nast)

> She came in without a wrap, and the length of her graceful body, which is "light sealskin-brown," was swathed in a blue tulle frock with a bodice of blue snakeskin, worn with slippers to match. The frock was cut excessively low in the back, with a huge diamond ornament at the waist. On her left hand, she wore an enormous diamond ring and, on the wrist of the same hand, a very impressive diamond bracelet. Her hair, which grows in tight curls, was plastered close to her head with white of egg and looked as though it were painted on her head with black shellac. This woman is like a living drawing by Aubrey Beardsley or Picasso. (51)

McMullin also depicts her daring finale costume, in which "she wears only a *diamanté*-trimmed *maillot* of tulle and red gloves with diamond balls hanging from the tips of her fingers" (51). His description thus juxtaposes costly luxury items, bright colors, sensuous textures, and cubist imagery; his words speak to a desire, characteristic of primitivist art, writing, and patronage, to see black bodies complemented and exposed by bold color and exotic textiles and by clothing that has movement, playing out Western fantasies of Darkest Africa.

Performers like Baker embodied these stereotypes and indulged audience fantasies. In *Negrophilia: Avant-Garde Paris and Black Culture in the 1920s* (2000), Petrine Archer-Straw talks about Baker's character from *La Revue Négre,* in which she portrays a "dancing native who steps out of the dream of a European explorer." Archer-Straw asserts that as Fatou, Baker "plays into the fantasy that whites create for her" (94), a role she accepted onstage and off, where she "was happy to . . . accept a gift of a monkey and later a leopard as her pet companions; and to present herself as Tahitian, if that was what her public desired."[1] The illustrator Paul Colin established this primitive image as part of Baker's brand, using stylized sketches to dramatize her curves and to enhance the contrast between her textured, colorful costumes and her smooth brown skin. Archer-Straw notes how, over time, Baker's performances shifted from a "focus on savagery" to a more polished and elegant image: by about 1930 she was promoted as "a picture of refinement—bejeweled, coiffured and dressed in designer clothes" (133).[2] This progression set a precedent for black women to achieve success through performance.

Other black female performers of the period reflect this paradoxical blend of high-end luxury clothing with primitivist performances, and their popularity, while perhaps not on the scale of Baker's, drew large crowds both in the United States and abroad. In his autobiography *The Big Sea* (1940), Langston Hughes describes Florence Embry of Harlem at the Grand Duc in Paris: "She was no Raquel Meller or Yvette Guilbert. But she was very pretty and brown, and could wear the gowns of the great Paris couturiers as few other women could" (160–61).[3] In Hughes's and other writers' depictions of these women, the observers stress the way white audiences fetishize the performer; however, they also emphasize the women's agency. Their performances afford them relative financial independence, as well as access to luxurious, gorgeous clothing.

The duality embodied by these performers is reflected in the popular fashions of the mid-1920s to the early 1930s. Fashion during this period celebrated such a bold use of color and texture. The period was heavily influenced by the 1925 Paris Exposition, generating a style that maintained its popularity in the 1930s. Daniel Delis Hill describes the influence of art deco on ready-to-wear, noting an "[e]mphasis on straightline forms of garment construction such as crystal pleats, triangular gores, diagonal yokes, handkerchief hemlines, and squared necklines," textiles that "reinterpreted traditional depictions of flora and fauna into hard-edged, stylized representations," and designs or trimmings composed of "diamonds, chevrons, and other rectilinear shapes" (45). While the Depression would eventually lead to more "sober" fashions in the 1930s, this period still celebrated the dramatic, with slender and elongated silhouettes (Hill 49), as well as backless gowns with "fussy detailing, including cascading ruffles, garlands of silk flowers, wings of accordion pleats, and oversized bows" (51). The fashion of the 1920s and 1930s, therefore, drew from graphic prints, risqué cuts, and African imagery to establish an iconic style. These fashions reflected a white modernist fascination with primitivism.

The scene described in the epigraph to this chapter, taken from Nella Larsen's novel *Quicksand* (1928), helps to show the psychological impact of primitivism on African American women. In this chapter, I contextualize some of the most popular fashions of the late 1920s and early 1930s within discussions of the Parisian avant-garde and its influence on American culture, particularly on the Harlem Renaissance. *Quicksand*'s Helga Crane, like several other characters I discuss in this chapter, illuminates a tension between embracing color, boldness, and sexuality and rejecting such exuberance for fear of reinforcing white racist stereotypes. Exploring this tension requires some historical context, including a brief discussion of the avant-garde, the emergence of Harlem Renaissance writers, and the relationship of these movements to a larger history of black women's fashion.

Scholars have various ways of defining the Parisian avant-garde and the art it stimulated, but most agree that it refers to a period of modern, experimental art dating back to the nineteenth century and gaining widespread popularity in the early 1900s. Colonial expeditions during the nineteenth century had brought artifacts from central and western Africa to Europe, where they were featured in museums. Fauvist and cubist artists likely visited these exhibitions, since they featured the geometric forms, masks, and other imagery in their artwork, catalyzing a new era of avant-garde painting and sculpture in Paris. Archer-Straw describes the movement as it flourished in 1920s Paris: "The artistic climate then was sensitive and experimental, as reflected in the *mélange* of modernist art styles. African art's influence on the Parisian avant-garde in the prewar years had stimulated such works as Picasso's *Les Demoiselles d'Avignon* (1907), and subsequently black forms were slowly absorbed into the Cubist vocabulary" (16). Archer-Straw notes the Parisians' desire to connect with "authentic" Africa; however, most of the blacks in Paris had distanced themselves from Africa: few were born there, and all had adopted white behaviors and customs in order to "dilut[e] their 'otherness'" (94). The Parisian avant-garde viewed "negro forms" as a means of "satisfy[ing] its own need for the 'exotic' and the 'real'"; according to Archer-Straw, "black culture . . . stood for a spiritual wholeness that had been obscured in an increasingly 'civilized' and mechanized environment by layers of material development" (18). The use of black imagery in French art and design thus "served as an antidote for easing the psychic and spiritual needs of its dislocated and disenchanted bohemian society" (18). Many Parisian artists and designers followed Picasso's example, blending African forms, images, and patterns into their compositions, fashion designs, jewelry, textiles, and interior décor (53, 71).

The works of Picasso and his cubist, fauvist, and futurist contemporaries had reached the United States as early as 1913, when they were featured in the Armory Show exhibition. Black and white audiences viewed the works of French avant-garde painters and sculptors, and the Parisian fascination with primitivism began to take root in American cities. In *The Big Sea,* Hughes explains the white modernist fascination with primitivism through the eyes of his former patron, Charlotte Osgood Mason (unnamed in the book), in a description that echoes Archer-Straw's discussion of the Parisian avant-garde: according to Mason, blacks had "mystery and mysticism and spontaneous harmony in their souls" and had the ability to connect the Western world with "the primitive." Mason felt blacks "had let the white world pollute and contaminate that mystery and harmony, and make of it something cheap and ugly, commercial and, as she said, 'white.' She felt that we had a deep well of the spirit within us and that we should keep it pure and deep" (316). Mason, like many other patrons during the Harlem Renaissance, championed any black art that indulged this white fascination with primitivism. Others shared Mason's view—not only patrons but also the many white urban dwellers who ventured to Harlem to dance at clubs and watch cabaret performances. According to the fashion historian Susan L. Hannel, "Harlem was perceived as a place where one could throw off the constraints of American morality" (63). Hannel's word choice is telling: only whites had this "American morality" to cast away—even temporarily. Implicitly, black culture existed outside conventional morality; it came to represent a purity of spirit that white visitors could temporarily enjoy.

The fascination with primitivism and the Parisian avant-garde generated fashions inspired by African images and patterns, as well as jazz and other creations of African American culture. In her study of jazz music's influence on 1920s fashion, Hannel shows how black culture shaped the silhouettes, materials, textiles, and movement of the mode. Even the musicians themselves inspired textile prints, as did "the active and improvisational nature of jazz" (58). The technology after World War I enabled printing patterns on affordable fabrics like cotton, and extended the style of graphic prints to a wider consumer base (Archer-Straw 72).[4] Popular African American dances altered the structure and length of evening wear: "The energetic nature of jazz dances like the Charleston and the Black Bottom no doubt contributed to the need for shorter evening dresses without sleeves, dresses with skirts, fringe and beading that would fly away from the body like the arm and leg movements required by the dances" (Hannel 58). Accessory designers created necklaces inspired by slave collars and African headdresses, as well as stacked enamel bracelets of red, green, and black; high-end furniture designers like Pierre Legrain would draw from both African imagery and cubism to create new styles that juxtaposed "gloss surfaces . . . with heavily grained woods . . . exotic fabrics and animal skins" (Archer-Straw 72, 76). The masks that had inspired Picasso would influence prints and textures throughout the 1920s, including the black chiffon dress with an art deco velvet cut pattern, trimmed with salmon ribbon and fur (believed to be coney), pictured in figure 13.

Although some black women, especially performers, took part in the African-inspired, colorful trends, other black women avoided these styles. This decision of whether to embrace or reject primitive fashions exposes a complex history of black women and clothing with its roots in slavery. When slaves were forcibly brought to the United States, they were expected to immediately shed their cultural norms of dress and accept Western styles, albeit of a drastically inferior quality.[5] During slavery, black women were presented with few, if any, options for self-expression through their clothing; slave narratives (including Frederick Douglass's famous narrative published in 1845) often describe the scant allotments of clothing distributed on a yearly or biyearly basis by slave masters. These narratives also highlight the poor quality of the clothing. In *World Clothing and Fashion* (2014), Mary Ellen Snodgrass explains that slaves were given clothing specific to their roles and duties, for example, household uniforms or long dresses with aprons for kitchen maids, or loose clothing for slaves laboring in the fields. She adds, "To discourage runaways, slave owners supplied skimpy work clothes and

FIGURE 13. Black chiffon dress with art deco velvet pattern, ca. 1925. (Museum at the Fashion Institute of Technology; gift of June Mayper, 74.43.1; photograph courtesy of The Museum at FIT)

insubstantial footwear hand sewn from cowhide and lined with cardboard" (20).[6] Despite such limited resources, even during the harsh conditions of slavery many black women found ways to express their creativity and desire for color and beauty through their headwraps and, occasionally, hats.

In *Hats and Headwear around the World* (2013), Beverly Chico notes the popularity of headwraps during the late nineteenth century, suggesting that they had been common among female slaves yet continued in popularity among black women after Emancipation.[7] During the post-Reconstruction period, black women would personalize their headwraps with bright colors and prints. However, by the twentieth century these wraps had become part of a white slave mythology, as evidenced by white representations of slave women in popular culture and food product brands. Chico suggests that black women began "donn[ing] large, eye-catching, flamboyant hats, possibly in a display of sophisticated style, with a sense of racial and ethnic pride" (228) to build cultural confidence and move forward from past struggles. According to Chico, black women continue to wear these hats to church services, particularly "within racially-segregated communities" (228). The association of these colorful hats with black culture has continued to the present day, and it retains some of its initial meaning: to convey ethno-racial pride and identity and to celebrate bright, bold style through personal expression.[8]

Slavery also influenced other aspects of African American fashion, especially the use of clashing colors and striped textiles. In *Flash of the Spirit* (1984), Robert Farris Thompson explains that the juxtaposition of bold, clashing colors and the use of narrow-strip textile dates as far back as the ninth century, having been used in Mande-related art in West Africa. The Mande traditions included "narrow-strip textile, enlivened by rich and vivid suspensions of the expected placement of the weft blocks," as well as metrical rhythm in the textile patterns to echo African music, striped cloth, and "deliberate clashing of 'high-affect colors' . . . in willful, percussively contrastive, bold arrangements" (207, 209). As the Mali empire expanded, its cultural traditions spread to other parts of West Africa, and other generations and cultures have improvised on those traditions, changing them over time (197); eventually they spread to the Americas. Thompson explains that "in most cases the practitioners of these traditions have no specific memory of Mande origins" (197)—in other words, African Americans today wearing similar color combinations or patterns recognize such styles as culturally distinctive, yet do not necessarily connect them with Mande art. The bold use of color—what Thompson calls "a love of aesthetic intensity" (209)—would be appropriated by 1920s mainstream fashion, yet it was already a part of early African American culture.

During the decades following Emancipation, an emerging generation of college-bound black students would shift away from these color palettes and prints in the interest of elevating their social status and public perception. Tanisha Ford probes the history of black women's fashion in the South in her work on SNCC organizers, focusing on the rising black middle class in the early twentieth century. Middle-class institutions like the historically black women's college Spelman University promoted a "brand of womanhood" that strove to erase stereotypes of hypersexuality, poverty, and other myths associated with past enslavement. Ford notes that after Reconstruction, "respectable college coeds wore clothing that covered much of the body, like long skirts or dresses and long-sleeved blouses, in simple colors or prints. . . . Gloves, hats, and post earrings were common accessories that lent a sense of refinement and sartorial elegance" (630). Such clothing, rather than establishing a distinct middle-class African American fashion (one that, like the colorful hats, would have its roots in Africa), instead emulated middle-class white women's fashion.

The turn of the twentieth century thus marked a tension in black women's fashion that has continued to the present. Some women embraced what they perceived as a colorful style rooted in an African past, expressive and elaborate; others viewed this colorful style as reinforcing dominant culture stereotypes of black women as sexual, primitive, or lacking in taste. The latter would actively seek cues from upper-class white women to fit dominant culture standards of womanhood. In her book *Ladies' Pages: African American Women's Magazines and the Culture That Made Them* (2004), Noliwe M. Rooks asserts, "At the end of the nineteenth century, for all women, fashion was discussed as a marker of class status; its function was part of a larger project aimed at refuting charges of African American moral inferiority, as well as distancing African American women from cultural associations with rape and sexual availability" (21–22). Only white women or light-skinned black women were featured in the first magazine aimed at a black female readership, a roughly sixteen-page periodical known as *Ringwood's Afro-American Journal of Fashion* (1891–94) which brought "the latest Paris fashions" and "dressmaking patterns," as well as relevant articles, creative work, and biographical sketches, to its audience (28). The journal positioned fashionable clothing as a means of elevating darker-skinned black women and those outside "the social elite," meanwhile "undoing that damage" of an enslaved past (45): "They [the owner, editors and writers] told their readers that fashion represented class and that middle-class status represented respect and cultural acceptance" (Rooks 26). Rooks attributes this emphasis on fashion as a status symbol to the magazine's proprietors, writers, and editorial board, "elite, politically savvy African American women associated with the African American women's club movement" (46). The magazine thereby focused on promoting racial uplift through the mechanism of personal style. She continues: "*Ringwood's Journal* crafted an 'uplift' strategy that related fashion to morality. An older, more 'established' group of African American women used the publication to disseminate their views about the meaning of fashion among themselves, as well as to their 'less fortunate' sisters" (48). Rooks also suggests that *Ringwood's Journal* fit into a larger rhetorical landscape that posited white, Victorian models of "ladyhood" as the only respectable options for women. The desire to fit these constructions of femininity reflected African American women's attempt to erase "dominant culture assertions of the group as primarily understood through their bodily associations with sex and rape," replacing them with those characteristics associated with the "cult of domesticity" (52–53).

In the seemingly innocent choice of clothing and style, black women unwittingly engaged in an amalgam of historical associations, racial implications, socioeconomic status symbols, and community pressures. On the more conservative end of the spectrum, women chose to avoid any racially inflected clothes or accessories that indulged white primitivist fantasies, though many did so with the conscious hope of appearing more like middle-class whites. Many Harlem Renaissance writers specifically criticized the snobbery of middle-class blacks from Washington, DC, in their writing. Langston Hughes calls this social group "as unbearable and snobbish a group of people as I have ever come in contact with anywhere," adding that though they lived lives of luxury and "dressed well," they seemed "altogether lacking in real culture, kindness, or good common sense" (207). Carl Van Vechten paints a similar portrait in *Nigger Heaven* (1926) with the character of Hester Albright, who looks down on Harlem and the "New Negro" while worshipping "the respectful elegance of Washington society" (66). The novel's protagonist, Mary, observes that Hester and members of the "Blue Vein Circle" were losing their influence within the black community: "Times had changed indeed when brains, rather than money, a lighter colour, or straight hair, was the password to social favour" (42–43). The stuffy, proper attitudes of these characters resemble the advice of black newspapers and magazines that cautioned against any boldness in dress: in 1926 the recurring column "Beauty Chats by Mme. Roberta Creditt Ole" in the *Pittsburgh Courier* cautioned, "A Paris authority says, that smart women are neither wearing very short skirts, nor very short hair" (Creditt Ole); however, an issue of *Vogue* from the same period contradicts these claims. These cautionary columns maintained the message that *Ringwood's Journal* had voiced several decades before: that the modest gown, the "tightly laced corset," and the "hat chosen to blend with an ensemble, evidence of fashionable taste, denoted a belated acceptance into a members-only 'cult of true womanhood'" (qtd. in Rooks

51–52). The rhetoric of these periodicals not only encourages black women to emulate Victorian ideals of white womanhood but also contradicts the rhetoric of modernity.

On the other end of the spectrum were the women who viewed the brilliant color and art deco prints of '20s and '30s fashion as an opportunity to stand out, to showcase their beauty and to take pride in their skin tone by accentuating it with the most flattering colors and textiles. Black male and female writers of the Harlem Renaissance championed this stylistic choice even in art that did not specifically concern itself with fashion. One of Hughes's earliest poems, "When Sue Wears Red," begins, "When Susanna Jones wears red / Her face is like an ancient cameo / Turned brown by the ages." He refers to her as "A queen from some time-dead Egyptian night." The reference to timeless beauty in Hughes's phrases "ancient cameo" and "queen from some time-dead Egyptian night" speak to a contemporary interest among African Americans in connecting contemporary beauty with something timeless—his imagery recalls, for example, Meta Warrick Fuller's bronze sculpture *Ethiopia Awakening* (1914). However, the poem's specific focus on Sue's clothes simultaneously conveys her elegance and imbues her with an air of agency, for the speaker implies that she chose this bright color to enhance her beauty and to dramatize the contrast between the garment and her skin.

Zora Neale Hurston creates a similar moment in her novel *Their Eyes Were Watching God* (1937), when the people in Eatonville watch a woman named Daisy walking through the center of town: "Daisy is walking a drum tune. You can almost hear it by looking at the way she walks. She is black and she knows that white clothes look good on her, so she wears them for dress up. She's got those big black eyes with plenty shiny white in them that makes them shine like brand new money and she knows what God gave women eyelashes for, too" (67–68). Hurston's imagery builds a striking contrast between Daisy's brilliant white clothing and her dark skin and eyes. Both of these features are rendered even more beautiful by the contrast. Like Hughes, Hurston indicates Daisy's personal agency in creating the impact on her gaping audience—her rhythmic walk implies her confidence, her knowledge that she is showing off her features in the most flattering way possible.

Such bold, striking styles were especially prominent among blues and jazz singers. Hughes, Carl Van Vechten, and Jessie Redmon Fauset frequently spotlighted the more glamorous and flamboyant styles of female performers. Later writers depicting this period would continue these representations of black female singers—Alice Walker, for example, details the brightly colored and risqué dresses worn by the blues singer Shug Avery in *The Color Purple* (1982), set during the 1930s: "She got on a red wool dress and chestful of black beads. A shiny black hat with what look like chickinhawk feathers curve down side one cheek, and she carrying a little snakeskin bag, match her shoes" (87). Perhaps inspired by these new fashion icons, newer African American periodicals like *Half-Century Magazine* (1916–25) were more permissive in their fashion and style advice. According to Rooks, *Half-Century* "sought to weave its story from a different, more 'modern' fiber that emphasized the cultural project of uplift in relation to fashion, race, and adornment in the context of African American migration out of the South" (64). Rooks explains that *Ringwood's* and other nineteenth-century periodicals seemed fixated on the past and looked to middle-class white women as a model of femininity; however, *Half-Century Magazine* embraced modern fashions as a venue for constructing a new identity for black women, especially those living in northern U.S. cities (64). The magazine targeted a broader audience by featuring a wider range of women—women of darker skin tones, for example, or more shapely women, women of different social classes, and women from rural regions or the Deep South. This latter category was pressured to observe norms of stylish, modern dress and behavior; the magazine even offered shopping services to aid them in this endeavor (74–75).

The contrast between these two black female perceptions of modern fashion—the conservative and the more flamboyant—shows up repeatedly in iconic Harlem Renaissance texts. For example, in Fauset's *Comedy, American Style* (1933), Olivia Cary, because of her obsession with passing for white, keeps a tight control over her daughter Teresa's behavior, including how she dresses: "As a rule her mother dressed her in pastel shades with the thought that in some way this brought out every possible delicacy of coloring and even of feature; refining her and taking away every possible vestige of connection with a cruder race" (45). Fauset shows the psychological result of this seemingly superficial repression: "Teresa usually presented something of the personality, if not the appearance, of a mouse. The light pinks and blues and tans of her mother's choice dulled the creaminess of her rather thick but perfect mat skin; they killed the sheen and the tone of her soft, abundant chestnut hair" (45). In her description, Fauset draws attention to the relationship between clothing and the color and texture of Teresa's skin and hair, indicating that the right balance of these variables induces a livelier, more confident personality.

Through the character of Teresa's friend Phebe Grant, Fauset reveals the ability of both designer and clothing to bring a woman to life, elevating her mood and encouraging her self-expression. For her farewell party before college, Teresa is permitted to choose her dress, and Phebe, an aspiring designer, aids her. Teresa's choice of materials hints at her craving for warmer tones and more sensuous fabrics: "She chose then a very soft, supple silk of the shade known as burnt orange . . . the blouse was made simply with round girlish neck and baby puff sleeves. A brown velvet girdle, fine and glowing, was to surround her slender waist and for her nice narrow feet there were bronze slippers and cobwebby bronze stockings" (45). The clothing transforms Teresa. Her friend Nicholas tells Phebe how different Teresa looks at the party, and Phebe responds, "[S]he was happy. . . . But her dress helped a lot" (50).

Fauset uses two opposing styles to represent the difference between dressing for an imagined white audience and dressing for oneself. In contrast, Carl Van Vechten, in his controversial novel *Nigger Heaven,*[9] presents a wider spectrum of fashion among black women living in Harlem. Mary, a librarian with a fascination for black culture, African sculpture, and a wide range of literature, dresses in a way that balances her more introverted, slightly prudish personality with her appreciation of color and modernity. She takes pride in her appearance, wearing blue silks and jerseys as well as other colors and textiles that highlight her skin tone: "The rich golden-brown colour of her skin was well set off by the simple frock of Pompeian-red crêpe which she wore" (25). Van Vechten's flattering portraits of Mary's wealthy friend Adora—allegedly based on A'Lelia Walker, Madame C. J. Walker's daughter (Borst 690)—reflects the rhetoric of *Half-Century Magazine,* for the text celebrates Adora's "beautiful and regal" appearance, her "almost black" skin, her "broad" nose, and her "thick" lips: qualities that, in the past, had been characterized as undesirable by white and black critics. To complete the regal portrait of Adora, Van Vechten describes her dress: "She was garbed in a pansy chiffon robe which matched the pansy lights in her lustrous eyes. Caught by an invisible chain around her ebony forehead gleamed a single pear-shaped emerald" (27–28). In contrast to Adora's elegant and expressive style, the uptight Washingtonian character Hester, despite wearing color, selects clothing with an old-fashioned and conservative feel: "Hester was wearing a gown of black and yellow striped satin, cut princesse, with very long, tight sleeves and a train. On another this robe might have appeared picturesque. Hester merely succeeded in looking more dowdy than usual" (153). Hester dresses to conform to the style of her desired Washington caste rather than in a way that properly flatters her distinct features.

Finally, the character Lasca Sartoris serves as a living embodiment of the white primitivist fantasy. Initially, Lasca is introduced as a paragon of African American beauty and wealth; she wears high-end designers like Poiret, Vionnet, and Reboux (64). Mary first sees her in a photograph at Adora's—a woman reclining on a couch draped in "a Spanish shawl, embroidered in fantastic flowers" (79): "The nose was delicate, the mouth provocative and sensual. Pear-shaped pearls depended from the lobes of the tiny ears. The black, wavy hair was combed severely back from the forehead, above the ears, and shingled. The lady was dressed in the smartest mode of the moment; moreover, Mary observed, she wore her clothes with that manner which is rare with women of any race or color" (79–80). Mary learns of Lasca via rumor and photographs, feeding the aura of mystery around her. Unlike Mary, Lasca exudes sexuality and modernity; she is daring, unrestrained, and—we later learn—destructive. When Lasca finally appears in person, she is introduced as "the most striking woman Mary had ever seen" (163). Her clothes accentuate her curves and force observers to imagine her naked: "A robe of turquoise-blue satin clung to her exquisite body, brought out in relief every curve. The dress was cut so low in front that the little depression between her firm, round breasts was plainly visible. Her golden-brown back was entirely nude to the waist. The dress was circled with wide bands of green and black sequins, designed to resemble the fur of the leopard" (163). The relationship of Lasca's clothing to her body, as well as her incorporation of high-end luxury materials, recalls Erickson's description of Josephine Baker and Paul Colin's illustrations. She frequently surfaces in exotic, stylized landscapes reminiscent of an Archibald Motley painting.

Hester and Lasca ultimately represent two extremes of black women's dress and, implicitly, models for behavior. Hester's style reads as too stiff and conservative; her clothing suggests that she focuses her efforts on blending into an elitist social caste that looks down on working-class blacks and their cultural products. Hester acts only in accordance with what her mother and her social group consider proper, and thus despite her financial independence lacks any independence of spirit. Lasca, on the other hand, is fully financially and socially independent, for she dresses and behaves exactly as she pleases—selfishly, outrageously, and indulgently. But like Hester, aside from appearing at Harlem social functions (ostensibly to meet new lovers), Lasca wants nothing to do with black culture or community. The text implicitly cautions against both extremes, or at least suggests that both exist on the fringes of black art and black community. The women in between—Adora, Olive, and Mary—strive to balance their independent desires with their deep love of community and cultural legacy.

One notable quality of all of the female characters in this novel is their financial independence. While Mary and her roommate Olive do not share the wealth of Adora, Hester, or Lasca, they nevertheless work respectable jobs and earn enough money to support themselves and to supply their own lavish wardrobes. Even the less respectable women in the novel earn a living as performers. In fact, the novel's women tend to fare far better financially than the men—many of whom (including protagonist Byron) cannot find employment. Other novels of the period (including Claude McKay's *Home to Harlem,* to which Van Vechten's work is often compared) contain similar portrayals of financially independent women and dependent male characters. The phenomenon has some basis in reality, for many African American women of the Harlem Renaissance developed careers—not only as cabaret or club performers but also as writers, cooks, entrepreneurs, and other professions. By modeling Adora on A'Lelia Walker, Van Vechten alludes to the first African American millionaire—also a woman.

Van Vechten's portrayal of financially independent women is especially useful when read in conjunction with Nella Larsen's novels *Quicksand* and *Passing,* both of which revolve around middle-class black women who subscribe all too willingly to prevailing wisdom, when they might meet different fates if their independent desires were fully realized. While much of the critical work on these novels has focused on Larsen's appropriation and revision of the "tragic mulatta" trope,[10] this critical approach has its limitations, especially since Larsen focuses primarily on issues of gender and social mobility within the black middle class.[11] As with Van Vechten's work, Larsen's novels convey polarized images of black fashion and style while revealing the impact of this polarization on black female consciousness and identity construction.

In most novels of transformation, women use stylish clothing to change their social castes; however, in *Quicksand* and *Passing,* women change their social castes to wear stylish clothing. In *Quicksand,* clothing represents identity options for black women. All of these options seem promising at first, but inevitably, each prescribed role limits individual identity and expression in some crucial way. Additionally, Larsen reveals how black women lack well-rounded role models who might help a young woman construct her own identity and find a fulfilling life path. Instead, the women who present themselves as role models want to mold the protagonist, Helga Crane, into a fledgling version of themselves, or else to use her in order to further their own social agenda. *Passing,* on the other hand, more explicitly addresses the black middle class during the height of the Harlem Renaissance. In this social circle, black women embrace a range of social and economic freedoms; however, Larsen reveals the way even this culturally conscious group emulates the harmful gender hierarchies and classist behavior that characterize the white middle class. In both novels, clothing serves to represent both the freedoms and the limitations of prescribed identities for black women.

Quicksand

Helga Crane is first introduced among her clothes, situated in a vista of luxurious lingerie: "In vivid green and gold negligee and glistening brocaded mules, deep sunk in the big high-backed chair, against whose dark tapestry her sharply cut face, with skin like yellow satin, was distinctly outlined, she was—to use a hackneyed word—attractive" (2). Her appearance is contrasted with her mood, for she lounges in her room battling "a surge of hot anger and seething resentment" (3). Helga works for Naxos, a school modeled after the Tuskegee Institute, and she despises the conformity and complacence of the institution. Immediately Larsen provides the defining elements of Helga's character, the traits that drive her actions throughout the novel. Helga nurtures a deep appreciation of beautiful clothes and luxury (6), yet she also craves social acceptance and approval.[12] She longs for a meaningful career, yet she finds hypocrisy and insult in each promising professional aspiration.

Helga's frustration with Naxos symbolizes a more widespread rhetoric against compromise during the Jim Crow period.[13] By working at Naxos, Helga feels complicit in promoting a mission of compromise, a mission voiced by the white preacher she heard earlier that morning who claimed that "Naxos Negroes knew what was expected of them. . . . They knew enough to stay in their places and that, said the preacher, showed good taste" (3). Because of Helga's anger at this speech, it is tempting to read her as an aspiring race leader, or at least as an intellectual and potential activist with a clear goal. However, Larsen intersperses Helga's reflections on the school with reflections about her appearance and wardrobe, suggesting that she conflates the conformist and complacent rhetoric of Naxos with a stifling of aesthetic expression.

Larsen first introduces this parallel when Helga recalls a speech by Naxos's dean in which the dean claimed, "'Bright colors are vulgar'—'Black, gray, brown, and navy blue are the most becoming colors for colored people'—'Dark-complected people shouldn't wear yellow, or green or red'" (17–18). Helga acknowledges the difference in station and respectability between her and the dean—especially because of the dean's social and familial connections, and Helga's status as "a despised mulatto" (18)—but in this moment of rebellion Helga reflects that "something intuitive, some unanalyzed driving spirit of loyalty to the inherent racial need for gorgeousness told her that bright colours *were* fitting and that dark-complexioned people *should* wear yellow, green, and red. Black, brown, and gray were ruinous to them, actually destroyed the luminous tones lurking in their dusky skins" (18). Helga's fashion instincts hearken back to Robert Farris Thompson's assertion that bold, clashing colors are deeply rooted in African and African American cultural aesthetics, however unconscious of their Mande origins the wearer might be. The dean's advice, meanwhile, resembles the archaic fashion tips of *Ringwood's Journal* and turn-of-the-century black newspapers, which called for black women to avoid striking colors or anything that would draw attention to their racial difference. Helga instinctually rejects the dean's advice, recalling the beauty of "a sooty black girl decked out in a flaming orange dress" (18), a dress the girl was forced to dye in the interest of appearing more ladylike and conventional.

The dean's litany against bright color and showy trimmings highlights the atmosphere of conformity at Naxos, cementing Helga's outsider status and stymieing any attempts at standing out or looking fashionable. Administrators, faculty, and students alike absorb the dean's views, and although Helga restrains her impulse to wear bold fashions, she feels judged for her appearance: "Too, they felt that the colors were queer; dark purples, royal blues, rich greens, deep reds, in soft, luxurious woolens, or heavy, clinging silks. And the trimmings—when Helga used them at all—seemed to them odd. Old laces, strange embroideries, dim brocades. Her faultless, slim shoes made them uncomfortable and her small plain hats seemed to them positively indecent" (18). Larsen conveys the mutual discomfort between Helga and her colleagues to provide a larger commentary about social tensions within the black community and especially among race leaders. These tensions reflect a clash of ideas about black women's fashion and what it conveys about standards of beauty and respectability: an adherence to dominant culture ideals of propriety versus a more experimental, expressive, and modern understanding of beauty and style.

Reflecting on this tension and discomfort solidifies Helga's decision to leave Naxos. Her decision appears radical on several levels. First, in rejecting Naxos, she must break off her engagement to James Vayle, thereby severing two connections to respectability and financial security in one gesture. Second, Helga turns away from a possibility for eventual fulfillment and, arguably, happiness. When she confronts the principal of the school, Dr. Anderson, about her intention to leave, he surprises her by implicitly supporting her unconventional style and cautioning her about the disappointment she will find by running away: "Some day you'll learn that lies, injustice, and hypocrisy are a part of every ordinary community" (20). He goes on to encourage Helga in her uniqueness: "What we need is more people like you, people with a sense of values, and proportion, an appreciation of the rarer things of life. You have something to give which we badly need here in Naxos" (20–21). For the moment, Dr. Anderson successfully persuades Helga, for he sees something in her as an individual that she hopes to cultivate herself—her "appreciation of the rarer things" symbolized by her love for color and art. Unfortunately, he counteracts the power of his initial plea by speaking of Helga's "dignity and breeding" (21)—two words that contradict her initial belief that Dr. Anderson understands her. Helga resents these words for the way they force her to feel ashamed of her mixed and illegitimate parentage.

Once Helga flees her career at Naxos, she arrives in Chicago with the hope of pursuing a more meaningful profession while having more opportunity for self-expression. Although Helga longs to wear stylish clothing, she understands how such clothing is interpreted, since she has an expert knowledge of clothing signifiers and thus knows how to dress appropriately: "She dressed herself carefully, in the plainest garments she possessed, a suit of fine blue twill faultlessly tailored, from whose left pocket peeped a gay kerchief, an unadorned, heavy silk blouse, a small, smart, fawn-colored hat, and slim, brown oxfords, and chose a brown umbrella" (31). Helga's selection of the "plainest" clothes speaks to the conventions of dress among respectable African Americans in the city. Larsen thus introduces Helga's paradox in finding new employment: she chooses to dress for the job search, yet her selection will attract jobs that force her into the same repressive role she rejected at Naxos.

Helga, Larsen reveals, only exercises freedom in selecting her more outlandish, expressive clothing when she wishes to convey an emotion or intention. For much of the novel, however, she negotiates her desires with the expectations of her current society. In Harlem she continues to tone down her style for the sake of blending in with the respectable black middle class—those engaged in the abstract project of racial "uplift" (52). However, when Helga discovers that her uncle has sent her a check and recommended that she leave Harlem for her white relatives in Denmark, she sees an opportunity to display her intentions, to express her desire to escape the dull social events of the black middle class, and she selects a costume for doing so: "There was that cobwebby black net touched with orange, which she had bought last spring in a fit of extravagance . . . both she and Anne had considered it too *décolleté,* and too *outré.* Anne's words: 'There's not enough of it, and what there is gives you the air of something about to fly,' came back to her, and she smiled as she decided that she would certainly wear the black net" (56). The outfit's design is modern and daring: it gives Helga the confidence to follow through with her intention.

Helga finally has an opportunity to wear brilliant color, risqué designs, and intricate jewelry when she travels to Denmark to live with her white aunt, Katrina. Initially, this change liberates her from the social constraints of black middle-class society, and the novelty of her aunt's circle of artistic friends amuses her and makes her feel valued. Having grown disillusioned with the fixation on race relations in Harlem, Helga feels grateful to escape into a landscape where, rather than being part of a controversial group, she can stand out as an individual—her nonconformity is celebrated rather than denigrated. Her aunt indulges her desire to stand out, to wear outrageous clothes.

Aunt Katrina's desire to see Helga in bright, exotic clothes and jewelry reflects the primitivist desire embedded in 1920s fashion design and the Parisian avant-garde. When Helga tries to select a garment for tea, which she assumes should be conservative and understated, her aunt suggests, "That black there, the one with the cerise and purple trimmings. Wear that." Helga protests, "But for tea, Aunt! Isn't it too gay? Too—too—*outré*?" (68). Helga appropriates the word that others have used to castigate her choices. Yet her aunt insists on the dress, and later has a dressmaker alter Helga's wardrobe to make it more vulgar: "At last, after much trying on and scrutinizing, it was decided that Marie should cut a favorite emerald-green velvet dress a little lower in the back and add some gold and mauve flowers, 'to liven it up a bit,' as Fru Dahl put it" (68). Marie and Katrina conspire to adorn Helga in enameled earrings, layered beads, and bracelets resembling manacles, making her feel "like a veritable savage" (69). By altering and exaggerating these clothes, the women remove Helga's agency and, implicitly, the freedom of self-expression she initially hoped to enjoy.

As Helga brings her aunt and uncle unprecedented popularity and secures the attention of the acclaimed artist Axel Olsen, her wardrobe grows even more colorful and exotic, resembling a nightclub scene from Van Vechten's *Nigger Heaven:*

> There were batik dresses in which mingled indigo, orange, green, vermilion, and black; dresses of velvet and chiffon in screaming colors, blood-red, sulphur-yellow, sea-green; and one black and white thing in striking combination. There was a black Manila shawl strewn with great scarlet and lemon flowers, a leopard-skin coat, a glittering opera-cape. There were turban-like hats of metallic silks, feathers and furs, strange jewelry, enameled or set with odd semi-precious stones, a nauseous Eastern perfume, shoes with dangerously high heels. (74)

Larsen's violent diction—words like "screaming," "blood-red," and "dangerously"—creates a dramatic contrast with her words conveying the luxury of these pieces: "chiffon," "batik," "glittering," "furs," "perfume." She conveys the dissonance between Helga and her clothes—a clash that parallels the dissonance between Helga and her acquaintances in Denmark.

When Olsen proposes to Helga, his approach lacks romance but instead reveals the nature of his interest in her: he tells her that she "disturbs" him, and Helga has "a stripped, naked feeling under his direct glance" (86). He says, "You have the warm impulsive nature of the women of Africa, but, my lovely, you have, I fear, the soul of a prostitute. You sell yourself to the highest buyer. I should of course be happy that it is I. And I am" (87). His observation is cruel and insulting, as well as untrue—Helga has no intention of accepting his hand. Her resistance stems from being both devalued and misunderstood. She relates the disconnect in their relationship to his painting of her, which she views with disapproval: "The picture—she had never quite, in spite of her deep interest in him, and her desire for his admiration and approval, forgiven Olsen for that portrait. It wasn't, she contended, herself at all, but some disgusting sensual creature with her features" (89). She reflects how "collectors, artists, and critics had been unanimous in their praise" and how viewers of the piece at an exhibition attempted to purchase the piece. The portrait becomes, for Larsen, a critical commentary on the avant-garde movement and its portrayals of exotic black women.

Helga's disconnect with Danish society drives her once again to New York, but after a heartbreaking confrontation with Dr. Anderson, Helga's disappointment drives her to greater extremes. Dr. Anderson, like Olsen, devalues Helga by sexualizing her and disregarding her independent spirit. As Helga fails to cope with the disappointment of this encounter, these feelings of worthlessness act in conjunction with the clothing she wears—in this case, a "clinging red dress" (112)—to make her especially vulnerable to yet another group's influence. This time, Helga is attracted by the uplifting singing of a church choir, a group that acts quickly to embrace her: "On the face of the dancing woman before her a disapproving frown gathered. She shrieked: 'A scarlet 'oman. Come to Jesus, you pore los' Jezebel!'" (112). The woman conflates the shocking color of Helga's dress with Helga herself, assuming from her clothing that she is a fallen woman. Unfortunately, this moment ends up trapping Helga into the most suffocating identity of all, as a childbearer for a southern preacher.

The choir and the small southern community employ a rhetoric of self-sacrifice to make Helga feel selfish or, worse, like a prostitute. Marrying the preacher seals Helga's fate by making her a mother and wife, with obligations she cannot shake. In addition, her choice changes her body: "For she, who had never thought of her body save as something on which to hang lovely fabrics, had now constantly to think of it" (123). Because Helga's body ceases to be "something on which to hang lovely fabrics," she loses, symbolically, her ability to express her individual desires.

Helga's poor decisions indicate a much larger problem: she has no clear role models, women who can confidently express themselves while remaining impassive in the face of public opinion. Larsen does present a fleeting possibility for a role model in the form of Audrey Denny. Audrey Denny surfaces during Helga's first tenure in Harlem as Dr. Anderson's date. Helga's friend Anne Grey identifies her with disapproval and disgust, noting that "[s]he certainly ought to be ostracized" (61) for her occasional association with white men. Helga, in contrast, thinks Audrey "lovely":

> She was pale, with a peculiar, almost deathlike pallor. The brilliantly red, softly curving mouth was somehow sorrowful. Her pitch-black eyes, a little aslant, were veiled by long, drooping lashes and surmounted by broad brows, which seemed like black smears. The short dark hair was brushed severely back from the wide forehead. The extreme *décolleté* of her simple apricot dress showed a skin of unusual color, a delicate, creamy hue, with golden tones. (60)

Audrey's apricot dress highlights her smooth pale skin, and her demeanor—"beautiful, calm, cool" (62) fills Helga with "envious admiration." Audrey, unlike Helga, can "placidly . . . ignore racial barriers and give her attention to people" (62). Helga notes that Audrey dances "with grace and abandon, gravely, yet with obvious pleasure." Audrey arouses Helga's admiration, not because of her beauty, but because of her calm self-assurance and the freedom with which she exposes her natural beauty. Unlike Helga, she dresses and acts without fear of social judgment.

Toward the end of the novel, as Helga lies ill in bed and laments that "[s]he had ruined her life" (133), she thinks of Audrey Denny as part of a stream of images, "placid, taking quietly and without fuss the things which she wanted" (129). Helga's reminiscence also includes images of the "gay fashionable frocks" associated with moments from her past. These memories help to characterize a larger social commentary, because clothing in this novel serves as a metaphor for the human spirit. As Helga has hidden her favorite styles, adapted her look for her community, or seen her relatives tailor and vulgarize her wardrobe, she has at the same time suppressed her desires and individual spirit. Larsen thereby portrays how black women are driven to act against their instincts for a host of reasons—to earn respect from peers and colleagues, to please their families, to secure husbands, or to prove their race loyalty—yet a fear of moral judgment proves to be the strongest influence. This same fear leads to the costliest sacrifices. *Quicksand* ends with Helga vowing to find an escape from her current life, only to find she is about to give birth to her fifth child.

Passing

Quicksand's commentary on marriage frames the novel, which opens with Helga choosing to end her engagement to James Vayle and closes with her regretting her marriage to the Reverend Mr. Pleasant Green. In *Passing,* through the characters of Irene Redfield and Clare Kendry, Larsen illustrates the way marriage encourages financial and social dependence on men while disrupting solidarity among black women; material luxuries (in this case, beautiful clothes and other trappings of middle-class life) tempt women into this position.

Both women have the resolve and determination to succeed as financially independent individuals. Unfortunately, neither Clare nor Irene seems to question—at least initially—that she must have a husband in order to feel whole and to have the luxuries she craves. Some critics of the novel have indicated that Larsen demythologizes, not whiteness itself, but white middle-class identity. In her analysis of *Passing,* Cheryl Wall argues that middle-class values and practices entrap the novel's heroines: "[Larsen] exposes the sham that is middle-class security, especially for women whose total dependence is morally debilitating" (109). Irene, obsessed with security and her façade of middle-class perfection, emulates the frigid sterility of a white middle-class housewife, resisting her husband's exploration of the deeper meaning of race and refusing to acknowledge her own unhappiness. In contrast, Clare—though she marries a white man and suppresses her racial identity—never ceases to recognize and pursue her desires. Irene judges her friend for choosing luxury and class over race loyalty, yet she is guilty of the same: "Each of these characters, like Clare, relies on a husband for material possessions, security, identity. Each reflects and is a reflection of her husband's class status. Clare's is merely an extreme version of a situation all share" (Wall 107). While the traditional tragic mulatta figure cannot define herself in terms of her racial community, the women of Larsen's novels, as Wall suggests, cannot negotiate individual identities owing to the (often conflicting) pressures of middle-class, gender, and racial restrictions. Clare and Irene differ, however, in their motivations for selecting their husbands. Irene does so because she never fails to challenge her community's expectation that she secure a respectable husband and a place within the black middle class. In contrast, Clare has rejected her community's expectation that she accept her inferior status as a servant, and in choosing to marry a white man, acts according to her own desires—in this case, her desire to live in luxury and to wear beautiful clothes.

Like Helga, Clare is introduced among clothes; however, Clare, somewhat prophetically, has to construct her own clothing from scraps. Irene introduces Clare through a memory of their childhood, as Clare patches together a "pathetic red frock" for her Sunday school picnic: ". . . a small girl sitting on a ragged blue sofa, sewing pieces of bright red cloth together, while her drunken father, a tall, powerfully built man, raged threateningly up and down the shabby room, bellowing curses and making spasmodic lunges at her which were not the less frightening because they were, for the most part, ineffectual" (143–44). Clare makes the dress in an act of defiance, rejecting for the moment poverty, social ostracism, and, implicitly, abuse from her father.[14] She does not want the dress to impress whites or to pass, but merely to appear respectable among other blacks. Though her materialist interests may initially characterize Clare as shallow, Larsen's exposure of Clare's past—her history of poverty and abuse—reveals the depth and intensity of her need for financial security and her desire for material luxuries and social status.

Clare's narrative in the novel offers a twist on the Cinderella story. She is born into poverty; her father works as a janitor, and she is forced to wear rags. Her white, middle-class great-aunts act like her wicked stepsisters, treating her like a servant, as Clare tells Irene with a touch of irony: "Being good Christians . . . when dad came to his tipsy end, they did their duty and gave me a home of sorts. I was, it was true, expected to earn my keep by doing all the housework, and most of the washing" (158). Clare looks back on this experience as her first glimpse of the white world. Despite her role as a servant, she comes into contact with the material comforts and society that, if she were to pass, would be within her reach.

Clare's marriage to Jack secures her role as an ironic Cinderella, for Jack functions symbolically as both her Prince Charming and Fairy Godmother. We first glimpse the adult Clare in the luxury of a high-end hotel, "a sweetly scented woman in a fluttering dress of green chiffon whose mingled pattern of narcissuses, jonquils, and hyacinths was a reminder of pleasantly chill spring days" (148), accompanied by her husband. Jack has rescued Clare from both poverty and servitude, and having gained an immense fortune from banking and gold speculation in South America, he provides her with the life of luxury and social status she has always craved. Unfortunately, he is also extremely racist, unaware of his wife's racial identity yet ironically referring to her as "Nig." Clare's acceptance of her own decision to pass lies not in her love for Jack but in her material and class-based comforts.

Whenever Clare appears with Jack, she blends perfectly and gorgeously into her luxurious surroundings: "Irene found herself in a sitting-room, large and high, at whose windows hung startling blue draperies which triumphantly dragged attention from the gloomy chocolate-coloured furniture. And Clare was wearing a thin floating dress of the same shade of blue, which suited her and the rather difficult room to perfection" (165). Clare's clothing—often described as "floating" or "chiffon"—incorporates the textiles commonly used during the late 1920s, but it lacks the graphic prints and bold colors so typical of the mode. Instead, the floral prints and delicate styles fit with her upper middle-class image and her role as Jack's wife. In this scene, Clare blends so seamlessly with her lifestyle that her dress literally matches the room.

Unfortunately, the beautiful façade of Clare's life fails to give her a sense of meaning. When she reaches out to Irene after seeing her at the hotel, she does so out of a longing for intimacy. In her letter she declares, "For I am lonely, so lonely . . . cannot help longing to be with you again, as I have never longed for anything before; and I have wanted many things in my life. . . . You can't know how in this pale life of mine I am all the time seeing the bright pictures of that other that I once thought I was glad to be free of. . . . It's like an ache, a pain that never ceases" (145). Given such an introduction, we may be tempted to assume that she is saturated with regret and pining for her native culture, feeling the first pangs of conscience when confronted with a friend from her black past. Instead, Larsen reveals that by submerging aspects of her past Clare limits her ability to express herself. Intimacy, then, means revealing one's whole self to another person—sharing secrets but also living and behaving in a way that expresses those inner desires. Irene, it turns out, is as lonely as Clare, but she lacks her friend's self-awareness. She wishes to pursue the intimacy of friendship without reflecting on her own life and the ways that she, too, feels lonely and unfulfilled.

On entering Irene's social circle in Harlem, Clare releases her inhibitions and uses her clothing to stand out rather than to blend in. When she joins

Irene for the Negro Welfare League dance, Irene releases a "little choked exclamation of admiration": "Clare, exquisite, golden, fragrant, flaunting, in a stately gown of shining black taffeta, whose long, full skirt lay in graceful folds about her slim golden feet; her glistening hair drawn smoothly back into a small twist at the nape of her neck; her eyes sparkling like dark jewels. Irene, with her new rose-coloured chiffon frock ending at the knees, and her cropped curls, felt dowdy and commonplace" (203). While Irene's dress, with its length and color, sounds more consistent with contemporary fashion, Clare's creates more drama. By wearing a long black gown and smoothing her hair back, Clare finally draws attention to her striking beauty rather than blending into the beauty of her surroundings. In Harlem, she feels she can reveal herself.

While in other passing novels (Johnson's *Autobiography of an Ex-Coloured Man* and Schuyler's *Black No More,* for example) protagonists face the threat of lynching if discovered, Clare Kendry's risks are predominantly material. For much of the novel, she manages to get the best of both worlds—the role of the exotic newcomer in the thriving Harlem social life, and all the material comforts and class status of white society. In her interactions with Irene, Clare wears gorgeous, often exotic clothes that, when contrasted to the snapshot of her childhood, make passing appear desirable. The emphasis on clothing and material culture in the novel reveals that while Clare's motivation for passing may seem superficial, her "having nature," as Irene calls it, has shaped her childhood and most of her life decisions. While on the one hand Larsen uses Clare's obsession with clothing to reveal the shallowness of her choice—reducing her life to a series of beautiful, picture-perfect images—on the other hand she paints these pictures as desirable.

For Clare, then, blackness is neither "a supportive 'birthright' to which [she] may serenely return" (Little 175) nor a dark family secret she stumbles upon during her childhood.[15] Instead, the black world in *Passing* is a world of glamour, fashion, excitement, and superficial public relations. Her choice to join Harlem society, according to Larsen's biographer George Hutchinson, is "epicurean" (299), for she wishes to go to parties and wear beautiful clothes without being forced to repress a part of her identity—or her physical beauty. The white world feels lonely, cold, and lifeless to her, while the African American world feels vibrant and diverting.

Through the Harlem social landscape, Larsen illustrates how both black and white culture can be performed, studied, or appropriated: in *Pass-*

ing, for example, she features just as many whites attending Harlem dance events, trying to blend into the scene, as she does blacks having tea parties or emulating other signifiers of white middle-class culture. The presence of whites in Harlem society helps contextualize the interaction between Irene and Clare. Larsen suggests these white socialites are primarily interested in mingling with an intellectual and artistic elite as well as indulging primitivist fantasies—and perhaps collecting artistic inspiration. Larsen dedicated the novel to Van Vechten and his wife Fania Marinoff; in both *Quicksand* and *Passing,* Van Vechten makes an appearance in the form of the character Hugh Wentworth. When Clare inquires about Wentworth's—and the other whites'—presence in Harlem, Irene responds, "A few [come] purely and frankly to enjoy themselves. Others to get material to turn into shekels. More, to gaze on those great and near great while they gaze on the Negroes" (198). Larsen exposes the irony that whites appear so eager for the society of blacks; the Harlem dances provide an arena for them to socialize with, even dance with blacks. Nevertheless, her tone is not judgmental, for she implies that not only whites but also black writers and socialites appropriate Harlem as a fantasy landscape. Irene, in fact, is depicted less sympathetically than Harlem's white patrons for her superficial claims to race pride.

Unlike Clare, Irene dresses in the mode, if a little more somberly than the mode demands. Her clothes and her mannerisms convey her respect for convention: even the details about how she rises from sitting, "smoothing out the tumbled green and ivory draperies of her dress with light stroking pats" (193), indicate a fussy propriety about her appearance. This sense of control intensifies as she tries increasingly hard to maintain the façade of her conventional life: "She went on pouring. Made repetitions of her smile. Answered questions. Manufactured conversation" (219). Much of Irene's life—her selection of a proper, black middle-class husband, her child rearing, her event-planning and fund-raising role within the Harlem nightlife, and her polite teas with members of her circle—reflects this propriety. She does not love her husband, and despite her judgment of Clare for abandoning her race, she does not care about her community. She "cares more for hollow and repetitive social functions than she does for any deep emotional attachment to the Black community" (Little 178). While Clare enjoys sitting in the Redfields' kitchen conversing with the black house servant, Irene refuses to break class barriers and treat the servant as a social equal.[16] Like the characters Wall has labeled "Helga's Harlemites" (after the *Quicksand* character), Irene and others of her ilk enjoy their roles in Harlem society for the implicit social clout these roles confer: "Indeed, though they claim their love for blackness, they imitate the values and ways of white folks down to the smallest detail" (Wall 100). Both Irene and Clare, therefore, remain a part of the Harlem nightlife scene as extensions of their archetypal roles rather than as an attempt to negotiate their identities: Irene uses the special events to socialize and make idle chat with whites and middle-class blacks, while Clare views them as opportunities to dress up and dazzle others with her beauty, to seduce those around her.

It is Irene's jealousy of Clare, not Clare's passing, that brings about the novel's tragic ending. Larsen alludes to this jealousy initially in the way Irene compares her appearance and clothing to Clare's, yet even these idle comparisons feel more loaded with meaning as Irene begins to suspect Clare of having an affair with her husband: "Irene couldn't remember ever having seen her look better. She was wearing a superlatively simple cinnamon-brown frock which brought out all her vivid beauty, and a little golden bowl of a hat. Around her neck hung a string of amber beads that would easily have made six or eight like one Irene owned" (220). Irene compares not only Clare's style but also her relative luxury to her own, and she envies her calm, "having" nature. As the novel reaches its climax, Irene mistakenly transfers her jealousy of Clare's seeming freedom to her jealousy of Clare's desirability. What Irene really envies is Clare's ability to do as she pleases, much like Helga Crane's envy of Audrey Denny in *Quicksand.* Yet as she sees Clare's increasing intimacy with her husband, Irene views Clare as a threat to her carefully controlled, middle-class life.

Irene's paranoia about Clare's soon-to-be-single status suggests she believes Clare will leave Bellew only to marry her own husband, Brian. Although Clare claims, "I'd be able to do as I please, when I please" (234) if she ceased her charade, Larsen implies that Clare would still need to rely on a man for financial security. Irene herself does not love Brian—"Strange, that she couldn't now be sure that she had ever truly known love. Not even for Brian" (235)—rather, she sees him as an abstraction, as "her husband and the father of her sons." Now Clare, too, intends merely to exchange her white husband for a black husband, if it means she may "do as she pleases." Irene observes of her friend, "She isn't stupid. She's intelligent enough in a purely feminine way. Eighteenth-century France would have been a marvelous setting for her, or the old South if she hadn't made the mistake of being born a Negro" (216). Clare knows the powers of her feminine wiles, and she recognizes the unfortunate dependency middle-class women (both black and white) have on men; thus she deliberately positions herself to make a seamless transition from the middle-class white world to the middle-class black world. However, she does not require the same social status or trappings of the middle-class social life that Irene craves. Instead, Clare believes that the Harlem community offers her an opportunity to celebrate her own beauty and to achieve genuine intimacy with her friends. As Mrs. Bellew, she is forced to maintain a charade with her husband and most of her acquaintances, and she must select her clothing and style carefully to avoid arousing suspicion about her racial identity.

Although Larsen does not debunk race as a legitimate biological classification, she does demythologize the popular idealization of whites and their society. She highlights the dullness and repression of white womanhood, yet reveals that even black middle-class women struggle with these restraints. Security surfaces as an illusion for both Clare and Irene, for both white and black women. Through these characters, Larsen offers a larger commentary—albeit a cynical one—on the Harlem Renaissance and its beautiful façade. Her narrative suggests that this period gave women the illusion of options, of other roles, and yet black women of deep creative potential nevertheless allowed context, social pressures, tradition, or even the social structures so endemic to white society to interfere with their paths to self-expression and self-discovery. The need to fit into a larger narrative, Larsen suggests, ultimately limits the artistic potential of not only black writers and artists but also all members of the black community.

While a variety of factors contributed to the end of the Harlem Renaissance—disillusionment with white patronage and conflicting visions and plans for "racial uplift," for example—most historians agree that the Depression ultimately brought an end to the period. The historian and curator Steven Watson explains, "The Crash ushered in a period in which white patrons attended to more immediately pressing financial matters than their support of Negro writers" (157). Watson observes how Harlem writers continued to thrive over the next few years, and even nightclubs maintained a steady business until Prohibition was repealed in 1933 (158). As the nightlife dwindled and the area progressed "from ghetto to slum" (158) in the wake of the Depression, Harlem lost its energy, the constant public interaction of white and black—however hierarchical and complicated that relationship may have been—and, at least for the time being, the optimism concerning a distinct black aesthetic, something that could exist independent of white influence. Reflecting back on the period, Langston Hughes would write, "It was a period when white writers wrote about Negroes more successfully (commercially speaking) than Negroes did about themselves" (228).

Hughes's remark, which appears in the section of *The Big Sea* entitled "When the Negro Was in Vogue," helps contextualize the fashion discussed in this chapter—the fashion that historians now associate more with the 1920s as a whole than with the Harlem Renaissance. The fashions described by Nella Larsen and Carl Van Vechten, the dresses with their low backs, their bright colors, their movement, their elaborate beadwork and fringe, were not exclusive to black women. Nevertheless, the authors of this period showcased the potential for clothing to enhance a woman's beauty in the specific context of her difference. Through the venue of clothing and accessories, the authors suggest, black women learned to embrace their otherness through their sense of what looked good on their figures or against their skin tones—even if these instincts were still, to an extent, mediated by the white gaze. Though it would be decades before black journalists developed and marketed a "black aesthetic" and distinct black style, the origins of this aesthetic had already emerged.

Conclusion

The Depression and the Dawn of American Designers

I see now that this has been
a story of the West after all.
—F. Scott Fitzgerald,
The Great Gatsby

In *Autobiography of an Ex-Coloured Man* (1912), James Weldon Johnson writes, "New York City is the most fatally fascinating thing in America. She sits like a great witch at the gate of the country, showing her alluring white face and hiding her crooked hands and feet under the folds of her wide garments, constantly enticing thousands from far within, and tempting those who come from across the seas to go no farther" (442). Johnson personifies New York in the familiar form of the Statue of Liberty,[1] yet casts this familiar symbol of hope as a temptress, a magnetic force attracting citizens from other parts of the United States and from around the globe. His image of New York also provides an apt metaphor for the American fashion industry in its early years: the industry thrived in New York for decades, a magnetic beacon for workers, designers, and consumers, before the Depression and World War II changed its course.

It is not surprising that New York emerged as the fashion capital of the United States as early as the nineteenth century. Edith Wharton's novels demonstrate how New York served as a foundation for an American elite who set the fashion trends for the rest of the country. Wharton also highlights how New York's geographical location made it a logical base for a developing transatlantic fashion industry: wealthy citizens could afford to sail to Paris for their wardrobes or to have new gowns shipped overseas, and Parisian design houses recognized opportunities for expanding their brands and profits by marketing designs to the United States. Wharton shows how the earliest fashion journalism developed first in Manhattan, often in the form of gossip magazines that followed the lifestyles of the wealthy elite.

Writers like Abraham Cahan and Anzia Yezierska illustrate why New York rose so quickly in the fashion industry, attributing its industrial climb to the mass immigration from Europe through Ellis Island during the late nineteenth and early twentieth centuries. These immigrants, Cahan asserts, provided cheap labor and helped engender the explosion of New York's garment industry. Wharton, Cahan, Yezierska, and Theodore Dreiser also indicate how the changing cityscape, with its rapid expansion and population growth, led to more mobility and contact among its citizens: women spent more time out of doors, socializing, passing shopwindows, and spending evenings out in society, and thus being fashionably attired became a more pressing concern. Dreiser shows how New York was one of the first cities to take advantage of fashion marketing and advertising, with its shop display windows, its billboards, and its clothing catalogs. Fitzgerald and writers of the Harlem Renaissance established New York as a cultural center, a place where individuals from different walks of life came into contact and generated new music, new art, and inevitably, new fashions. If America as a body represented a land of opportunity, a place for upward mobility and self-transformation, then New York was its heart center.

Many of these characters drawn in by the allure of the big city, however, would reveal their disillusionment with its glamorous façade. In Wharton's novels, Lily sinks into poverty and takes her own life; the Countess Ellen Olenska returns, heartbroken, to Europe. Cahan's David Levinsky finds himself rich but lonely, longing for his life as a poor yeshiva student in Russia. Sister Carrie achieves her dream of becoming a wealthy, glamorous actress, only to find herself alone and restless, alienated from friends and potential suitors. Helga leaves New York twice in *Quicksand,* unable to stomach what she perceives as its hypocrisy. *The Great Gatsby*'s Nick Carraway abandons his life in New York to move back west. Just over a decade after the novel's publication, Fitzgerald would move west as well, to Hollywood.

After the Crash of 1929, American fashion mirrored the path of these prominent figures in American literature: it moved west. In American literature, the West has often represented a fresh start, a new horizon, the ultimate potential of national expansion. During the 1930s and early 1940s—arguably one of the darkest periods for Western civilization—the American West, its culture, its business, and its fashion were thriving in unexpected ways. Though today New York continues to represent the center of fashion in the United States, the city and the industry itself works in symbiosis with a Hollywood celebrity culture that emerges predominantly from the West Coast.[2]

Democratic Fashion in the American West

In the decades leading up to the 1930s, the United States had built a cultural identity through its literature, music, art, and technological innovation; however, U.S. cultural identity has always struggled with its duality as a producer of great art and a panderer to popular tastes. From an elitist perspective, since its earliest days as an independent nation, the United States has blended its contributions to high art with its steady stream of popular culture. Yet from a cultural studies perspective, such dualities do not—or should not—really exist. The United States has proclaimed since its beginnings that it collapses such boundaries, that Old World divisions and hierarchies should not exist.

In his introduction to Nathaneal West's *The Day of the Locust,* Alfred Kazin argues, "Like all good Hollywood novelists, West saw the place as a symbol of whatever is most extravagant, spoiled, and uncontrolled in American life. But more than any other novelist preoccupied with Hollywood's specialized styles, West apprehended the American future in all these people who thought they had discarded their past" (xvii). Kazin observes that West recognized the 1930s as "an era not only of mass taste . . . but of uncertain control." Nathaneal West's novel, as well as the detective fiction of Raymond Chandler and many other works of the 1930s and early 1940s, illustrates the heightened sense of nationalism, the rise of American popular culture, and the emergence of a thriving American style and fashion industry during the period between the wars.

Fashion magazines of the 1930s reflect similar tensions, for they recognized that the American fashion industry was finally getting global recognition for its styles and designers, but they questioned whether the industry could thrive without the inspiration of Paris. "Nationalism is the fetish of the day," proclaims a *Vogue* editorial from April 15, 1933. The author asks: "Will the American designers come into their own? Will we place a moral ban on French ideas and develop a new national style?" ("Fashion: New York Couture" 33). The author of the editorial seems dubious, claiming that buyers can consistently find the more creative, artistic clothing designs in Paris. Nevertheless, the author acknowledges that America must play a larger role in the fashion landscape.

To some extent, the United States had already become a major component of a transatlantic fashion landscape, for several reasons. First, it provided an enormous consumer base, composing "the largest international groups of Paris high-fashion clients" (Pouillard 320). Second, Parisian production, unlike American production, was localized and "rooted in craftsmanship" (320). Because of the expense and limits of Parisian production, some American companies were authorized by the French couture houses to reproduce their high-end designs in New York (Pouillard 320). Third, American fashion journalism had gained an international acclaim and influence, especially in the case of *Vogue,* which in 1920 engendered a French affiliate, *Vogue Paris.* And finally, American ingenuity in technology and manufacturing had introduced some important inventions that would have an impact on the fashion world, including B. F. Goodrich's invention of the zipper in 1923, which would facilitate the design of side-zip dresses in the 1930s (Hill 50–51), and Carl Jantzen's 1915 invention of the lightweight knits that would be used in his first swimwear in 1920, effectively "chang[ing] bathing into swimming" (Hill 161). Each of these influences characterized Americans as extremely interested in fashion, but in a specific way: Americans wanted to make fashion more accessible, more comfortable and user-friendly, and more connected with their own lives. Generally speaking, Americans loved the sophistication of Paris fashion, but they also looked for ways to make it their own.

Because the French and American consumer base had different ideas about the role fashion played in their lives, their tastes diverged around the period between the two world wars. In her study of "design piracy" during this period, Véronique Pouillard explains, "In France, the creation of a system protective of fashion was a branch of high art, whereas, in the United States, fashion was perceived in functional terms, and thus its designs were not protected. Under French law, fashion creators were held in the same high regard reserved for artists, while American law assigned them a lower status" (321). I would suggest that while Americans were indeed more concerned with function, they certainly cared about the aesthetic elements of fashion, as well as the cachet of wearing a piece designed and produced by a haute couture house. However, Americans also celebrated and continue to celebrate the designer who can take an expensive, exclusive look and make it more affordable, more comfortable, and more practical while retaining its elegance and refinement.

Such an understanding of the distinction between French and American fashion reflects common perceptions of the United States as a place of mass culture, without the refinement and elegance of Europe. Pouillard confirms how consumers on a global scale have recognized Paris fashion as high art since the early days of the Chambre Syndicale, when the first talented craftsmen showcased their technical expertise and understanding of "ancient traditions" in dress and design. These designers could draw from the treasures of the art community and cityscape that surrounded them (322). Pouillard adds that "the proximity of the royal court, and later of socialites' and artists' circles, created sustained demand," while tourists helped build an international clientele and a buzz about the glamour and luxury of this fashion destination.

American fashion, in contrast, was seen as an imitation of Paris—most of its designers were not known by name until the 1930s, and the industry was known more for its technological innovations, its manufacturing power, and its marketing potential than for the elegance and creativity of its designers. In addition, while Paris maintained a strict hierarchy that distinguished between the haute couture designers of the Chambre Syndicale, other high-end couturiers, and the various ready-to-wear retailers, the U.S. market (especially its advertisers and fashion journalists) blurred these distinctions (Hill 67). Sandra Stansbery Buckland, a professor of fashion merchandising, argues, "French couturiers were celebrities who created artistic, custom models for their wealthy clients. Most American designers worked anonymously, interpreting Paris designs for ready-to-wear manufacturers who targeted middle-income consumers" (100). Paris designers were considered artists; the Americans, mediators and mass producers. In the 1930s, however, this polarization began to change.

In the wake of the Great Depression, American designers helped to bolster a nationalist rhetoric of inventiveness and resourcefulness. As both increasing "tariff difficulties" and limited budgets for buyers reduced the market for Paris imports ("Fashion: New York Couture" 33), the American fashion industry began to solidify its foothold as a system connected to, yet separate from, the Parisian industry, challenging Paris as the center of the fashion world for the first time.

During the 1930s fashion magazines and retailers seemingly conspired to champion American designers as well as a distinctly American fashion aesthetic (Pouillard 336). One of the most well known efforts to familiarize the American public with U.S. designers was Lord & Taylor's 1932 promotion of American designers, an initiative pioneered by then vice president Dorothy Shaver (Hill 56). While Shaver's campaign, entitled "American Fashions for American Women," acknowledged Paris's continued role as leader of the fashion world, it nevertheless helped establish American designers like Elizabeth Hawes, Annette Simpson, and Clare Potter as known entities in the New York fashion world (Buckland). Over the next few years, *Vogue* advertisements began promoting more American brands, making designers like Hattie Carnegie and Peggy Hoyt household names (Hill 58).

With American designers gaining traction in the fashion market, mainstream fashion in the United States took its most democratic form: it became less costly, available to a wider consumer base, more comfortable, and heavily influenced by the American lifestyle and American innovation. According to the costume historian Patricia Campbell Warner, the American woman's "look" that first appeared during the Depression represented the convergence of "three major developments" in the United States: first, the popularization of "sportswear," or "the clothing initially designed specifically for sport" that became daily casual wear; second, "the new ideals of beauty that were closely connected to the lithe, sporting look, created in large part for and by Hollywood movies"; and third, "the role those movies played in selling new fashion ideas and goods to the movie-going public" (79–80). American literature of the 1930s and early 1940s reflects these developments outlined by Warner. Hollywood novels like *The Day of the Locust* revealed the sportswear style entrenched in American culture as well as the way Hollywood inspired new standards of beauty and style. The United States also witnessed a new relationship between American novels and fashion during this period: novels that would be adapted into films and then subsequently inspire fashion trends.

Even after Hollywood started to have an impact on the fashion world, many journalists dismissed this impact as temporary, like so many American fads. The mass tastes of the United States could not compete with the long-standing, high-art fashion world of Paris. The author of the 1933 *Vogue* editorial observes, "A few purely American fashions have been launched through Hollywood, . . . which automatically makes them 'mass' styles, short-lived. But, largely, it is the American designer's job to look over the shoulder of Paris, to come home and write his or her own versions of the mode, as it has been established there" ("Fashion: New York Couture" 34). In other words, any ingenuity arising from Hollywood, or from American designers for film, is destined to be a passing fad because such designs do not derive from Parisian ingenuity. With seeming reluctance, the author goes on to note that this particular issue of *Vogue* has deviated from the magazine's traditional coverage by featuring some New York designers and their spring collections. However, the author quickly clarifies, "Many of these people have sponsored new fashion ideas practically simultaneously with Paris, the result of something in the air, perhaps, intangible or actual" (34). These designers' moments of genius, in other words, are actually just a coincidental channeling of Parisian designers' trend forecasting for the season.

Certainly the author has a point. Even sportswear, often considered the iconic American style because of its casualness and comfort, originated with Jean Patou and Coco Chanel in the 1920s and their introduction of "menswear trousers, sailor's gobs, shorts, and pyjamas" (Hill 55). Similarly, early Hollywood films boasted beautiful costumes designed by Parisian couturiers—in many cases, specific actors established and maintained an ongoing design relationship with one particular couture house. However, environment played a large role in boosting American designers' influence over the direction of Hollywood style and, eventually, American fashion. First, Hollywood's location in Southern California, with its "warm weather, sunshine and casual living" (Warner 92), ensured that the sportswear and resort wear looks would prove more than a passing trend; in fact, the weather and lifestyle of this region helped popularize trousers and, later, shorts, as casual wear. During the early 1930s, *Vogue* began to juxtapose Parisian designs of sportswear and resort wear with looks created by American designers. One of the most popular ensembles of the period was silk pajamas, like those featured in figure 14, which offered a way to blend luxury and glamour with the breezy, casual feel of the West.

Second, as noted above, the Depression limited the number of Parisian

FIGURE 14. Elizabeth Hawes, silk lounging pajamas, 1939. (Brooklyn Museum Costume Collection at the Metropolitan Museum of Art, gift of the Brooklyn Museum, 2009; gift of the estate of Elinor S. Gimbel, 1984, 2009.300.1008a–c; image courtesy of Art Resource, NY)

garments imported during the 1930s (and the war would stop them altogether in the early 1940s), yet films and moviegoing gained popularity during the Depression. Warner notes, "If we consider that by 1930, between 90 and 110 million people in the United States out of a total population of 117 million went to the movies *every week,* it is not hard to accept that movies wielded a considerable influence" (82). Although Americans continued to peruse fashion magazines, catalogs, and other print media, the visual impact of film would change the nature of fashion consumption. Some movie stars maintained clear connections with well-known Parisian couturiers or other recognizable labels, yet the larger impact was one of style rather than designer brands. Americans saw the chic, effortless looks of the stars, and they emulated these looks.

Hollywood Fashion in Literature

The literature of this period reflects the trendsetting so prevalent in the American West. In *The Day of the Locust,* protagonist Tod Hackett captures the look of Southern California with its casual, colorful style. Tod has arrived in Hollywood to design film sets and costumes while working on his painting *The Burning of Los Angeles.* In the opening of the novel, as Tod surveys the "evening crowd" on Vine Street, he notices people wearing "sports clothes which were not really sports clothes": "Their sweaters, knickers, slacks, blue flannel jackets with brass buttons were fancy dress. The fat lady in the yachting cap was going shopping, not boating; the man in the Norfolk jacket and Tyrolean hat was returning, not from a mountain, but an insurance office; and the girl in slacks and sneaks with a bandanna around her head had just left a switchboard, not a tennis court" (22). Tod's judgmental eye makes the clothing seem ridiculous and impractical. However, such clothing represents the pinnacle of democratic fashion in the United States. American designers and consumers embraced the sportswear trend with the logical assumption that sports clothing is designed and manufactured to provide optimal comfort and durability. Its practical function thus anticipated its adoption for casual wear among a public that spends so much time outdoors in warm weather. This clothing also has a sign exchange value, for it conveys the luxury of leisure, and it implies physical health and activity. Such clothing hearkens back to *The Great Gatsby*'s Tom Buchanan wearing his polo outfit to dinner, taking pride in his physique and displaying self-assurance in his wealth. While Tod Hackett views the crowd in its sportswear as a sign of the apocalypse, the scene actually heralds U.S. fashion autonomy and Hollywood's assertion of a new, functional fashion aesthetic.

The novel's fashion thereby serves to limn the landscape of nationalistic mass taste that Tod critiques, but it also reveals West's knowledge of contemporary fashion and its relevance for shaping his quasi-comedic femme fatale, Faye Greener. In each description of Faye, West describes her clothing in detail—in fact, clothing is so important to Faye that at various parts of the novel she prostitutes herself for a glamorous wardrobe. She believes such a wardrobe will help her achieve her dream role. Whenever Faye appears in the novel, she is described from the vantage point of one of the sycophantic male characters. In each instance, the character experiences initial awe at her beauty, and then describes her clothing as though to analyze the way it collaborates with her appearance to achieve such an impact. At her father's funeral, for example, Tod observes, "She had never looked more beautiful. She was wearing a new, very tight black dress and her platinum hair was tucked up in a shining bun under a black straw sailor" (119). In another instance, she greets Tod and her benefactor, Homer, "in a new flower print dress and picture hat. . . . She was much more than pretty. She posed, quivering and balanced, on the doorstep and looked down at the two men in the patio. . . . She looked just born, everything moist and fresh, volatile and perfumed" (140). West's emphasis in these descriptions does not rest on the expense or style of the garments, but on their ability to showcase Faye. Faye shows her knowledge of contemporary clothing trends—in one scene, for example, she appears in "a pair of green silk lounging pajamas" (161), one of the biggest trends of the period and locale because they fused comfort with luxury in an effortless way. Yet more importantly, the clothing illustrates the value of personal style. Personal style—the ability to project one's persona through a combination of garments and accessories while simultaneously showcasing oneself in a pleasing way—became the ultimate hallmark of American fashion, and indeed of democratic fashion. The move from conformity to expressive individualism paved the way for a range of new fashion icons, a range of looks and modes from which to choose, and a range of new, innovative American designers.

As American novels of the 1930s recorded American innovation and autonomy through fashion, these novels also initiated a trend of fashion through adaptation. While earlier novels, most famously, perhaps, *The Great Gatsby,* would be adapted many decades later and inspire historical revivals of the novel's contemporary fashions, these adaptations occurred with more immediacy in the 1930s and early 1940s. One of the most famous film adaptations of the twentieth century, Victor Fleming's film version of Margaret Mitchell's *Gone with the Wind* (book 1936, film 1939), became the inspiration for one of the first retro fashion trends of the century. That same year saw prom dresses reminiscent of the antebellum South, layered with rustling crinoline skirts (Hill 62). Jane Mulvagh explains that this historical revival trend stemmed from a collective sense of "nostalgia," or a "yearn[ing] for the luxury and precise social etiquette of the past" (122). *Gone with the Wind*'s historical commentary and mythologizing of the antebellum period fit with the escapist trend of Hollywood films, and this escapism bled into the realm of fashion. Throughout the Depression and the early war years, Hill notes, "eveningwear reflected a marked interest in fanciful escapism with revivals of Renaissance and rococo finery" (62). Mulvagh notes that such "fancy-dress escapism lingered on in the subconscious throughout the war until its reappearance as the inappropriately titled 'New Look' of the late forties" (122). The marked split between the dramatic evening wear of the 1930s and early 1940s and the simple, casual day wear makes it easy to forget this continuity. Retro fashion, and nostalgic escapism, would remain a staple of both Hollywood film and American fashion.

Hollywood would also draw film and fashion inspiration from other literary genres of this period, including the hard-boiled detective fiction of Raymond Chandler. In his book *Creatures of Darkness* (2000), Gene Phillips mentions the popularly held belief that "film noir has lived in greater intimacy with its literary sources than any comparable trend in cinema" (6). Like many writers of this phase of detective fiction, Chandler "was less interested in the solution of a mystery than in portraying his detective-hero's encounters with the evils of modern society in a vivid and compelling fashion" (2). The dark, brooding protagonists battling their own demons in harsh urban landscapes, their sexual tension with femme fatale characters, and the backdrop of drinking, violence, pornography, and murder lend themselves to the cinematic visions in black and white and the sharp, tailored looks of the time. Chandler published his first novel, *The Big Sleep,* in 1939, and it was adapted into a feature film in 1946. The film expanded the role of Vivian, played by Lauren Bacall, who imbued the role with smoldering haughtiness and helped establish the femme fatale look of 1940s film noir. Even today people associate Bacall's role in the film with her striking, tailored ensembles—especially her houndstooth suit paired with a beret and black sweater.

Characters like Vivian, Faye, and *The Big Money*'s Margo Dowling (also an aspiring Hollywood starlet) helped to establish the beautiful temptress as a fashion icon who would later become the femme fatale in film. In the years between World War I and World War II, according to Mulvagh, "The sophisticated temptress became a feminine ideal and sex appeal was a woman's front-line weapon. The fashionable woman of the midthirties was slender, long-legged, small-breasted, narrow-hipped, heavily painted, and sexy" (12). Indeed in *The Big Sleep,* Chandler devotes more than half a page to describing Vivian's long legs as Philip Marlowe "stare[s] at her legs in the sheerest silk stockings" (17). The elongated, narrow look of the temptress fit with the 1930s and early 1940s mode: it helped make women look taller and more elegant on camera; it used less fabric than the more dramatic, large-skirted looks of the fantastical evening wear, and it fit with the tailored sportswear look so popular at the time.

American Fashion and the War Years

Within a year of *The Big Sleep*'s publication, the Paris border was closed, and the United States was on its own for fashion design. Rationing, necessity, war, and Hollywood shaped the looks of the late 1930s and early 1940s. Actresses like Joan Crawford had already helped popularize the tailored look of American ready-to-wear designers with her "tailored suits with padded shoulders" (Hill 54), and Katherine Hepburn and Marlene Dietrich had helped to make tapered pants a wardrobe staple of American women (54). California design establishments, including White Stag, Catalina, and Jantzen, gained fame for women's sportswear, while New York firms became known for "cosmopolitan styles of urban dress" (Mulvagh 124). By 1940, after years of rationing, Paris already had narrower, more tailored silhouettes (64), and the L-85 regulation by the War Production Board ensured that for the duration of the war, silhouettes would be narrower, jackets would fall no lower than the hips, and pant legs would be narrower and more tailored to the body. Excess trimmings, wide cuffs, scarves, sashes—all of these embellishments would disappear from the mode for the time being (Hill 71). Paris offered no new hat trends in 1940, and U.S. designers championed their favorites: the Gibson Girl boater, Winston Churchill bowlers, and the swagger fedora (170)—a staple of the film noir genre. American ready-to-wear designers maintained the slimmer silhouettes during the war years, incorporating military styles and trench coats into the mode.

With no imports coming in from Paris, American designers were truly "on their own," and they responded to the call of duty. Henri Bendel of Lafayette, Louisiana, who opened his New York store in 1895, was the first retailer to brand himself. While he sold Paris brands, he was also an original designer of hats, accessories, and clothing, and he expanded to ready-to-wear in 1931 (Hill 60). Elizabeth Hawes had already established herself in the design market through her creations for Dorothy Shaver and other New York style mavens, as had Muriel King (Fashion: "New York Couture" 34). Shaver and other major retailers brought new American designers to the forefront, but the designers also participated in their own self-promotion. Main Rousseau Bocher, better known as Mainbocher, returned to the United States from Paris in 1940 (Mulvagh 128), and ultimately became an iconic fashion house for designing clothing for Wallis Simpson (Hill 70). Norman Norell and Claire McCardell became known for their tailoring and sportswear, respectively (Mulvagh 128). The best designers are described in *Vogue* as having both range and humility; for example, the April 1933 *Vogue* editorial refers to Hattie Carnegie designing for Joan Crawford and working with luxury items like fur while also "turn[ing] out a Boston dowager, than which there is none more dignified, in a masterly fashion" (96). Adaptability, versatility, empathy—these were the traits of the successful American designer. Of course, innovation would continue to be the hallmark of the truly iconic designer. Charles James, whom Christian Dior would cite as one of his major influences, gained consumer and media attention during this period for his incredibly complicated, structured designs. To this day he is known as "America's First Couturier."

During this period, women went to work. *Vogue* began to publish articles advising women on what ensembles were best for career wear, beginning as early as 1930 with editorials like, "A Sound Plan for the Year-Round Wardrobe of the Woman with a Job." One *Vogue* cover from 1943, pictured in figure 15, reads, "Take a Job! Release a Man to Fight!" The woman pictured looks tailored, polished, and effortless. Rather than looking at the camera, she examines a paper reading "Women in Necessary Civilian Jobs." This cover was part of a national Labor Day initiative in which magazine covers featured nationalist messages encouraging women to work so that their husbands could serve in the war. While the lighting in the image is somber, the woman looks confident, and her pose is even slightly masculine—like a man casually perusing a newspaper.

Studying this fascinating transformation of women from World War I to World War II makes the changes after the war seem especially jarring. For decades American fashion had mapped women's gradual liberation, their increasing freedom for sexual expression, their emergence within an American workforce. Hemlines were raised; undergarments grew less restrictive;

FIGURE 15. *Vogue* cover, September 1, 1943. (John Rawlings, *Vogue*; image courtesy of Condé Nast)

pants, shorts, and even bathing suits were integrated into casual and resort wear. Magazine covers showed women flexing, shouting, reading, playing sports, driving, and working.

The authors discussed in this volume echo these fashions and their corresponding social and political changes. From the restrictions of Victorian Edith Wharton heroines, in their tightly laced corsets and voluminous, expensive gowns, to the ready-made fashions of immigrants hoping to assimilate, to the daring chemises and tailored pants of liberated modern women, the canonical American writers reveal the paradigm shift from Old World Parisian couture to American democratic fashion.

Democratic Fashion after the War

What happened to fashion after the war? Why did the Victorian silhouette return, and why did the voluminous escapist evening styles of the 1930s prevail over the more comfortable casual wear?

If we look at the general arc of fashion in the United States from the 1870s, when *The Age of Innocence* was set, to the present, we can read fashion as increasingly democratic. In the introduction I define democratic fashion as "the expression of American ideals of freedom and democracy through the American fashion industry, as reflected in the accessibility of fashion to all citizens, in fashion's facilitation of individual self-expression or personal style, and in the comfort and ease of the clothes themselves, allowing for freedom of movement for its wearers." The canonical works examined in this volume exemplify this general arc: over the years, fashion extends to a larger demographic, transcends lines of class and race, and affords increasing opportunities to express one's personality and lifestyle through a range of stylish garments and accessories. Fashion grows increasingly pluralistic.

Scholars of fashion and cultural studies, though, caution against reading myths of progress into fashion. Marcia A. Morgado notes how, during the modernist period between the world wars, fashion reinforced a prevailing belief in myths of progress: "it appeared to give tangible form to the newest, most up-to-date technological innovations and social ideas" (44). However, she notes that postmodernists found such a validation of progress "simply a façade": "In postmodern culture fashion is explained in terms of changes of a superficial nature. Akin to performativity, it speaks to change merely for the sake of change or, less benignly, as change solely for the sake of commerce" (44). I argue that on a macrolevel (looking at the general arc of American fashion), fashion in the United States has grown increasingly democratic; however, on the microlevel, from year to year, it presents an illusion of change.

Looking at *Vogue* covers immediately before and after the war reveals a break in the arc of democratic fashion. In May 1947, for example—the same year that Christian Dior revealed his "New Look"—*Vogue* featured a brides issue with a disturbing cover image. The cover, designed by Irving Penn, features a sleeping woman's face reflected in a mirror, as well as a plate with two kumquats (which look eerily like large pills). The cover is the epitome of passiveness and submission. The carnations in the vase seem to be wilting, the placement of the kumquats give the impression that the woman has fainted for lack of nourishment (her sleeping position certainly does not look comfortable). The word "Brides" in the bottom left corner of the page, especially when combined with the image, offers a helpful social commentary on the subservient role of women after the war. Incidentally, the June 1,

1947, cover of *Vogue* would also feature a sleeping woman, this time from the waist up, lying flat on a beach.

The drastic shift to such a passive mode of femininity mirrors the gender norms of the postwar period, as well as the fashion ethos of Christian Dior, who famously claimed, "I brought back the art of pleasing" (Hill 77). His New Look heralded a "return to femininity" with its use of corsets and dropped hemlines, its "full drapery, gathers, pleats, gores, flounces, and oversized bows" with matching accessories for every look (Hill 75–77). The postwar period marked a "return to normalcy" during which businesses, colleges, advertisements, television programs, and the fashion industry conspired to put women back in the home (77). Mulvagh suggests that many women were complicit in this shift: "In an understandable reaction to the demands of war, women now wanted to masquerade as decorative ladies of leisure, retreating into the styles of the past. Longing to cast aside the mean fashions of the war, they welcomed the lavishness of the Paris line: a softened silhouette, a defined, normal waistline and a longer hemline" (180). Every Dior collection, Mulvagh adds, "seemed to be more complicated, more constricting and more artificial" (181). The financial and physical demands of this clothing, and the domestic roles that accompanied them, would be described by female writers of the 1950s and early 1960s, including the feminist authors Betty Freidan and Sylvia Plath.

Despite this seeming step backward in the arc of American fashion, the first half of the twentieth century had made its mark on fashion history, and the energetic push back of democratic fashion would reveal itself even in the most conservative moments of the 1950s. Many women resisted their domestic roles, while others, having accepted them, were disillusioned and restless. Meanwhile, the designers of the postwar era changed the industry in important ways: fashion became more international (Hill 91), more ready-to-wear designers came to the forefront in the United States, and new silhouettes were introduced, including Dior's A Line, which has retained its popularity over the decades (Hill 86). Dior's lasting impact on the fashion industry has not been the desire to restrict and confine women to the home, but to present an aesthetic of femininity and fantasy, much like the prewar designs of Vionnet and Charles James.

Fantasy would, in fact, continue to be a central element of the fashion industry. The Victorian style of Dior masterpieces like his "Junon" dress (now part of the Metropolitan Museum of Art's Costume Institute) may echo the ensemble of a Wharton heroine, but today such gowns would be considered expensive indulgences of fashion royalty—usually Hollywood celebrities. Rather than feeling obligated to wear such a gown on a regular basis, the women who choose these looks do so for the dramatic impact. Hollywood, in turn, has continued to transform fashion's role in American culture. While fashion would continue to serve as a vehicle for self-transformation, it would also become more of a vehicle for experimenting with different personal identities, much like a Hollywood actress tries on different film roles or types (a temptress, a housewife, a career woman), discards some, and maintains an association with others. This experimentation with performing identities differed from earlier discussions of performance in that they were not always hierarchical—that is, women did not solely perform a role for the sake of upward social mobility, but instead as a step toward identity construction.

In the decades following World War II, Americans would find style icons in other arenas of popular culture and various countercultures, eventually allowing individuals to carve out personal styles that relate not only to personal aesthetic preferences and gender roles but also to anything from musical taste to political leanings. During these years, American popular culture presented icons more prevalently than magazines and other print media. It offered different personality types, style images, roles to be emulated through clothing. Literature of the postwar era would reflect such experimentation as it engaged questions of multiculturalism and narrated the ethos of various American countercultures.

More recent American literature extends this experimentation into different arenas. In transgender memoirs, writers like Leslie Feinberg and Aleshia Brevard convey the sense of power or confidence inspired by the forbidden dress of the other gender. In the dystopian literature of the past few decades, American novels predict gloomy futures in which all Americans are doomed to dress the same and fashion has become a luxury of independence denied the average citizen, as in Canadian author Margaret Atwood's *The Handmaid's Tale* (1985), set in futuristic Boston, or Suzanne Collins's popular young adult trilogy *The Hunger Games* (2008). In these novels, personal expression through fashion is so controversial, so forbidden, that it can lead to the execution of the wearer—or the designer.

Even though these novels help illustrate the deep personal, social, and sometimes political meaning that clothing can help generate, many would consider the performance of identity through clothing superficial and inauthentic, and such claims continue to frame debates about contemporary fashion. Does fashion help us find ourselves, or does it encourage us to hide ourselves? Does it encourage, as many contemporary critics of the fashion industry claim, dissatisfaction with one's body and physical appearance, or does the range of styles and cuts encourage acceptance of one's natural beauty? Most of these American novels champion the possibilities of democratic fashion, even as they navigate the failings and trappings of the beauty industry. American novels of transformation suggest that the opportunity to try on identities, to perform a role without committing to it for life, is the ultimate sign of freedom—and, perhaps, an ideal of American nationalism.

Notes

Introduction

1. Barthes distinguishes between "real clothing" (the garment itself), "image clothing" (the photographic image of a garment), and "written clothing" (the written description of a garment), noting that "the being of the written garment resides completely in its meaning, it is there that we stand the greatest chance of discovering the semantic pertinence in all its purity" (8); in other words, fashion journalism is unencumbered by "practical or aesthetic function" but exists only to signal to its readers what purchases will make them fashionable (4–8).

2. From *CeciStyle Magazine,* May 14, 2013: Johnson, "Gatsby Fever" (cecinewyork.com).

3. With this phrase I refer to the popular TLC television program *What Not to Wear,* in which fashion gurus Stacey London and Clinton Kelly "arrest" unsuspecting individuals sporting unfashionable attire and instruct them in creating more fashionable, lifestyle-appropriate looks for themselves. The series originally debuted in the UK on the BBC with stylists Trinny Woodall and Susannah Constantine.

4. Though no broad-spectrum study of fashion in American literature by a single author currently exists, other scholars have published essays and books on specific authors, which I reference in this volume. Some of these works include Rachel Bowlby's 1985 book *Just Looking: Consumer Culture in Dreiser, Gissing, and Zola;* Clair Hughes's, Maureen Montgomery's, and Katherine Joslin's writings on fashion in Edith Wharton's novels; Katherine Keyser's book *Playing Smart: New York Women Writers and Modern Magazine Culture* (2010), and Katherine Stubbs's work on clothing in Anzia Yezierska's fiction. Cynthia Kuhn and Cindy Carlson have edited a collection of essays on fashion in literature, ranging from *Beowulf* to Toni Morrison's *Jazz;* only a proportion of the volume focuses on American literature and fashion.

5. Several scholars use the term "performative" to describe a property of fashion, including Bowlby and Barbara Vinken, among others. This term should not be confused with Judith Butler's concept of "gender performativity" introduced in *Gender Trouble* (1990), since the performativity discussed in these texts involves a deliberate manipulation of surface signifiers to achieve a desired public persona; the characters maintain an active awareness of their role-play as well as the hidden components of their individual identities. In her book *Fashion Zeitgest* (2005), Vinken discusses fash-

ion's performative power, evaluating "fashion as a poetological activity . . . [that] not only confirms and economically functionalizes the division of gender and class; it constructs and subverts them by stripping them bare— . . . and reveals them as an effect of construction" (4). While Vinken's assessment of fashion's performative quality has a pejorative connotation in that it ultimately deepens divisions of gender and class (at least, before the post-1970s era she terms "postfashion"), I am looking at this performative function as empowering, a move that potentially allows an individual to explore multiple identities and roles as a move toward individual identity construction.

6. The dandy is a notable exception to this general trend, and merits discussion as he emerges in some of these narratives (arguably, e.g., in the figure of Drouet in *Sister Carrie*). Vinken notes that the plainness of men's clothing during the nineteenth century helped to underline the female role as evidence of her husband's wealth: "'His' eternally inconspicuous dark suit provides the ideal matt background before which 'she' can spring into life, with the brilliance of silk, the sparkle of jewels, the shimmer of naked skin, and the ivory of the *décolleté*" (5). Though the options for men's fashions and the utilitarian properties of women's fashions would expand over the course of the twentieth century, men's business and formal wear in the United States and Europe has not altered drastically since Beau Brummell introduced the modern suit in the early 1800s (Gunn 153).

7. Barthes does not work to define "real Fashion" but "written" or "*described*" fashion, an institution of industrial society that relies on a collection of "calculating" clothing producers who "blunt the buyer's calculating consciousness" by cloaking the fashion object with a "veil"—"in short, a simulacrum of the real object [that] must be created, substituting for the slow time of wear a sovereign time free to destroy itself by an act of annual potlatch" (xi–xii). By imposing this expiration date on the object, the producers of fashion and its commercial venues can ensure an endless cycle of production and consumption.

8. Veblen argues that dress affords the clearest example of conspicuous "waste of goods" as well as of "indication of our pecuniary standing to all observers at the first glance" (167). To indicate leisure class status, he explains, one's dress "should not only be expensive, but it should also make plain to all observers that the wearer is not engaged in any kind of productive labour" (170).

9. In *The Face of Fashion,* Craik expands definitions and studies of fashion to non-Western societies, noting that in both Western and non-Western cultures "clothes construct a personal *habitus*" (4). She continues: "A fashion system embodies the denotation of acceptable codes and conventions, sets limits to clothing behavior, prescribes acceptable—and proscribes unacceptable—modes of clothing the body, and constantly revises the rules of the fashion game" (5).

10. The sociologist Tim Edwards explains, "Style may simultaneously refer to the 'what' and the 'way' of fashion—its design and how it is worn. This is at once collective, for what we understand as stylish is clearly culturally learned, and individual, as some people are simply perceived as having more style than others" (3–4).

11. Diana Crane contrasts the limitations imposed by fashion trends with the freedom of expression and choice afforded by clothing options: "Clothes as artifacts 'cre-

ate' behavior through their capacity to impose social identities and empower people to assert latent social identities. On the one hand, styles of clothing can be a strait-jacket, constraining (literally) a person's movements and manners, as was the case for women's clothing during the Victorian era. . . . Alternatively, clothing can be viewed as a vast reservoir of meanings that can be manipulated or reconstructed so as to enhance a person's sense of agency" (2).

12. Silk has maintained its role as a signature textile for high fashion for several reasons: its durability and strength, its natural sheen and reflective properties, its resistance to static electricity, its soft and smooth texture, its versatility, and its organic makeup.

13. "Until that time the woman of society would choose a material, and send it to the fashion designer with an idea for its cut. For Worth, however, the cut of the dress, the material and the pattern of the cloth belonged inseparably together. The result was that fashion production was concentrated in one house" (Vinken 20).

1. The Free Spirit in the Gilded Age

1. See, e.g., Kassanoff's "Extinction, Taxidermy, Tableaux Vivants."

2. "That the alleged beauty, or 'loveliness,' of the styles in vogue at any given time is transient and spurious only is attested by the fact that none of the many shifting fashions will bear the test of time. When seen in the perspective of half-a-dozen years or more, the best of our fashions strike us as grotesque, if not unsightly" (Veblen 178).

3. Ewen and Ewen explain, "The restrictive practices [of nineteenth-century fashion] placed women on a pedestal, above concerns of trade and carnality, yet it produced generations of women whose concerns were mobilized around issues of the body. As the predominant ideology denied women any pleasures of the flesh, it simultaneously fixated on female flesh, molding it and restricting it" (101).

4. According to Jane Mulvagh, "A sartorial chameleon, the Edwardian lady would change her appearance five or more times a day, wearing a boudoir gown while taking breakfast, a tailored suit for shopping, a serge skirt and blouse if remaining at home, a dress for luncheon and a more formal gown or suit in the afternoon for receiving a guest or calling for tea. During the early evening she wore a tea gown; then for dinner she changed again into formal evening wear—a gown invariably decorated with elaborate lace fichus and beadwork, worn with a headdress, fan, lavish jewelry and gloves. Special outfits were needed if a woman wished to participate in sporting events, go motoring, or attend specific social occasions such as weddings, the races or a function at court" (3).

5. In her treatment of the novel, Clair Hughes reiterates Lily's need for such adaptability: "To survive in New York's Gilded Age, with its post-bellum standards of conspicuous consumption and waste, and its inheritance of an increasingly hypocritical moral code, Lily must maintain a protean ability to accord with her surroundings" (388).

6. Jacques Doucet was a high-end Parisian fashion designer whose clothes were popular during the late nineteenth and early twentieth centuries.

7. In *Edith Wharton and the Making of Fashion,* Joslin suggests that Lily's costume

here echoes Wharton's own preference for aesthetic dress: "Photographs taken of Wharton in tea gowns and shirtwaists reveal, as we have seen, her own comfort in wearing reform apparel. Reading dress, we note that Lily Bart's costume in the tableau vivant scene . . . is an example of reform or aesthetic dress very like fashions being designed about the same time by Mariano Fortuny, an artist born in Spain and raised in Paris who worked in Venice as a painter, costume designer, and architect" (79).

8. Joslin observes the irony of this request: "The truth is that she has performed as a displayer of goods throughout the novel and has changed garments to fit into various scenes, dressed in a red crêpe de chine for card playing, a gray 'devotional-cut' gown to lure Percy Gryce on his way to church, and a woodland ensemble for her walk in the woods with Lawrence Selden" (*Making of Fashion* 77).

9. Montgomery notes how, in the eighteenth century, refined women read, painted, embroidered, or entertained small private parties for leisure, yet during the next century their leisure would grow more public, serving primarily to advertise their wealth: "Women had to work hard at displaying leisure and making sure that the display was noticed, particularly as newspaper scrutiny raised the ante. But while there was increasing surveillance of women at leisure and mounting pressure to make their leisure signify distinction, the other side to this was that women were able to have fun, indulge new desires, enjoy the attention and admiration that came from display, and have access to resources in order to put on an effective 'show'" (11).

10. Regarding the two women's cleavage, Joslin remarks, "The fact that no man at the opera gets a view of May's bosom marks her sexual value in Old New York society. And it is a prize not lost on the hero Newland Archer. From the moment at the opera when he sees May's tucker and Ellen's clasp, we note, he moves to secure his engagement to May. . . . His fascination with Ellen, the old-fashioned clasp and exposed bosom aside, has more to do with notions of independence: a woman's right to be as free as a man and, even more so, the idea of his *own* independence from the stultifying culture that surrounds and defines him" (*Making of Fashion* 122–23).

11. "By 1884, Liberty & Company opened a dress department and joined other reformers in arguing for simplicity of line, one that follows the natural contours of a woman's body in styles that became associated with Art Nouveau. Liberty & Company advertised their apparel as the expression of a woman's self-reliance and personal taste. . . . Indeed, the company by 1920 assured customers that their dresses, especially the distinctive Empire or Directoire cut, would 'never go out of style'" (Joslin, *Making of Fashion* 134).

12. Newland's reaction to Ellen's home resembles the narrator's reaction to Mrs. Hazeldean's home in the "1870s" chapter of Wharton's later work *Old New York* (1924): "What is there in the atmosphere of such houses that makes them so enchanting to a fastidious and imaginative youth? Why is it that 'those women' (as the others call them) alone know how to put the awkward at ease, check the familiar, smile a little at the over-knowing, and yet encourage naturalness in all? The difference of atmosphere is felt on the very threshold. The flowers grow differently in their vases, the lamps and easy-chairs have found a cleverer way of coming together, the books on the table are the very ones that one is longing to get hold of" (305).

13. A *New York Times* editorial from December 10, 1871, entitled "Fashionable Gossip from Paris," describes a similar ensemble at a major fashion event: "Mlle. Doucet wore a black silk toilet, the skirt of which was covered with flounces, and the tunic was trimmed with a very stylish guipure fringe. . . . A black velvet polonaise, bordered with Canadian sable, and a charming black velvet bonnet, completed the toilet." Other pieces from the *Times* and the *Chicago Tribune* from around the same time note the popularity of dyed monkey fur and velvet polonaises.

14. Veblen analyzes the adoption of the corset by the leisure class, arguing that "the corset is, in economic theory, substantially a mutilation, undergone for the purpose of lowering the subject's vitality and rendering her permanently and obviously unfit for work. It is true, the corset impairs the personal attractions of the wearer, but the loss suffered on that score is offset by the gain in reputability which comes of her visibly increased expensiveness and infirmity" (172). In other words, the corset functions by announcing simultaneously the woman's wealth and her leisure.

15. "She was taller than most women depicted in illustrations of the era, many times shown at about the same height as her male companions. Her facial features were solidly articulated: heavy-lidded eyes, sometimes with a defiant glint, arched eyebrows, full lips, and a strong jawline. Her hair was most always piled atop her head in twists, rolls, and chignons, usually casual in look but sometimes formal when appropriate. She played golf, hunted, canoed, bicycled, and rode horseback—often hatless and jacketless in only a shirtwaist. She also dined with titled aristocrats and wore sumptuously accoutred evening gowns" (Hill 23).

16. Ewen and Ewen also emphasize this connection between fashion and the increased mobility within city environs during the late nineteenth century: "The modern city was a magnetic arena of motion and diverting display. Activity was its conspicuous spectacle, and the city made the insularity of the home ideal more and more anachronistic. Against the sensate allurements and attractions of urban pageantry, the notion of the home as an unsullied fortress became harder and harder to justify to its appointed keepers. Motion was the social language of a cosmopolitan tableau, and that language began to leave its explosive charge within female activity and dress. By the 1890s, the bicycle, for example, had become a vehicle of diversion and purpose for both men and women; altered styles of female adornment became not only statements of politics, but functionally requisite" (113).

17. Hill calls the skirt and shirtwaist the first versions of "separates" (23).

2. *The Social Climber in the Era of Ready-Mades*

1. During the Depression, Americans could not afford to import French designs as they had in the past; in addition, in 1932 Lord & Taylor vice president Dorothy Shaver started showcasing American designers (Hill 56).

2. Daves notes that higher-end shirtwaists retailed for $150 and more (30), the equivalent of over $4,000 today.

3. Gelfant uses the word "see" rather than "notice" when describing Carrie's response to fashion and other hallmarks of her consumerist society, asserting that "the

simple sequence of seeing, wanting, and buying constitutes a deterministic structure of desire underlying naturalistic novels, like *Sister Carrie,* and advertisements psychologically programmed to motivate the modern consumer" (179–80).

4. Donald Pizer has argued that Carrie is not "introspective," that like Hurstwood, she never "examines the decisions leading to [illegal or immoral] acts in relation to whether they are right and wrong. The two figures are rather in these decisions principally acting out the deepest levels of their temperaments and desires" (166). Though Carrie does, as Pizer suggests, act instinctually out of desire, her pursuit of desire requires her to strategize, to analyze and think critically.

5. In her analysis of the novel, Gelfant argues that the introduction of plate glass as a means of displaying wares helped engender consumerist desire: "In effect, plate glass changed the concept of shopping from satisfying to creating desire, and turned shopkeepers into 'amateur psychologists' delving into the secrets of human behavior" (180).

6. Humphries observes, "While Drouet's and Hurstwood's selfish attention to appearances has led them to neglect reading Carrie deeply and has pointed her towards external satisfactions for her desires, Ames's appearance, his deep engagement with her appearance, and his 'analytical' praise, have 'thrilled' her by pointing her desires towards those inner qualities of hers which are 'worthy of discussion'" (51).

3. *The Immigrant in the Era of Simplicity*

1. "As fashion became a staple among women who entered into the outer world of work, designs that were predicated on docility and enforced leisure became patently restrictive. Among rich women, sport and city life denoted a need for more mobile styles. Among poor women it was wage labor. If the first generations of ready-to-wear had provided working-class women the opportunity to emulate the fashions of the rich, by the 1920s fashion had begun to emulate the logic of industrialism" (Ewen and Ewen 150).

2. Lori Harrison-Kahan suggests this transformation began even earlier, attributing to Chanel and her contemporaries the shift to the more menswear-inspired look and emphasis on comfort: "Between 1906 and 1916, styles changed from the Victorian corset to modernist designs that were more functional with less ornamentation. After World War I, women designers such as Gabrielle 'Coco' Chanel looked to men's wear for inspiration not only because of the comfort it provided, but also because of the independence and power it represented" (314).

3. Corset advertisements in *Vogue* during the early 1920s often referenced the "liberating" qualities of the newer models. Some companies, like P.N. Practical Front Corsets, would contrast current flexible and comfortable corset styles with earlier, more constricting styles.

4. Mulvagh explains, "The First World War thrust Chanel's functional ideals into the limelight as simplicity became characteristic of wartime clothing. As governments were forced to utilize the hitherto unrecognized talents of women, their clothing nec-

essarily evolved to suit a new purpose. The wartime silhouette was far easier to move in than the ankle-binding, long, narrow or draped skirts of previous seasons. . . . The variety of garments available was reduced and fewer lavish evening gowns were now created. Those that were made were destined for the American market, where social life was largely unaffected" (10).

5. Chanel "was the first haute couture designer to consider the functional aspects of dress, rationally deconstructing women's dress through cut, fabric and simplicity of design. Her work deliberately disrupted and overturned social class indicators in so far as it discarded the dominant concept of conspicuous consumption as a means of achieving status" (English).

6. In her essay on the role of fashion and design in the works of Yezierska and Jessie Fauset, Harrison-Kahan recognizes Chanel for her ability to blend conventional elements of women's fashion with contrasting elements: "In addition to mixing elements of masculine and feminine dress, Chanel unconventionally combined fabrics that were previously not used together. Thus fashion becomes a material metaphor for the bringing together of seemingly contradictory elements" (314).

7. Scholars offer a range of interpretations of this Stokes-Dewey figure: Ann Shapiro emphasizes the maturity of these men—a quality Yezierska associates with the wisdom of a father figure (82); Carol Schoen highlights the importance of these figures as instructors who can educate the heroines in the ways of the dominant culture (10); Stubbs notes how these men embody the contemporary style of the dominant culture which the heroines seek to emulate (165); Delia Konzett delineates the role of the male characters' social reform institutions in bringing the immigrant daughter out of the sphere of the mother, viewed as a barrier to assimilation; and Gay Wilentz suggests these characters serve as a means for Yezierska to critique the hypocrisy of the social reformers of the era (xviii). Mary Dearborn, much of whose scholarship on Yezierska has focused on her romance with Dewey, notes, "Their relationship became an obsessive subject in almost all of her fiction, in which she portrayed cold, rational, successful American-born men who are initially attracted to the ethnic heroines for their warmth and intensity. The ethnic heroine sees in this possible union the chance to 'open up' her culture to America, and the possibility of Americanization for herself" (112).

8. As Shapiro argues, Yezierska's heroines are drawn to older men, who represent financial security, maturity, and wisdom (thus the potential to educate the heroines) and are a replacement for the patriarchal Jewish father.

9. Pavletich notes how Pessah realizes her mistake when she and Barnes have entered the library: "Pessah immediately senses the differences between herself and the librarian dressed in grey. What had pleased her and seemed right to her in the context of her own choice is made into a source of difference and shame when played out within the power dynamics of middle-class Anglo-Saxon cultural, emotional, and fashion-related reserve" (90).

10. Yezierska expressed a concern about the inconsistency between the content and the delivery of Dewey's socialist message. In an article for *The Bookman,* she

praises Dewey's message yet observes, "Unfortunately, Professor Dewey's style lacks flesh and blood. It lacks that warm personal touch that would enable his readers to get close to him" ("Prophets of Democracy" 497).

11. Stubbs offers two reasons for this material culture focus on women: for one, she notes that men's ready-made clothing was more concerned with function, whereas "women's ready-made clothing was advertised as decorative and imitative" (162); and secondly, she cites the "visibility and perceived sexual availability of young working-class women in American society; such women . . . might, it was feared, snare a man of a higher social class" (163).

12. Harrison-Kahan describes him as "a Division Street tailor who took advantage of women's needs to create deceptive appearances, establishing his reputation by crafting designs that make heavy women look thin and skinny girls fat" (317).

4. *The Modern Woman and the Slim Silhouette*

1. In *Appearance and Identity,* Llewellyn Negrin agrees with this assessment of the functionality and affordability of Chanel's clothing: "Against the exclusivity of the one-off designs of other *haute couture* designers, Chanel introduced designs that could be mass produced and that used relatively inexpensive materials, such as jersey. Their simplicity and lack of decoration also enhanced their affordability as well as their practicality. This was epitomized by her famous range of black dresses, whose pared back minimalism was compared to the standardized design of Henry Ford's Model T car" (127).

2. The term comes from Judith Halberstam's *Female Masculinity* (1998). Halberstam argues, however, that a meaningful analysis of masculinity should not assume its conflation with power and privilege. She asserts, "Masculinity . . . becomes legible as masculinity when it leaves the white male middle-class body" (2).

3. Butler discusses this poststructuralist understanding of gender and sex in her work *Bodies That Matter* (1993). She refutes the notion that gender is entirely socially constructed whereas sex is biological; instead, she asserts that "['sex'] is not a simple fact or static condition of a body, but a process whereby regulatory norms materialize 'sex' and achieve this materialization through a forcible reiteration of those norms" (xii).

4. In his 2010 biography of Faulkner, Philip Weinstein describes the original expedition: "In 1925 he had been aboard an abortive cruise on New Orleans's Lake Pontchartrain. Rain assailed the party, the yacht's motor gave out, and they were unable to move. Hordes of mosquitoes descended on them. The same event, reconfigured, gives *Mosquitoes* its plot. More broadly, Faulkner was sorting out his New Orleans experience—what he had come to know of its artistic and intellectual pretensions—into a ship of fools" (28).

5. In *Unbelievable Happiness and Final Sorrow,* Ruth A. Hawkins notes that the novel mirrors Hemingway's honeymoon with Pauline, and the characters reflect Hemingway as well as his wives Hadley, Pauline, and Mary (79, 253).

6. Froehlich argues that Jordan is a lesbian "passing" as a heterosexual woman in the novel, and that this "passing" helps to build a "familiarity" between her and the narrator Nick Carraway (who, she argues, is also a homosexual).

7. Some scholars have also associated her name with the performer Josephine Baker, noting Fitzgerald's references to Jordan's darkly tanned skin concealed by powder (122), the homosocial overtones of her relationship with Daisy, and her tendency to stand as though she were posing. Froehlich notes how Josephine Baker frequently appears "as a representative cultural icon in [Fitzgerald's] later work," and asserts a connection between this icon and Jordan Baker in *Gatsby:* "Jordan Baker's name itself identifies her as queer—referring not only to the automobiles that are, of course, so closely associated with (male) wealth and power in the novel, but also with Josephine Baker, a racially and sexually transgressive figure" (85).

8. Clemente explains of the pink suit: "It's a detail that modern readers remember because of its connotations with gender and sexuality, but in its historical context, the color was about class and about showiness" ("My Big Idea").

9. In her analysis of the novel's color symbolism, Maia Samkanashvili suggests that whiteness in the novel has two connotations—purity and privilege. She observes that "the different shades of white indicate that Daisy may not be an embodiment of purity and that privilege may have a corrupting effect, at least when it is used to veil or whitewash misdeeds" (32).

10. "The young Faulkner's versifying recurrently joins hands with the aim of impressing or seducing its intended female reader—usually Estelle (mostly absent between 1918 and the late 1920s) but also, at least twice, Helen Baird (the young woman to whom he proposed in the mid-1920s and who turned him down flat)" (Weinstein 21).

11. Angela Jenny Durante Ellison explains, "As industrialization flourished and hard labor moved indoors, a tan became a sign of time for leisure. The raging vogue for tanned skin, beginning in the 1920s, made sun-tanning oils a necessary part of beauty regimes for white women, the consequences of which are coming to light today."

12. Pat's remark is likely an allusion to a propaganda poster from World War I, in which a girl with short, curly hair, wearing a sailor suit, proclaims, "*Gee*!! I wish I were *a man*. I'd join the Navy!"

5. *The Black Middle Class and the Primitive*

1. Mae Gwendolyn Henderson has also underlined Baker's agency in embodying a vision of colonialist and primitivist desire: "Baker's early stage performances . . . mirror and arguably constitute colonial desire as a longing for otherness imagined in terms of sexual and colonial conquest. It was the manipulation of such 'utopian' imagery . . . that allowed Baker to exercise control and agency in the marketing of her image in an entertainment economy and cultural circuit based on the production and consumption of otherness" (1).

2. While Baker wore these colorful, often flamboyant costumes in her stage performances, her costumes in films more closely resemble the more subdued modern mode discussed in chapter 4. In his discussion of Baker as a "New Woman," Tyler Stovall observes, "Quite apart from her costumes during her performances, in her films Josephine Baker dressed in the modern style pioneered by Coco Chanel, with skirts up to the knee and boyishly slimming dresses" (5).

3. Hughes's observation is particularly ironic given how whites had historically parodied blacks who dressed in stylish, upper-class clothing. In their book *Stylin'* (1998), Shane White and Graham White note, "Whites' descriptions of African Americans were usually set in a framework of failed imitation, of a clumsy, inept and inappropriate black translation of whites' mores into blacks' own lowly situation" (92).

4. Archer-Straw describes the popularity of Sonia Delaunay's printed fabrics in the context of textile print technology: "Her independent status as a designer benefited from the popularity of printed fabric, which after the war provided an alternative to the woven silks and woolen textiles that had previously been the mainstay of the clothing industry. Printing on fabric was new. It was also cheap, since it required materials such as cotton, previously considered an inferior fibre" (72).

5. White and White explain, "African slaves were thrust into a society with its own set of ideas about the appropriateness of clothing for various social groups, ideas that, in the fineness of their discriminations between various forms of European apparel, bore little relation to those current in the slaves' native lands" (8).

6. White and White corroborate this assertion, noting that the distinction between slaves' and masters' clothing helped reinforce their respective social castes: "it was clearly intended that slaves would wear loose-fitting garments made of the coarsest available cloth" (9).

7. In 1786 Louisiana governor Esteban Miró enacted a law requiring free woman of color to wear *tignons* (headwraps) to denote their status in society (Bell 19).

8. The history behind black women's church hats has been chronicled in Michael Cunningham and Craig Marberry's book *Crowns* (2000), a book later translated into a "gospel musical" by Regina Taylor.

9. Van Vechten's Harlem Renaissance contemporaries responded to the novel in a polarized fashion. Some writers, including Langston Hughes, praised the novel, while other writers and leaders of the time not only cast aspersions on its artistic merit but also found the novel offensive and deeply problematic. W. E. B. Du Bois wrote in *Crisis:* "His women's bodies have no souls; no children palpitate upon his hands; he has never looked upon his dead with bitter tears. Life to him is just one damned orgy after another, with hate, hurt, gin and sadism" ("On Carl" 517).

10. Cheryl A. Wall, for example, reads the novels in terms of how they revise this trope; Jonathan Little considers *Passing* in conjunction with other "tragic mulatto/a" narratives.

11. Wall also rejects, or at least questions, the label of "tragic mulatta" for this character, arguing that the term is too reductive to account for Larsen's sophisticated treatment of the dual gender and racial restrictions for black women (97).

12. Helga's nonconformist identity has led recent scholars to read her as a queer character. Keguro Macharia, for example, reads Helga's rejection of black nativist identity and constructions of black authenticity as a rejection of racial and gender normativity: "Helga doesn't simply fail; she fails to cohere as a normative subject as defined through nativist guidelines" (256). In a different queer reading of the novel, Johanna M. Wagner questions the critical tendency to read Helga in terms of her heterosexual desire, arguing instead that Helga's attempts to confine herself to heteronormativity stem from her lack of kinship, of both familial and social belonging.

13. We can trace this rhetoric to W. E. B. Du Bois's canonical sociological book *The Souls of Black Folk* (1903). In chapter 3, "Of Mr. Booker T. Washington and Others," Du Bois refers to Washington's 1895 speech, the Atlanta Exposition Address, as "The Atlanta Compromise" because of the way it sought to appease southern whites and to encourage blacks to accept second-class citizenship.

14. In his discussion of the novel's use of irony, Jonathan Little argues that Larsen implies Clare is abused: "Clare is generally a pathetic figure as a child, and there are some hints of her having suffered sexual and physical abuse at the hands of her father" (175). Little suggests that Clare's covetousness of the status and wealth of her bourgeois black friends and her history of abuse motivate her immersion in white society: "Clare's background of grinding obsession and physical abuse shaped her decision to pass for white and improve her circumstances" (176).

15. George Hutchinson argues, "Clare Kendry is not a 'tragic mulatto.' . . . Clare undergoes no tragic struggle over a discovery that she is black, nor is she tragically prevented from marrying a white suitor because of the unbreachable barrier separating the races. To Clare, there is nothing tragic about being black. She makes no profound sacrifices, no deeply ethical choice for one race over the other. Her choices are entirely selfish and epicurean; she does what pleases her" (299).

16. Jennifer DeVere Brody observes, "Irene . . . is guilty of treating African-Americans not as individuals but as objects of her own ability to serve and have power over them" (1055).

Conclusion

1. Felipe Smith notes how Johnson conflates the image of the Statue of Liberty with the image of New York City and the white woman by "condensing the gendered national space, America, into a gendered urban space, New York City, and then into the gendered icon universally associated with the myth of America's nurturance of the immigrant dispossessed—the Statue of Liberty" (320).

2. Anna Wintour, the artistic director of Condé Nast and editor-in-chief of *Vogue*, has acknowledged on multiple occasions the impact that American celebrity culture has on the fashion world, and in fact made her mark on the iconic magazine by shifting its focus from supermodels to the style and glamour of American celebrity culture.

Works Cited

"About Women's Cloaks: New York Has the Lion's Share of the Cloak Trade of the Country." *Chicago Daily Tribune (1872–1922)*: 25. 10 Nov. 1889. *ProQuest.*

Archer-Straw, Petrine. *Negrophilia: Avant-Garde Paris and Black Culture in the 1920s.* New York: Thames & Hudson, 2000.

Barnard, Malcolm. *Fashion as Communication.* London: Routledge, 2002.

Barthes, Roland. *The Fashion System.* Translated from the French by Matthew Ward and Richard Howard. London: Jonathan Cape, 1985.

Bassett, John Earl. "Faulkner's 'Mosquitoes': Toward a Self-Image of the Artist." *Southern Literary Journal* 12.2 (Apr. 1980): 49–64. *JSTOR Journals.*

Bell, Caryn Cossé. *Revolution, Romanticism, and the Afro-Creole Protest Tradition in Louisiana, 1718–1868.* Baton Rouge: Louisiana State University Press, 1997. *eBook Collection (EBSCOhost).*

Borst, Allan G. "Signifyin(g) Afro-Orientalism: The Jazz-Addict Subculture in *Nigger Heaven* and *Home to Harlem.*" *Modernism/Modernity* 16.4 (Nov. 2009): 685–707. Web.

Bourdieu, Pierre. *Distinction: A Social Critique of the Judgment of Taste.* Translated by Richard Nice, with a new introduction by Tony Bennett. London: Routledge, 2010.

Bowlby, Rachel. *Just Looking: Consumer Culture in Dreiser, Gissing, and Zola.* New York: Methuen, 1985.

Brody, Jennifer DeVere. "Clare Kendry's 'True' Colors: Race and Class Conflict in Nella Larsen's *Passing.*" *Callaloo* 15.4 (Autumn 1992): 1053–65.

Brown, Phil, ed. *In the Catskills: A Century of Jewish Experience in "The Mountains."* New York: Columbia University Press, 2002. *eBook Collection (EBSCOhost).*

Buckland, Sandra Stansbery. "American Design 1900–1946: Moving from the Shadows to Leadership." *Fashion American Style, 1900–1999.* Ed. Buckland, Leslie Stoel, and Gayle Strege. Columbus: Ohio State University, Fashion Studies Collection, 2001. N.p. Web.

Bullock, Maggie. "Fashion Spotlight: Baz Luhrmann's Leading Lady." *Elle* 3 May 2013. Web.

Butler, Judith. *Bodies That Matter: On the Discursive Limits of "Sex."* 1993. New York: Routledge, 2011.

———. *Gender Trouble: Feminism and the Subversion of Identity.* New York: Routledge, 1990.

Cahan, Abraham. *The Rise of David Levinsky.* 1917. New York: Penguin Books, 1993.

Cather, Willa. *My Ántonia.* 1918. Boston: Houghton Mifflin, 1995.

Chametzky, Jules. *From the Ghetto: The Fiction of Abraham Cahan.* Amherst: University of Massachusetts Press, 1977.

Chandler, Raymond. *The Big Sleep.* 1939. New York: Vintage, 1988.

"Cheap Jewelry for Men." *The Washington Post (1877–1922):* 9. 23 Feb. 1890. *ProQuest.*

Cherry, Shai. "Judaism, Darwinism, and the Typology of Suffering." *Zygon: Journal of Religion & Science* 46.2 (2011): 317–29. *Academic Search Premier.*

Chico, Beverly. *Hats and Headwear around the World: A Cultural Encyclopedia.* Santa Barbara, CA: ABC-CLIO, 2013. *eBook Collection (EBSCO Host).*

Clemente, Deirdre. Interview by Mark Adams. "Weekly Chat: UNLV's Deirdre Clemente on Fashion Consulting for 'The Great Gatsby.'" *Las Vegas Weekly* 11 May 2013. Web.

———. "My Big Idea: Decoding Gatsby's Costume Drama." *Harper's Bazaar UK* 7 May 2013. Web.

Cole, Stewart Grant, and Mildred Wiese Cole. *Minorities and the American Promise: The Conflict of Principle and Practice.* New York: Harper, 1954.

Craik, Jennifer. *The Face of Fashion: Cultural Studies in Fashion.* New York: Routledge, 1994.

Crane, Diana. *Fashion and Its Social Agendas: Class, Gender, and Identity in Clothing.* Chicago: University of Chicago Press, 2000.

Creditt Ole, Mme. Roberta. "Beauty Chats." *The Pittsburgh Courier (1911–1950):* 7. City ed., 26 June 1926. *ProQuest.*

Cunningham, Michael, and Craig Marberry. *Crowns: Portraits of Black Women in Church Hats.* New York: Doubleday, 2000.

Cunningham, Patricia A., and Linda Welters, eds. *Twentieth-Century American Fashion.* New York: Berg, 2005.

Daves, Jessica. *Ready-Made Miracle: The American Story of Fashion for the Millions.* New York: Putnam, 1967.

Dearborn, Mary V. "Anzia Yezierska and the Making of an Ethnic American Self." *The Invention of Ethnicity.* Ed. Werner Sollors. New York: Oxford University Press. 105–23.

Dos Passos, John. *The Big Money.* 1933. Boston: Houghton Mifflin, 2000.

Dreiser, Theodore. *Sister Carrie.* 1900. New York: Signet Classic, 2000.

Du Bois, W. E. B. "On Carl Van Vechten's *Nigger Heaven.*" *W. E. B. DuBois: A Reader.* Ed. David L. Lewis. New York: H. Holt, 1995.

———. *The Souls of Black Folk.* 1903. *Three Negro Classics.* New York: Avon Books, 1965. 207–389.

Eby, Carl P. "'Come Back to the Beach Ag'in, David Honey!': Hemingway's Fetishism of Race in 'The Garden of Eden' Manuscripts." *Hemingway Review* 14.2 (Spring 1995): 98–117.

———. *Hemingway's Fetishism: Psychoanalysis and the Mirror of Manhood.* Albany: State University of New York Press, 1999.

Edwards, Tim. *Fashion in Focus: Concepts, Practices and Politics.* New York: Routledge, 2011.

Ellison, Angela Jenny Durante. "Body and Dress." *Berg Encyclopedia of World Dress and Fashion,* vol. 3: *The United States and Canada.* Ed. Phyllis G. Tortora. New York: Berg, 2010. *New York Public Library.* Web.

English, Bonnie. *A Cultural History of Fashion in the Twentieth Century: From the Catwalk to the Sidewalk.* New York: Berg, 2007.

Ewen, Stuart, and Elizabeth Ewan. *Channels of Desire: Mass Images and the Shaping of American Consciousness.* Minneapolis: University of Minnesota Press, 1992.

"Fashion: Advance Sketches with Lots of News about Resort Fashions." *Vogue* 15 May 1932: vi, vii. *ProQuest.*

"Fashion: Chanel Designs Again." *Vogue* 15 Feb. 1954: 82–85, 128, 129. *ProQuest.*

"Fashion: New York Couture." *Vogue* 15 Apr. 1933: 33–35, 96, 99. *ProQuest.*

"Fashion: The Brim Roll." *Vogue* 1 Apr. 1913: 60. *ProQuest.*

"Fashion: The Debut of the Winter Mode." *Vogue* 1 Oct. 1926: 55–69, 152, 154, 166, 168, 170. *ProQuest.*

"Fashionable Gossip from Paris." *New York Times (1857–1922):* 5. 10 Dec. 1871.

"Fashions from the New York Point of View." *Vogue* 1 May 1922: 37–39, 130. *ProQuest.*

Faulkner, William. *Mosquitoes.* 1927. New York: Liveright, 1997.

Fauset, Jessie Redmon. *Comedy: American Style.* 1933. Ed. Cherene Sherrard-Johnson. New Brunswick: Rutgers University Press, 2010.

"Features: Now that we have Adopted Golf." *Vogue* 21 June 1894: 270–71. *ProQuest.*

Fitzgerald, F. Scott. *The Great Gatsby.* 1925. New York: Scribner, 2003.

Ford, Tanisha C. "SNCC Women, Denim, and the Politics of Dress." *Journal of Southern History* 79.3 (2013): 625–58. *Academic Search Premier.*

Froehlich, Maggie Gordon. "Jordan Baker, Gender Dissent, and Homosexual Passing in *The Great Gatsby.*" *Space Between: Literature and Culture, 1914–1945* 6.1 (1 Jan. 2010): 81–103. *Humanities International Index.*

Gelfant, Blanche H. "What More Can Carrie Want? Naturalist Ways of Consuming Women." *The Cambridge Companion to American Realism and Naturalism.* Ed. Donald Pizer. New York: Cambridge University Press, 1995. 178–210.

Gerard, Bonnie Lynn. "From Tea to Chloral: Raising the Dead Lily Bart." *Twentieth-Century Literature* 44.4 (1998): 409.

Geyh, Paula E. "From Cities of Things to Cities of Signs: Urban Spaces and Urban Subjects in *Sister Carrie* and *Manhattan Transfer.*" *Twentieth-Century Literature* 52.4 (Winter 2006): 413–42. *Academic Search Premier.*

Gold, Michael. *Jews without Money.* 3rd ed. New York: Public Affairs, 2008.

Gunn, Tim. *Tim Gunn's Fashion Bible.* New York: Gallery Books, 2012.

Halberstam, Judith. *Female Masculinity.* Durham: Duke University Press, 1998.

Hannel, Susan L. "The Influence of American Jazz on Fashion." Welters and Cunningham 57–77.

Harmon, Charles. "Cuteness and Capitalism in 'Sister Carrie.'" *American Literary Realism* 32.2 (Winter 2000): 125–39. *JSTOR Journals.*

Harrison-Kahan, Lori. "No Slaves to Fashion: Designing Women In the Fiction of Jessie Fauset and Anzia Yezierska." Kuhn and Carlson 311–31.

Hawkins, Ruth A. *Unbelievable Happiness and Final Sorrow: The Hemingway-Pfeiffer Marriage.* Fayetteville: University of Arkansas Press, 2012.

Hemingway, Ernest. *The Garden Of Eden.* Preface by Charles Scribner Jr. New York: Collier Books, 1986.

———. *The Sun Also Rises.* 1926. New York: Scribner, 2003.

Henderson, Mae Gwendolyn. "Colonial, Postcolonial, and Diasporic Readings of Josephine Baker as Dancer and Performance Artist." *The Scholar & Feminist Online* 6.1–6.2 (Fall 2007/Spring 2008): 1–8. S&F Online.

Hill, Daniel Delis. *As Seen in Vogue: A Century of American Fashion in Advertising.* Lubbock: Texas Tech University Press, 2004.

Hillis, Marjorie. "Fashion: A Seat at the Paris Openings, Spring 1923." *Vogue* 15 Apr. 1923: 39–49, 132. *ProQuest.*

———. "Fashion: Fitting the Flat Back to the Full Figure." *Vogue* 15 Nov. 1923: 44–45, 128. *ProQuest.*

Huggins, Nathan Irvin. *Harlem Renaissance.* New York: Oxford University Press, 1971.

Hughes, Clair. "Consuming Clothes: Edith Wharton's *The House of Mirth.*" *Fashion Theory: The Journal Of Dress, Body and Culture* 9.4 (2005): 383–406. *Academic Search Premier.*

Hughes, Langston. *The Big Sea: An Autobiography by Langston Hughes.* 1940. New York: Hill and Wang, 1993.

Humphries, David T. "'The Shock of Sympathy': Bob Ames's Reading and Re-reading of Sister Carrie." *Dreiser Studies* 32.1 (2001): 36–55. *Academic Search Premier.*

Hurston, Zora Neale. *Their Eyes Were Watching God.* 1937. New York: Harper Perennial Modern Classics, 1998.

Hutchinson, George. *In Search of Nella Larsen: A Biography of the Color Line.* Cambridge, MA: Belknap Press of Harvard University Press, 2006.

"J.C. Ribbons Ad." *Cloak and Suit Review* 18 (July–Sept. 1919): 187. *HathiTrust.*

Johnson, Ceci. "Gatsby Fever." *CeciStyle Magazine.* Ceci New York. 30 Sept. 2013. Web.

Johnson, James Weldon. *Autobiography of an Ex-Coloured Man.* 1912. *Three Negro Classics.* New York: Avon Books, 1965. 391–511.

Joslin, Katherine. *Edith Wharton.* New York: St. Martin's Press, 1991.

———. *Edith Wharton and the Making of Fashion.* Durham: University of New Hampshire Press, 2009.

Kassanoff, Jennie A. "Extinction, Taxidermy, Tableaux Vivants: Staging Race and Class in *The House of Mirth.*" *PMLA* 115.1 (Jan. 2000): 60–74.

Kazanjian, Dodie. *Vogue: The Covers.* New York: Abrams, 2011.

Kelly, Rebecca J. "Fashion in the Gilded Age: A Profile of Newport's King Family." Welters and Cunningham 9–32.

Keyser, Catherine. *Playing Smart: New York Women Writers and Modern Magazine Culture.* New Brunswick, NJ: Rutgers University Press, 2010.

Konzett, Delia Caparoso. "Administered Identities and Linguistic Assimilation: The Politics of Immigrant English in Anzia Yezierska's *Hungry Hearts.*" *American Literature* 69.3 (Sept. 1997): 595–617. *Academic Search Premier.*

Kosak, Hadassa. *Cultures of Opposition: Jewish Immigrant Workers, New York City, 1881–1905.* Albany: State University of New York Press, 2000.

Kuhn, Cynthia, and Cindy Carlson, eds. *Styling Texts: Dress and Fashion in Literature.* Youngstown, NY: Cambria Press, 2007.

Larsen, Nella. *Quicksand* and *Passing.* Ed. Deborah E. McDowell. New Brunswick: Rutgers University Press, 1986.

Leach, William. *Land of Desire: Merchants, Power, and the Rise of a New American Culture.* New York: Pantheon Books, 1993.

Little, Jonathan. "Nella Larsen's *Passing*: Irony and the Critics." *African American Review* 26.1 (Spring 1992): 173–82.

Macharia, Keguro. "Queering Helga Crane: Black Nativism in Nella Larsen's *Quicksand.*" *MFS: Modern Fiction Studies* 57.2 (2011): 254–75. *MLA International Bibliography.*

MacPhee, Laurence E. "*Great Gatsby*'s Romance of Motoring: Nick Carraway and Jordan Baker." *Modern Fiction Studies* 18 (Summer 1972): 207–12. *Humanities and Social Sciences Retrospective: 1907–1985 (H. W. Wilson).* Web.

McMullin, John. "Features: A Night in Paris." *Vogue* 1 June 1927: 49–52, 150. *ProQuest.*

Michaels, Walter Benn. "'Sister Carrie''s Popular Economy." *Critical Inquiry* 7.2 (Winter 1980): 373–90. Web.

Montgomery, Maureen. *Displaying Women: Spectacles of Leisure in Edith Wharton's New York.* New York: Routledge, 1998.

Morgado, Marcia A. "Coming to Terms with *Postmodern:* Theories and Concepts of Contemporary Culture and Their Implications for Apparel Scholars." *Clothing & Textiles Research Journal* 14.1 (1996): 41–53. *Supplemental Index.*

Mulvagh, Jane. *Vogue History of 20th Century Fashion.* New York: Viking, 1988.

Negrin, Llewellyn. *Appearance and Identity: Fashioning the Body in Postmodernity.* New York: Palgrave MacMillan, 2008.

O'Meara, Lauraleigh. "Medium of Exchange: The Blue Coupe Dialogue in *The Great Gatsby.*" *Papers on Language & Literature* 30.1 (1994): 73. *MasterFILE Premier.*

Palmer, Alexandra. *Couture and Commerce: The Transatlantic Fashion Trade in the 1950s.* Vancouver: University of British Columbia Press, 2001.

Pavletich, JoAnn. "Anzia Yezierska, Immigrant Authority, and the Uses of Affect." *Tulsa Studies in Women's Literature* 19.1 (Spring 2000): 81–104.

Pfeiffer, Pauline. "Features: Madame in Search of Her Youth." *Vogue* 1 Jan. 1922: 51, 51, 88, 90. *ProQuest.*

Phillips, Gene D. *Creatures of Darkness: Raymond Chandler, Detective Fiction, and Film Noir.* Lexington: University Press of Kentucky, 2000.

Pizer, Donald. "An Evolutionary Reading of Sister Carrie." *"The Game as It Is Played": Essays on Theodore Dreiser.* New York: Peter Lang, 2013. 165–72.

Poiret, Paul. "Fashion: Poiret on the Philosophy of Dress." *Vogue* 15 Oct. 1913: 41. *ProQuest.*

Pouillard, Véronique. "Design Piracy in the Fashion Industries of Paris and New York in the Interwar Years." *Business History Review* 85.2 (2011): 319–44. *Scopus.*

Rohy, Valerie. *Impossible Women: Lesbian Figures and American Literature.* Ithaca: Cornell University Press, 2000.

Rooks, Noliwe M. *Ladies' Pages: African American Women's Magazines and the Culture That Made Them.* New Brunswick, NJ: Rutgers University Press, 2004.

Ross, Robert J. S. "Bread and Roses: Women Workers and the Struggle for Dignity and Respect." *WorkingUSA: The Journal of Labor and Society* 16 (March 2013): 59–69. *Business Source Premier.*

Samkanashvili, Maia. "Uses of Symbols and Colors in *The Great Gatsby.*" *Journal of Education* 2.1 (2013): 31–39. Web.

Schoen, Carol B. *Anzia Yezierska.* Boston: Twayne Publishers, 1982.

Schuyler, George. *Black No More: Being an Account of the Strange and Wonderful Workings of Science in the Land of the Free.* 1931. Reprint. New York: Modern Library, 1999.

Shapiro, Ann R. "The Ultimate *Shaygets* and the Fiction of Anzia Yezierska." *MELUS* 21.2 (Summer 1996): 79–88.

Simmel, Georg. "Fashion." *American Journal of Sociology* 62.6 (1957): 541. *Publisher Provided Full Text Searching File.*

Smith, Emily Esfahani. "The Early Years of *Vogue.*" *Acculturated: Pop Culture Matters* 26 June 2013. acculturated.com.

Smith, Felipe. *American Body Politics: Race, Gender, and Black Literary Renaissance.* Athens: University of Georgia Press, 1998.

Snodgrass, Mary Ellen. *World Clothing and Fashion: An Encyclopedia of History, Culture, and Social Influence.* Armonk, NY: M. E. Sharpe, 2014.

Stabb, Jo Ann C. "Influence of the Arts." *Berg Encyclopedia of World Dress and Fashion,* vol. 3: *The United States and Canada.* Ed. Phyllis G. Tortora. New York: Berg, 2010. *New York Public Library.* Web.

Steele, Valerie. *Women of Fashion: Twentieth-Century Designers.* New York: Rizzoli International, 1991.

Stevenson, N. J. *The Chronology of Fashion: From Empire Dress to Ethical Design.* London: A&C Black, 2011.

Stovall, Tyler. "The New Woman and the New Empire: Josephine Baker and Changing Views of Femininity in Interwar France." *The Scholar & Feminist Online* 6.1–6.2 (Fall 2007/Spring 2008): 1–7. S&F Online.

Stubbs, Katherine. "Reading Material: Contextualizing Clothing in the Work of Anzia Yezierska." *MELUS* 23.2 (Summer 1998): 157–72.

Thompson, Robert Farris. *Flash of the Spirit: African & Afro-American Art and Philosophy.* New York: Random House, 1984.

Tischleder, Bärbel. "The Deep Surface of Lily Bart: Visual Economies and Commodity Culture in Wharton and Dreiser." *Amerikastudien/American Studies* 54.1 (2009): 59–78. *JSTOR Journals.*

Van Slooten, Jessica. "Fashion, Money, and Romance in *The House in Mirth* and *Sister Carrie.*" Kuhn and Carlson 249–67.

Van Vechten, Carl. *Nigger Heaven.* 1926. Urbana: University of Illinois Press, 2000.

Veblen, Thorstein. *The Theory of the Leisure Class.* 1899. New York: Dover, 1994.

Vinken, Barbara. *Fashion Zeitgeist: Trends and Cycles in the Fashion System.* Oxford: Berg, 2005. *eBook Collection (EBSCOhost).*

Wagner, Johanna M. "(Be)Longing in *Quicksand:* Framing Kinship and Desire More Queerly." *College Literature* 39.3 (2012): 129–59. *MLA International Bibliography.*

Walker, Alice. *The Color Purple.* 1982. New York: Pocket Books, 1985.

Wall, Cheryl A. "Passing for What? Aspects of Identity in Nella Larsen's Novels." *Black American Literature Forum* 20.1/2 (Spring–Summer 1986): 97–111.

Warner, Patricia Campbell. "The Americanization of Fashion: Sportswear, the Movies and the 1930s." Welters and Cunningham 79–98.

Watson, Steven. *The Harlem Renaissance: Hub of African-American Culture, 1920–1930.* New York: Pantheon Books, 1995.

Weinstein, Philip. *Becoming Faulkner: The Art and Life of William Faulkner.* New York: Oxford University Press, 2010.

Welters, Linda, and Patricia A. Cunningham, eds. *Twentieth-Century American Fashion.* New York: Berg, 2005.

West, Nathaneal. *The Day of the Locust.* 1939. Introduction by Alfred Kazin. New York: Penguin Group, 1983.

Wharton, Edith. *The Age of Innocence.* 1920. New York: Macmillan, 1993.

———. *A Backward Glance by Edith Wharton.* New York: D. Appleton-Century, 1934.

———. *House of Mirth.* 1905. Ed. Janet Beer and Elizabeth Nolan. Ontario: Broadview Editions, 2005.

———. *Old New York.* 1924. New York: Simon & Schuster, 1995.

———. *The Unpublished Writings of Edith Wharton.* Ed. Laura Rattray. London: Pickering & Chatto, 2009.

Wharton, Edith, and Ogden Codman. *The Decoration Of Houses, by Edith Wharton and Ogden Codman, Jr.* New York: C. Scribner's Sons, 1902.

White, Shane, and Graham J. White. *Stylin': African American Expressive Culture from Its Beginnings to the Zoot Suit.* Ithaca, NY: Cornell University Press, 1998.

Wilentz, Gay. "Introduction." *Salome of the Tenements.* By Anzia Yezierska. 1923. Urbana: University of Illinois Press, 1995. ix–xxvi.

Yezierska, Anzia. *Bread Givers: A Novel.* 1925. New York: Persea Books, 1999.

———. *Hungry Hearts and Other Stories.* 1920. New York: Persea Books, 1991.

———. "Prophets of Democracy." *The Bookman: A Review of Books and Life* 52.6 (Feb. 1921): 496–99. *ProQuest.*

———. *Red Ribbon on a White Horse.* 1950. New York: Persea Books, 1981.

———. *Salome of the Tenements.* 1923. Urbana: University of Illinois Press, 1995.

Index

Recent Books in the Cultural Frames, Framing Culture Series

Rachel Hall
Wanted: The Outlaw in American Visual Culture

Stephanie L. Hawkins
American Iconographic: "National Geographic," Global Culture, and the Visual Imagination

Stephanie Harzewski
Chick Lit and Postfeminism

Samuel Chase Coale
Quirks of the Quantum: Postmodernism and Contemporary American Fiction

Eric Aronoff
Composing Cultures: Modernism, American Literary Studies, and the Problem of Culture

James J. Donahue
Failed Frontiersmen: White Men and Myth in the Post-Sixties American Historical Romance

Jinny Huh
The Arresting Eye: Race and the Anxiety of Detection

Ann Brigham
American Road Narratives: Reimagining Mobility in Literature and Film

Lauren S. Cardon
Fashion and Fiction: Self-Transformation in Twentieth-Century American Literature